International Contracts
and Payments

International Contracts and Payments

Edited by

P. Šarčević

Professor of Law, Faculty of Law
University of Rijeka, Croatia
Visiting Professor, holder of
John D. Drinko-Baker and Hostetler Chair
Case Western Reserve University
School of Law, Cleveland, Ohio

P. Volken

Professor of Law, Faculty of Law
University of Fribourg, Switzerland

Graham & Trotman/Martinus Nijhoff
Members of the Wolters Kluwer Academic Publishers Group
LONDON/DORDRECHT/BOSTON

Graham & Trotman Limited
Sterling House
66 Wilton Road
London SW1V 1DE
UK

Kluwer Academic Publishers Group
101 Philip Drive
Assinippi Park
Norwell, MA 02061
USA

© Graham & Trotman Ltd, 1991
First published in 1991

British Library Cataloguing-in-Publication Data
International contracts and payments.
 I. Šarčević, O. (Peter), *1941-* II. Volken, P.
 342.62

 ISBN 1-85333-615-7

 0185177

Library of Congress Cataloguing-in-Publication Data
International contracts and payments / edited by P. Šarčević. P. Volken.
   p.   cm.
   Includes index.
   ISBN 1-85333-615-7
   1.   International finance–Law and legislation. I. Šarčević,
Petar.   II. Volken, Paul.
   K1005.6.I59   1992
   341.7'51—dc20

91-36836
CIP

Computer typeset by Graham & Trotman Ltd
Printed and bound in Great Britain by Hartnolls Ltd, Bodmin, Cornwall

Contents

Foreword

In our day and age of constant change, lawyers are continuously confronted with new problems which threaten the expansion of international trade. This applies above all to changes in the global monetary system. Since the abandonment of the Bretton Woods agreement and the adoption of a floating exchange rate system, the international monetary markets have been plagued by instability and thus unpredictability. As Sir Joseph Gold said in his new book *Legal Effects of Fluctuating Exchange Rates*, "a characteristic of such a system is that it makes predictability of exchange rate behaviour extremely difficult".

It was partly to protect their economies from the volatility of the international monetary markets that the EC countries took the initiative and created a European monetary system. An important aspect of this development was the creation of the European currency unit (ECU). In Chapter One Hugo J. Hahn analyzes the ECU, comparing it with the IMF's special drawing right (SDR). Other countries were more susceptible to the adverse effects of the instable conditions. Dependent on borrowed money to keep their economies going, numerous countries accumulated unmanageable external debts. Disenchanted with past attempts to deal with the international debt crisis, debtor countries and their credtiors desperately need new debt management strategies. In Chapter Two Andre W. G. Newburg presents proposals for adapting restructuring and loan agreements to international debt management strategies.

International trade could not function without international instruments of payment and efficient techniques for transferring interbank funds across borders. Thus the unification of legal rules in the field of international payments is of paramount importance. Already well known for its unification efforts, the United Nations Commission on International Trade Law (UNCITRAL) is preparing a Model Law on International Credit Transfers. In his analysis of the Model Law in Chapter Three, Eric Bergsten shows how the introduction of electronic techniques into the banking process has affected the rules governing interbank funds transfers. Other topics related to unification include international documentary credits, contract guarantees and bills of exchange. These are discussed respectively by Ljudevit Rosenberg, Lars A. E. Hjerner and Reinhard Welter in Chapters Four, Five and Six.

The final two Chapters deal with related topics of particular importance for the conclusion of contracts involving international financial transactions. Chapter Seven is devoted to conflict-of-laws issues which should be taken into account in international financial transactions. Discussing the limitations of party autonomy, Peter Šarčević emphasizes that numerous differences exist in comparative legislation and judicature even in regard to commonly accepted legal rules such as party autonomy. In the Eighth and final chapter Paul Volken analyzes the intricate and sophisticated role of legal opinions written by expert lawyers, showing how extremely important they are in international financial transactions.

The preparation of this book would have been impossible without the help of various individuals and institutions. In particular, we would like to thank the EC, the Swiss National Fund and the German DAAD for their support. Thanks also go to Susan Šarčević for making the English language revisions.

The Editors
September 1991

Abbreviations

ABAJ	*American Bar Association Journal*
BEA	Bills of Exchange Act
BGBl.	Bundesgesetzblatt
BGE	Entscheidungen des Bundesgerichts (Switzerland)
BGH	Bundesgerichtshof (Germany)
BGHZ	Entscheidungen des Bundesgerichtshofs (Germany)
BIS	Bank for International Settlement
Bus.Law.	*The Business Lawyer*
Cal.St.B.J.	*California State Bar Journal*
Clunet	*Journal de droit international*
Cornell L. Rev.	*Cornell Law Review*
DB	*Der Betrieb*
Duke L. J.	*Duke Law Journal*
EBA	ECU Banking Association
EC	European Communities
E.C.R.	*European Court Reports*
ECU	European Currency Unit
EDI	Electronic Data Interchange
EFTA	European Free Trade Association
EIB	European Investment Bank
EMCF	European Monetary Cooperation Fund
EMS	European Monetary System
EUA	European Unit of Account
Harv.Int'l.L.J.	*Harvard International Law Journal*
ICC	International Chamber of Commerce
IFLR	*International Financial Law Review*
IMF	International Monetary Fund
Inst. on Sec. Reg.	Institute on Securities Regulation
Int.Law	*The International Lawyer*
IPRax	*Praxis des Internationalen Privat- und Verfahrensrechts*
ISO	International Organization for Standardization
JBl	*Juristische Blätter*
J. of Commerce	*Journal of Commerce*
Lloyd's Rep.	*Lloyd's Law Reports*
Mass. L. Q.	*Massachusetts Law Quarterly*
MESA	Mutual ECU Settlement Account
NJW	*Neue Juristische Wochenschrift*
OJ	*Official Journal of the European Communities*

OJEC	*Official Journal of the European Communities*
Pacific L. J.	*Pacific Law Journal*
RabelsZ	*Rabelszeitschrift für ausländisches und internationales Privatrecht*
Rec. des Cours	*Recueil des Cours de l'Académie de droit international*
RIW/AWD	*Recht der internationalen Wirtschaft*, bis 1974: *Aussenwirtschaftsdienst*
SDR	Special Drawing Right
SJIR	*Schweizerisches Jahrbuch für Internationales Recht*
SWIFT	Society for Worldwide International Financial Telecommunication
UCC	Uniform Commercial Code
UCP	Uniform Customs and Practice for Documentary Credits
UNCITRAL	United Nations Commission on International Trade
WLR	*Weekly Law Reports*
WM	*Wertpapiermitteilungen*
WuB	*Wirtschafts- und Bankrecht*
Yale L. J.	*Yale Law Journal*
ZIP	*Zeitschrift für Wirtschaftsrecht*

Contributors

Eric BERGSTEN, Professor of Law and Secretary of the United Nations Commission on International Trade Law (UNCITRAL) at Vienna, Austria

Hugo, J. HAHN, Professor of Law, University of Würzburg, Germany; Chairman of the ILA Monetary Committee

Lars A. E. HJERNER, Professor of Law, University of Stockholm, Sweden; Member of the ICC Institute of International Business Law and Practice

Andre W. G. NEWBURG, General Counsel, European Bank for Reconstruction and Development, London

Ljudevit ROSENBERG, Emeritus Professor of Law, University of Zagreb, Croatia

Petar ŠARČEVIĆ, Professor of Law, University of Rijeka, Croatia; Director of Studies of the International Association of Legal Science

Paul VOLKEN, Professor of Law, University of Fribourg, Switzerland

Reinhard WELTER, Attorney-at-Law; Collaborator at the Institut für Internationales Recht des Spar-, Giro- und Kreditwesens of the University of Mainz, Germany

1

The European Currency Unit (ECU) and the Special Drawing Right (SDR): Legal Assessment of a World-wide and a Regional Basket Unit

Hugo J. Hahn

I. THE ECU

1. Definition

The ECU is defined as the sum of different amounts denominated in the currencies of the member states of the European Communities (EC)[1] and determined in accordance with a standard basket formula.[2] The share of each currency in the basket is determined by criteria reflecting the economic weight of this particular state. Until now the Council has only used its power twice to adjust the share of the individual currencies.[3] This was in 1984 when the Greek drachma was incorporated into the basket and again in September 1989 when the peseta and the escudo were introduced.[4] Every working day of the stock exchange the value of the ECU is calculated in U.S. dollars and the currencies of the member states by the Commission and published in the *Official Journal of the European Communities*.[5]

---

[1] 0.6242 German mark; 0.08784 pound sterling; 1.332 French francs; 151.8 Italian lire; 0.2198 Dutch guilder; 3.301 Belgian francs; 0.13 Luxemburg franc; 0.1976 Danish kroner; 0.008552 Irish pound; 1.44 Greek drachmas; 6.885 Spanish pesetas; 1.393 Portuguese escudos.

[2] Council Regulation (EEC) No. 3180/78 of 18 December 1978 and Council Regulation (EEC) No. 2626/84 of 15 September 1984; *Texts Concerning the European Monetary System*, published by the Committee of Governors of the Central Banks of the Member States of the EEC (Basle 1985) p. 74.

[3] Resolution of the European Council of 5 December 1978, A. 2.3, *Texts*, p. 14; Council Regulation No. 3180/78, Art. 2, *ibid.* 74.

[4] *Bundesgesetzblatt* (Federal Republic of Germany) Pt. II (1985) p. 1679. Joint Declaration Annexed to the Accession Treaty of Portugal and Spain.

[5] R. W. Edwards, Jr., *International Monetary Collaboration* (Dobbs Ferry NY 1985) p. 117.

International Contracts and Payments (Šarčević, Volken, eds.; 1 85333 615 7; © Graham & Trotman, 1991; pub. Graham & Trotman; printed in Great Britain), pp. 1-24.

2. The ECU as a Unit of Account

Since the Community did not have its own currency, in 1950 the unit of account which was used nationally as the domestic currencies of the members assumed the function of common denominator at Community level.[6] Originally, the Community had used the unit of account of the European Payments Union which had a uniform definition for all domains of EC activity and was equal in value to the U.S. dollar measured in terms of gold. This uniform method of valuation, however, was discarded as a result of the breakdown of the system of fixed exchange rates. Different rates were then introduced for specific topical domains whenever necessary, thus leading to the parallel application of various units of account for different operations. In order to establish a common denominator, the European Unit of Account (EUA)[7] was established in 1975 along the lines of the special drawing right in the International Monetary Fund (IMF). The EUA was defined as a closed basket of nine Community currencies.

Introduced in 1979, the ECU was not intended to replace the EUA although it had the same definition as the latter.[8] At first it was used only in certain domains; however, after 1981 it became the comprehensive substitute of the EUA in all respects. Today it is factually the unique unit of account in the Community.[9] As such it is used in accordance with the legal instruments governing EC accounting procedures, in the budget of the Community,[10] in Community relations with the African, Pacific and Caribbean states under the Lome Conventions,[11] in the European Development Fund, in the accounts of the European Investment Bank (EIB) and finally in the context of the common agricultural policy.[12]

The consequences of using the ECU as a unique unit of account may be observed by noting the actions of the EIB. Regarding the ECU as a means of establishing a European monetary identity, the EIB instituted the ECU as its unit of account[13] on 1 January 1981, thus emphasizing that its banking operations were in compliance with the prevalent trend. Currently the ECU is the unit of account for all loans provided by the bank[14] and is increasingly being used as the money of payment for loans denominated exclusively in ECU as well as for those in which the ECU constitutes one of the elements in a cocktail of currencies. Moreover, the EIB accepts refinancing loans denominated in ECU. By using the ECU as a unit of account internally, the EIB promotes its use as a denominator and means of payment *vis-à-vis*

---

[6] H. J. Hahn, "Wertsicherung im Recht der Europäischen Gemeinschaften", *Gedächtnisschrift Sasse* vol. I (Baden-Baden 1981) pp. 441, 443 *et seq.*

[7] *Ibid.* 441 and 452.

[8] Resolution of the European Council of 5 December 1978, A. 2.1, *Texts*, p. 14.

[9] *The ECU* Office for Official Publications of the European Communities (Luxemburg 1987) p. 7.

[10] *OJEC* N. L 345 (20 December 1980).

[11] O. Wulff, *Entwicklungshilfe zwischen Völkerrechtsordnung und Weltwirtschaftssystem* (Baden-Baden 1986) pp. 117, 133 *et seq.*

[12] Hahn, "L'Utilisation publique des monnaies composites (ECU/DDS)" in P. Kahn (ed.) *Droit et monnaie* (Paris 1988) p. 239 n. 13.

[13] EIB Statute, Art. 4; J. Käser, "Währungsrecht und Europäische Investitionsbank" in Hahn (ed.) *Integration und Kooperation im Europäischen Währungswesen* (Baden-Baden 1980) p. 65.

[14] *European Investment Bank, 25 Years 1958-1983*, published by EIB (Luxemburg 1983) pp. 93 *et seq.*, p. 101.

individuals and co-operations in credit transactions. This has led to the emergence of a private ECU market as an outgrowth of its official use in the Community.[15]

On the other hand, the denomination of EIB loans in ECU entails a value maintenance effect. Exchange rate risks, in particular those resulting from a devaluation of the currency of payment, are assumed by the debtor while the prospect of profit for the creditor bank due to revaluation remains limited. This is possible due to the fact that the stability of the ECU exchange rate *vis-à-vis* the currencies in the basket and frequently in relation to other currencies as well is relatively greater than is generally the case when devaluation occurs among basket currencies themselves. Fluctuations often occur which offset one another and, at any rate, the extent of the possible effects is proportional to the share of that particular currency in the basket. Such risk-splitting operates in whatever domain the ECU becomes prevalent, in particular where uniform prices have to be determined for the Community's economic policy or obligations under Community law regarding *border-crossing* trade and accounting have to be specified in figures.[16]

3. The ECU in the European Monetary System (EMS)

As defined here, the ECU is "at the centre of the EMS".[17] It is used as a denominator (*numéraire*) for the exchange rate mechanism, as the basis for a divergence indicator and as a unit of account (denominator) for operations in both intervention and credit mechanisms. Finally, it is also used as a means of settling obligations between monetary authorities in the European Community.

In the exchange rate mechanism, each currency has a central rate in relation to the ECU. These central rates are co-ordinated with one another, thus establishing a bilateral exchange rate of each currency in relation to each of the other participating currencies. The result is a parity grid of bilateral exchange rates which amounts to a regional system of fixed exchange rates in the sense of the optional possibility introduced by the Second Amendment of the IMF Articles of Agreement in favour of member states. Fluctuation margins of 2.25% (6% for the peseta) are established around these exchange rates. Once these upper or lower limits are passed, central banks are obliged to intervene in the foreign exchange market with other currencies participating in the EMS. A divergence indicator enables tensions between EMS currencies to be detected very early. It is calculated on the basis of the difference between the ECU value of a currency on that day and its central rate, also expressed in ECU.[18]

In anticipation of unlimited compulsory interventions when the fluctuation margins are exceeded in either direction, the central banks of EMS members have mutually granted one another very short-term credit facilities of unlimited amount,

[15] The accounts held for the EC by banks in Brussels and Luxemburg are denominated in ECU as they are used to finance the EC budget.

[16] Hahn, "L'Utilisation publique des monnaies composites (ECU/DDS)", pp. 237, 239 nn. 19 and 20 for further references.

[17] Resolution of the European Council of 5 December 1978, A 2.1, *Texts*, p. 14.

[18] *Ibid.* A 2.2 and 2.3, A 3. For comments and further references see Hahn, "L'Utilisation publique des monnaies composites (ECU/DDS)". With the exception of Spain and Portugal, EC Member States participate in the EMS. It should, however, be noted that the United Kingdom and Greece do not apply the exchange rate mechanism. This explains the fictitious central rates for the pound sterling and the drachma.

thus guaranteeing sufficient quantities of currencies for intervention. Debts arising from the use of these short-term facilities are denominated in ECU so that each central bank bears the risks involved in a modification of its national currency's central rate in terms of ECU. If the creditor's currency is revalued, the reimbursement of a debt in ECU requires a smaller amount of that currency from the debtor. If the debtor's currency is devalued, the other currencies, including that of the creditor, are revalued against the ECU. The revaluation of the other currencies mitigates the debtor's increased cost caused by the devaluation of his own currency. For the purpose of financing balance of payments difficulties, short-term financial support from central banks and medium-term assistance by member states were already available prior to the establishment of the EMS. Although both facilities have now been incorporated into the EMS, the ECU served as a unit of account only for medium-term assistance, its use in short-term monetary support being limited to exceptional cases only.[19]

In terms of volume, intramarginal optional interventions effected before the limits of the central rates are reached have become much more important than compulsory interventions. Thus far, U.S. dollars have usually been used in such intramarginal operations instead of EMS currencies.[20]

In view of the "highly desirable objective" of setting up a "scheme for the creation of closer monetary co-operation leading to a zone of monetary stability in Europe", exchange rate adjustments are still admissible. It is mainly the bilateral central rates which are involved in such negotiations. Their adjustment causes a change in the value of the amounts comprising the basket, thus necessitating new central rates for the revalued or devalued currencies. Since the central rates are linked to the ECU as a measure of reference, the modification of one currency's central rate inevitably requires that new central rates in ECU be established for all the other currencies as well. Therefore, adjustment of the central rates requires the mutual agreement of the states concerned.[21] From that angle, the autonomy of states in regard to establishing exchange rates remains untouched. Admittedly, obtaining the required mutual agreement from all participating states may delay an unavoidable adjustment and thus could appear to threaten genuine monetary autonomy. From the German point of view, the effects on monetary stability caused by a delay in readjusting central rates are clearly discernible. Interventions by the *Bundesbank* in favour of other IMF currencies require an increase in banking liquidities to offset the corresponding increase in the foreign exchange assets required by the institute of issue. If this situation occurs too frequently, this may call for the reappraisal of German monetary policy as it could result in a contradiction between the

---

[19] Agreement of 13 March 1979 between the Central Banks of the Member States of the European Economic Community establishing Operating Procedures for the European Monetary System, Articles 6-16 *et seq.*, *Texts*, pp. 23, 27-32; for comments see Edwards, *International Monetary Collaboration*, pp. 328, 332, 337, 355.

[20] Agreement between EC Central Banks of 13 March 1979, Articles 2.1 and 2.2, *Texts*, p. 25.

[21] Resolution of the European Council of 5 December 1978, A 1.1, *Texts*, p. 14; on successive realignments from 1985 to 1987 see Hahn, "L'Utilisation publique des monnaies composites (ECU/DDS)" pp. 241-242 with references. "Mutual" agreement is required by virtue of this Resolution of the European Council, A 3.2, *Texts*, p. 14.

international obligation of the *Bundesbank* to intervene and its statutory duty to maintain the domestic value of the German mark in accordance with Section 3 of the *Bundesbank Act*.[22]

4. The Official ECU

The official ECU is created from deposits of 20% of the gold holdings and 20% of the dollar reserves currently held by the central banks by means of rotating three-month swap arrangements with the European Monetary Cooperation Fund (EMCF), which then credits each participating central bank with an amount of ECUs corresponding to those deposits.[23] The ECUs thus obtained are specified on the balance sheets of the central banks as assets only, and not as gold holdings and dollar reserves contributed to the EMCF. Since the ECU assets are simply substituted for the holdings in gold and dollars,[24] the circulation of the ECUs does not increase the respective reserves. At least with regard to the gold, the operation may lead to additional liquidity as the central banks generally calculate the value of their gold on the basis of the former official gold price, whereas the current market price is used to determine the amount of ECUs to be provided. This process of substitution may then take on the traits of a remonetization. By reference to the network of agreements establishing the EMS and the ECU, the private ECU retains the value defined by the official ECU. However, the remaining characteristics of the two differ legally as well as in terms of their practical use. Private law ECU operations will be treated later.[25]

From the beginning, the official ECU was the means of settlement for balances from financial operations in the domain of very short-term credit facilities by means of which the funds required for obligatory interventions are acquired. Originally, a debtor balance could be settled, in whole or in part, by remittal of ECUs except that a creditor's central bank was not bound to accept settlement in ECUs in excess of 50% of the claim and could demand that the remainder be paid by transferring other reserve assets. Since September 1987, however, central banks accept settlements in ECUs exceeding 50% and up to 100% unless this would create a disequilibrium in the composition of reserves or lead to excessive debtor or creditor positions in ECUs. Thus there is an obligation to accept the official ECU, though admittedly a limited one. Upon agreement of the central banks directly concerned, it is already possible to arrange very short-term financing of intramarginal interventions in currencies of the EMS through the intermediary of the EMCF.

---

[22] Under that provision the Bank is bound to maintain the currency's domestic rather than its external value; for particulars see Hahn, "Die Deutsche Bundesbank im Verfassungsrecht", 113 *Bayerische Verwaltungsblätter* (1982) pp. 33 and 36. The factual developments described in the text are based on the reports of the *Deutsche Bundesbank* (1985) pp. 75 *et seq.*; (1986) pp. 71 *et seq.*

[23] Resolution of the European Council of 5 December 1978, A 3.8, *Texts*, p. 16; Agreement between EC Central Banks of 13 March 1979, Article 17, *Texts*, p. 25; Decision No. 12/79 of the Board of Governors of the EMCF of 13 March 1979, Article 2, *Texts*, p. 50; comment by Edwards, *International Monetary Collaboration*, pp. 320 *et seq.*

[24] e.g. balance sheet of the Deutsche Bundesbank, 31 December 1986, Appendix to report of the *Deutsche Bundesbank* for 1986, pp. 112 *et seq.*

[25] J. Gold, "Substitution in the International Monetary System", *Legal and Institutional Aspects of the International Monetary System*, vol. II (Washington DC 1984) p. 308; see comments on this process in *Texts*, pp. 31–36. On this development, see also *BIS, 56th Annual Report* (9 June 1986) pp. 156 *et seq.*; also Hahn, "L'Utilisation publique des monnaies composites (ECU/DDS)", pp. 243–244.

Automatic access to such currencies has not been granted. However, in order to acquire the foreign currencies needed for intervention, since July 1985 the intervening bank may mobilize its ECU assets by exchanging them within specific limits against U.S. dollars held by other EMS central banks,[26] thus strengthening the function of the official ECU as reserve assets. The same result can now be achieved when the EMS central banks arrange transactions with other central banks and international monetary institutions which the EMCF has accorded the status of "other holder".[27] At the meeting of the EEC central bank governors on 8 September 1987, it was agreed that intramarginal interventions in EMS currencies could be financed from very short-term credit facilities by the intermediary of the EMCF, provided the central bank issuing the intervention currency agreed in advance.

The President of the *Bundesbank* considers two elements to be particularly important: intramarginal operations in German marks can only take place with the prior consent of the German institute of issue and such interventions may also be financed by the intermediary of the EMCF. For their part, the French Finance Minister and the Governor of the *Banque de France* have stressed that the financing of intramarginal interventions[28] needs to be well-founded. This results in permanent uncertainty in regard to the burden of proof. This seems all the more so since the *Bundesbank* feels that it should not make decisions on such matters, even statutorily well-founded ones, without taking into account the monetary interests of France, the most important economic partner of the Federal Republic.

According to numerous observers, however, the official ECU continues to have certain weaknesses. To begin with, its very existence appears to be rather precarious as it depends on the extent to which central banks are inclined continuously to renew the swap operation with the EMCF involving gold and dollar reserves. In addition, past experience has shown that the global volume of ECUs created in this manner varies considerably, depending primarily on the initial price at which the gold was purchased and on developments of the U.S. dollar exchange rate. Finally, since the obligation to accept the ECU is restricted, the official ECU cannot be directly used as a financial means of intervention, even *vis-à-vis* central banks.[29]

Admittedly, there is no unconditional obligation to accept the ECU in payment of a monetary obligation, thus justifying the view that the official ECU does not constitute money in the legal sense of the term. On good grounds, the view prevails that objects which are given and accepted in compliance with an obligation by mutual agreement and not as legal tender under the command of a public authority cannot be considered money in the legal sense of the term. On the other hand, the EC member states have retained monetary sovereignty. When the EEC was instituted, the procedure chosen prevented the transfer of corresponding powers to an organ of the Community. The issuing of coins denominated in ECU thus appears to be insignificant when considering the monetary nature of the ECU. It is a different matter, however, when it comes to the use of the ECU as a unit of account in operations between individuals and private enterprises in which the EC

---

[26] About 40% of the total ECUs; "The Role of the SDR in the International Monetary System", *IMF Occasional Paper No. 51* (Washington DC 1987) p. 47. Practical experience is described in *BIS, 56th Annual Report*, p. 157.

[27] Decision No. 18/85 of the Board of Governors of the EMCF of 12 November 1985, *Texts*, pp. 59-61.

[28] *Deutsche Bundesbank, Auszüge aus Presseartikeln* (1987) Nos. 66 and 68, pp. 1-2 and 3 respectively.

[29] Hahn, "L'Utilisation publique des monnaies composites (ECU/DDS)", p. 243, nn. 43-49.

denominator is treated as if it were money. This raised the important question of whether national monetary authorities should encourage such tendencies, including the fiction of the ECU as quasi money.[30]

Since the EMS came into force, repeated attempts to strengthen the role of the official ECU have led only to the results mentioned above. In accordance with a resolution of the European Council of 5 December 1971, EMS provisions and procedures should have been consolidated in a final system no later than two years (transition period) after commencement of the project. This would have entailed the creation of a European Monetary Fund as well as full utilization of the ECU as a reserve asset and means of settlement.[31] It is understandable that radically different solutions have always been proposed regarding the concrete form which these projects should take, especially in respect of the institutions. As a result, numerous economic and political reasons continue to bar the opening of the final phase of the EMS.[32]

Thus the question arises as to how the official ECU can be strengthened pragmatically in its major functions as a reserve medium and means of payment. Furthermore, how can potential and thus additional institutional changes be accomplished in the same context and how can the circulation of separate official and private ECUs be unified? Thus far it has been suggested that foreign exchange reserves be permanently pooled, that ECUs be assigned in exchange for the national money of the central bank receiving them, or that the ECU be created *ex nihilo*, as was done with the SDR in the IMF, as this would render the ECU available as needed. The same proponents feel that co-operation between EMS central banks should make intramarginal operations denominated in ECU not only possible but also obligatory.[33]

The creation of a permanent pool of foreign exchange reserves and a Community institution with autonomous control over the volume of ECUs would eliminate structural limitations of the EMS and effect partial transfer of sovereignty held by national instances until now. It is true that the *Bundesbank* constantly points out that such proposals might not be compatible with the purpose of the EMS, i.e., to create a zone of monetary stability in Europe, and that they might conflict with its obligation to maintain the value of the mark.[34] Nevertheless, it is likely that the obstacles standing in the way of establishing a European monetary authority under Community law shall be mastered. However, impediments resulting from national law could require a constitutional amendment[35] to the *Grundgesetz* in the Federal Republic. In EMS member states which have no constitutional clause guaranteeing independence of the central bank *vis-à-vis* the executive, other constitutional obstacles might have to be coped with, albeit for different reasons.

[30] *Ibid.*

[31] *Texts*, p. 13. BIS, *58th Annual Report* (13 June 1988) cites examples (pp. 179-185, 195-196).

[32] See *BIS, 58th Annual Report*, pp. 165 *et seq.*, 180 *et seq.*

[33] For reference see Hahn, "L'Utilisation publique des monnaies composites (ECU/DDS)", pp. 244-245.

[34] Report of the Deutsche Bundesbank for 1986, pp. 68-71.

[35] L. Gramlich, *Europäische Zentralbank und Art. 24 Abs. 1 GG* (Baden-Baden 1979) pp. 169 *et seq.*; also id., *Bundesbankgesetz, Währungsgesetz, Münzgesetz, Kommentar* (Cologne 1988) pp. 39 *et seq.*, 4 Bundesbankgesetz, Marginal No. 12.

For the purpose of instituting a parallel European denominator as a new category of foreign exchange, it has been proposed from various quarters that the circulation of official and private ECUs be unified by admitting private banks as "other holders", that interventions on the free foreign exchange market be denominated in official ECUs, that investment banks be refinanced by the intermediaries of holders of official ECUs, that minimum reserves in private ECU deposits be obligatory or that banking clearing systems be co-ordinated with the settlement scheme for balances of the EMCF in official ECUs. It has even been suggested that the ECU be separated from the basket and transformed into an entirely independent money.[36]

II. Special Drawing Rights (SDR)

1. Definition

The SDR is defined as a basket consisting of fixed amounts of the five most important currencies.[37] The share of each currency reflects the size of the issuing country's exports of goods and services and the currency's official holdings in the monetary reserves of other IMF members. The composition of the basket and the share of the currencies are reviewed every five years. The value of the SDR is established every day in more than forty currencies and published twice monthly in the IMF *Survey*. Originally the SDR was defined in the IMF Articles of Agreement as the countervalue of 0.888671 grams of fine gold (= 1 U.S. Dollar). After the breakdown of the Bretton Woods system and the factual emergence of the official gold price, this definition became unusable. From 1 July 1974 to 31 December 1980 the value of the SDR was determined by a basket of 16 currencies. Thereafter the basket was reduced to five currencies.[38]

2. The SDR as a Unit of Account

The SDR is the unit of account of the IMF in which it administers the contributions of member states, their quotas, reserve positions in the Fund and drawings as well as loans extended to the Fund, the Fund's deposit at the Bank for International Settlement, the foreign exchange assets of member states and the amounts deposited into trust funds held by the Fund. The IMF Articles of Agreement specify the cases in which the SDR has to be used as a unit of account. Even where this is not mandatory as in agreements for borrowing by the Fund, it has been the general practice of the Fund to denominate its liabilities and claims in SDRs, thus avoiding any exchange rate risk. If the Fund received a currency through a loan without denominating its obligations in SDRs, that loan would nonetheless be made available to members in terms of SDRs. In that case, the Fund would have to bear the risk arising from a change in the value of the SDR in relation to the currency in which the particular loan was denominated.[39]

[36] For references see Hahn, "L'Utilisation publique des monnaies composites (ECU/DDS)", pp. 245-246.

[37] 0.452 US dollar; 0.527 German mark; 33.4 Japanese yen; 1.020 French francs; 0.0893 pound sterling; *IMF Annual Report 1986*, 51 referring to Executive Board Decision No. 6631-(80/145) G/S.

[38] Edwards, *International Monetary Collaboration*, pp. 176 *et seq.*

[39] For references see Hahn, "L'Utilisation publique des monnaies composites (ECU/DDS)", p. 247 and nn.

Outside the jurisdiction of the Fund, the SDR has gained recognition as a unit of account for the purpose of financial obligations or for limiting responsibility in a growing number of international conventions. The SDR has partially replaced gold and various categories of gold francs (*Franc-or*). Its use is not limited to international, in particular multilateral organizations and conventions although it is constantly referred to in a worldwide context since the breakdown of the Bretton Woods system. There are several reasons for the choice of the SDR as a unit of account; however, as in the case of the ECU, the main incentive arises from the greater stability in value generally provided by such a basket[40] compared with the fluctuations of its constituent currencies. Of course, the important share of the freely floating U.S. dollar in the denominator certainly entails economic risks and even arouses protests of a political and psychological nature from time to time. On the other hand, the value of the SDR has never been modified in relation to the currencies in the basket by successive adjustments which, in the case of the ECU, were a regular phenomenon for some time in the recent past.[41]

3. Maintenance of the Exchange Value of a Currency in Terms of the SDR

Article IV Section 2 (a) and (b) of the IMF Articles of Agreement authorize each state to choose freely the exchange arrangements which it considers suitable and to determine the external value of its money. It only has to inform the Fund forthwith about its choice and subsequent modifications. If a state decides in favour of a fixed exchange rate, it may peg its currency against the SDR as a means of reference for maintaining the exchange value of its legal tender. In that case, the bilateral exchange rates *vis-à-vis* other currencies are determined by the value of these currencies in relation to the SDR. At present, only a limited number of member states have linked their currency to the SDR. They have acknowledged variable margins of fluctuation as a result of pegging their currency against the IMF composite.[42]

4. The Official SDR

The official SDR, which is allocated by the Fund among its member states in proportion to their quota,[43] was deliberately designed to create reserve assets. The creation of SDRs was the result of economic discussions held at the beginning of the sixties. Numerous experts were of the opinion that the availability of reserve assets, namely gold and U.S. dollars, was no longer guaranteed in sufficient amounts for the future. This led to the conclusion that in order to increase the volume of monetary reserves worldwide, a reserve asset neutral to the incidence of inflation should be sought. This view prevailed over others which favoured stepping up the speed of

---

[40] Edwards, *International Monetary Collaboration*, p. 635 with further references.

[41] J. Gold, *SDRs Currencies and Gold: Sixth Survey of New Legal Developments*, IMF Pamphlet Series No. 40 (Washington DC 1983) pp. 8 *et seq.*

[42] Their low two-digit figure reveals the limited attractiveness of pegging currency against the SDR; this has been acknowledged in publications of the Fund. See e.g. *IMF Annual Report 1986*, p. 68.

[43] Articles XV, sect. 1 and XVIII, sect. 1 of the IMF Articles of Agreement. Allocation in itself does not entail the creation of domestic money, merely an increase in international liquidity; Hahn, "L'Utilisation publique des monnaies composites (ECU/DDS)", p. 248.

monetary circulation by taking recourse to the international capital markets. The Second Amendment to the IMF Articles of Agreement finally obliged members to co-operate with the Fund in order to make the SDR the principal reserve asset in the international monetary system.[44] This objective, however, has not been attained. One of the reasons for this is the fact that the Fund has no control over the capital markets which have become the principal source of international liquidity. Moreover, the evolution of the international monetary system has raised doubts about the weight of the arguments which led to the creation of the SDR, in particular the system of floating exchange rates in connection with the growing liberalization of capital movements as well as the emergence of other currencies which are now acknowledged as reserve assets in addition to the U.S. dollar.[45] Nevertheless, the SDR may have a complementary function as a safety net in case unpredicted developments arise.

The official SDR is created by allocation to Fund members participating in the SDR system, as decided by the Board of Governors. The volume of the allocation depends on the long-term worldwide need for a supplement to existing reserve assets free of the inflationary effects on existing currencies.[46] The postulate of allocating SDRs for the purpose of making them the principal reserve asset is as incompatible with the IMF Articles of Agreement as the request for an allocation of SDRs exceeding the limit determined in the particular quota, even if such a request takes the form of a demand for development aid (link). At present, the majority vote required to reallocate the SDRs cannot be obtained on the Board of Governors.[47]

In addition to Fund members participating in the SDR scheme, "other holders" may receive SDRs although such allocation is not provided for in the Articles of Agreement.[48] As of now, four central banks, three intergovernmental monetary authorities and nine development aid institutions are using SDRs as "other holders". Their respective functions determine the character and volume of their recourse to the IMF basket unit. The Fund has adopted standard terms and conditions for the use of the SDR by "other holders" in order to assimilate the basket device to a genuine currency as far as this is legally possible. Individuals and corporations may not receive official SDRs but may use them as a unit of account in private law transactions.[49]

From a formal point of view, there is a distinction between transactions and operations involving SDRs, depending on the goal to be attained.[50] SDRs are exchanged against other monetary assets in a number of transactions. A participant in the SDR scheme agrees to accept SDRs from any other participant upon designation by the Fund and to provide that member with an equivalent amount of

---

[44] Articles VIII, sect. 7 and XXII of the IMF Articles of Agreement.

[45] For this reason the BIS carries out constant monitoring; e.g., see *BIS, 58th Annual Report* (13 June 1988) pp. 185 *et seq.* and *passim*.

[46] Articles XVII and XVIII, sect. 2 and 4 of the IMF Articles of Agreement.

[47] See Edwards, *International Monetary Collaboration*, pp. 213 *et seq.*, 645 *et seq.*; Hahn, "L'Utilisation publique des monnaies composites (ECU/DDS)", p. 259. Comments on relevant developments can be found in annual reports of the Fund and member central banks.

[48] Article XVII, sect. 3 of the IMF Articles of Agreement.

[49] D. Lefort, "Problémes juridiques soulevés par l'utilisation privée des monnaies composites", p. 115 *Clunet* (1988) 370, with further references.

[50] Articles XIX and XXX (i) of the IMF Articles of Agreement; Hahn, "L'Utilisation publique des monnaies composites (ECU/DDS)", p. 250.

a freely usable currency which may be its own or that of another member if deemed by the Fund to be freely usable, as set forth in Article XXX (f) of the IMF Articles of Agreement. The obligation of the Fund to designate the participant and the obligation of the designated participant to accept SDRs are the two pillars of the SDR system as they secure its liquidity. Its smooth functioning thus presupposes that no specific group of members be permanently receivers or givers of SDRs.[51] Any other uses of the SDR are described as operations.[52] A series of obligations of the participants *vis-à-vis* the Fund can be carried out in SDRs, including important recourse to the Fund's means by drawing on credit facilities and purchasing their proper currency against SDRs. In addition, for the purpose of increasing the possibilities of using official SDRs, the Fund has rendered several decisions permitting SDRs to be used between members in payment of financial obligations, in swap or forwarding operations and as the denomination of loans, sureties or gifts. It should be noted that liabilities denominated in ECU may be settled between official holders of SDRs in the latter denomination. This has already been accomplished by two central banks in respect of a debt arising from the EMS credit mechanism.[53] The Fund does not participate in operations involving "other holders", thus showing that viable SDR markets can develop between participants and "other holders" without its support. On the other hand, individuals and private corporations are not allowed to participate in operations and transactions involving SDRs. Thus SDRs cannot be used for immediate interventions in the monetary market although, as has been shown, they are in several respects a monetary reserve asset in the full sense of the word.[54]

In addition to its functions as a reserve asset and *numéraire* (denominator) of value, the official SDR is used as a means of transferring value. Yet it is not money in the legal sense, and there is no duty to accept it as legal tender in any type of transaction.[55] On the other hand, such a duty ensues from relevant IMF provisions in three types of situations illustrated by the following examples. A participant is obliged to accept an unlimited amount of SDRs when it repurchases its own currency in connection with a drawing under Article V Section 7 of the IMF Articles of Agreement; it is limited to a certain amount when a freely usable currency is exchanged against SDRs under the procedure of designation (Article XIX Section 4); when quotas are changed, the Fund has to accept 25% of the increase in SDRs unless the Board of Governors decides otherwise (Article III Section 3 (a)). It is even doubtful whether the SDR can qualify as "bank money"[56] (*Buchgeld, monnaie scripturale*) in the usual sense. Indeed, quite intentionally the term *allocation* stresses that the process of creating SDRs does not have the characteristics usually prevailing when *Buchgeld* is created.[57] Thus it cannot be taken for granted that the SDR can be classified according to the category of international "bank money". Accordingly,

[51] BIS, 58th Annual Report (13 June 1988) pp. 189 *et seq.*

[52] Edwards, *International Monetary Collaboration*, pp. 203, 205 *et seq.*, with further references.

[53] Hahn, "L'Utilisation publique des monnaies composites (ECU/DDS)", p. 250 n. 92.

[54] K. W. Dam, *The Rules of the Game (Reform and Evolution in the International Monetary System)* (Chicago 1982) pp. 291, 307 *et seq.*, 328 *et seq.*, 341 *et seq.*

[55] F. A. Mann, *The Legal Aspect of Money*, 4th ed. (Oxford 1987) p. 507, with further references.

[56] *Ibid.* 507, "book entry".

[57] Gold, *SDRs Currencies and Gold*, p. 8; id., *SDRs, Currencies and Gold: Fifth Survey Legal Developments*, IMF Pamphlet Series No. 36 (Washington DC 1981) p. 41.

the SDR cannot be explained by recourse to traditional concepts. As a result the practitioner has to decide on a case by case basis whether the SDR is currency, i.e., whether it is money within the meaning of provisions outside the law of the Fund - a difficult avenue of interpretation indeed.[58]

The present position of the SDR has been criticized, notably by central banks. As to its function as a reserve asset, the reproaches concern, in particular, the following points: the limited obligation of its acceptance; the absence of anonymity in relevant transactions and operations; the fact that the composition of the basket does not reflect the proper commercial and financial weight of specific countries; the exclusion of individuals and corporations from transactions and operations involving the SDR. In order to circumvent the legal duty of keeping the circulation of official and private SDRs separate without amending the IMF Articles of Agreement, it has been suggested that a system of clearing be established in which the official SDR could be used in the form of central bank assets to compensate balances in the accounting system of private debts denominated in SDRs. This would favour the use of the SDR as a means of payment, a function which is necessary in order to transform the IMF basket into the principal reserve asset of the Fund. The Fund does not oblige its members to support such a development by enacting appropriate measures in their respective national legislation. This explains the difference between the SDR and the ECU, i.e., the lack of essential encouragement to integrate the circulation of private and official SDRs and, by the same token, to support the general uses of the two categories of SDRs.[59]

A comprehensive and comparative assessment of ECU and SDR shows that though their distinctive features are based on different concepts of monetary policy, similar reservations and hopes have accompanied the two units since their emergence. These circumstances have led to striking similarities which conclusively confirm the transformation of money and its functions. To begin with, notwithstanding certain distinctive features, official ECUs and official SDRs are used as a means of maintaining, measuring and transferring value although the transfer of value suffers from the possibility of non-acceptance. It is the lack of compulsory acceptance which places the ECU and the SDR functionally below money in the legal sense. This lacuna is frequently regarded as an obstacle, however, quite often as an advantage as well. This proves that practice is not ready to waive acceptance as an essential element of legal tender, even if the public discussion on the nature of "bank money" seems to lose sight of it from time to time.

Such shortcomings in terms of the essential elements of money do not at all diminish the great importance of the ECU and the SDR as units of account. Therefore it can again be concluded that money and concrete currencies can no longer be considered unique subjects of legal thought because they alone possess all the specific functional traits of legal tender. The ECU and the SDR share the general characteristics of real money, i.e., their availability as a unit of account and, accordingly, as a means of measurement. Although the ECU and the SDR operate primarily in their own official circuits, they also make themselves felt outside these networks by functioning as instruments for measuring value in lieu of national currencies. It should be taken into account that this is likely to or will necessarily

---

[58] Hahn, "L'Utilisation publique des monnaies composites (ECU/DDS)", p. 251.
[59] *Ibid.*

have an impact on the concept and role of money in terms of law. There is an ultimate reservation to be made here. Units of account defined in accordance with the standard basket method are at the same time *mensura et mensuratum*. Neither the ECU nor the SDR can be considered a unique instrument for measuring value as they only represent the value of the currencies in their basket. From this point of view and in the light of a comparative and retrospective assessment regarding gold clauses, it seems justified to say that international practice uses national currencies more than ever. Maintaining the value of these currencies, however, remains the responsibility of the issuing states.

III. The Private Use of Monetary Composites

By way of introduction it may be noted that the volume of private transactions in which the SDR is used as the denominator of value still seems to be modest. The main subject of the following discussion is the private ECU which has become the main feature of an entire clearing and payment system.[60] It is true that, as in the case of the EMS *numéraire*, private obligations defined by reference to the SDR are governed by such rules as the creditor and debtor may invoke, and not by the provisions dealing with that composite within the IMF.[61] Whereas commercial transactions in ECUs have become an everyday occurrence, by and large recourse to the SDR as a means of payment for SDR denominated claims is still rather exceptional. In view of this, the following analysis is limited to the private ECU.

Following the cautious beginning of the European Unit of Account (EUA) in 1975, the ECU emerged as a notable denominator in border-crossing private monetary obligations by 1981.[62] Viewed against the background of international credit operations in their entirety, the relatively rapid growth of ECU denominated assets has given the EMS *numéraire* a rather insignificant share only in that ensemble. This holds true for short-term as well as for medium- and longer-term transactions, including Euro-operations. Notwithstanding the relatively limited dimension of its use, the ECU should no longer be dismissed as a kind of institutional curiosity for a number of reasons.[63] In the first place, a series of initiatives has been launched by Community institutions, national governmental authorities and market participants. Both individually and jointly, these entities have secured a place for the ECU in the markets ahead of Euro-currency assets in sterling, French francs and Dutch guilders, but behind the volume of assets of Euro-dollars, Euro-DMs and Euro-Swiss francs.[64] Moreover, the growth of the ECU can be assessed as particularly strong when viewed in the context of the slowdown in overall growth of bank credit and ECU bond sales.[65]

One of the most important factors contributing to the rapid growth of the ECU as a unit of account in international financial transactions has probably been its relative stability. Consisting of a basket of currencies, it is likely to fluctuate less than

---

[60] See description in "The Clearing and Payment System for the Private ECU", *EIB, Information No. 50* (October 1986) pp. 1 *et seq.*

[61] Lefort, "Problémes juridiques", p. 381.

[62] *The ECU*, p. 7.

[63] *BIS, 55th Annual Report* (10 June 1985) p. 128.

[64] Ibid. 129

[65] *BIS, 56th Annual Report* (9 June 1986) pp. 100 *et seq.*

individual EEC currencies against other EEC currencies or the dollar. Similarly, its interest rate is bound to be more stable. As a means of risk aversion, the ECU can therefore offer advantages to both borrowers and investors at a time when the exchange and interest rates of the dollar are prone to strong fluctuation.[66] The ECU denomination seems to have attracted predominantly firms and entities as borrowers from countries with high domestic nominal interest rates for which it provides a less expensive alternative to borrowing in dollars. It also appears that in some EEC countries an increasing amount of foreign trade is being invoiced and even partly settled in ECUs, thus resulting in a certain amount of ECU borrowing to finance trade.[67] The ECU provides a convenient means of diversifying investments not denominated in dollars without having to accept the relatively unattractive interest rates of continental low inflation currencies such as the Swiss franc and the German mark.[68] Another important factor contributing to the increased use of ECUs is the official sponsorship and encouragement. Institutions of the European Communities and public sector entities of EEC member states have issued a substantial share of ECU denominated bonds. At the same time, there has been some easing of foreign exchange regulations to permit residents to invest in ECU bonds in precisely those countries which had been reluctant to do so, e.g., France and Italy.[69]

In order to assure continued growth of the ECU banking credit market, lending operations should be expanded beyond the few countries where such transactions have already made their mark, notably in Italy and France, and its non-bank deposit base should be broadened outside the Benelux countries. Furthermore, the present policy according to which exchange rates between EMS members are more stable than those between these currencies and the U.S. dollar should be continued as this affects first and foremost the ECU bond market. This in turn is linked not only to the performance of the American currency but also to the sustained convergence in respect of price stability among EC governments and the national economies for which they are responsible. Indeed, with the international monetary scene plagued by large and frequent currency fluctuations, the ECU has definitely benefited from this convergence of economic policies. Strict adherence to the exchange rate mechanism of the EMS and the agreements concluded thereunder are disciplinary factors which have helped reduce the inflation differentials prevalent when the EMS began to function. This development has led to the solid tenure of the exchange rate between the currencies participating in that mechanism.[70] Moreover, Community initiatives have contributed to the growth of the ECU as a denominator. The market for ECU denominated securities has profited when issues made by or on behalf of the Community or EC bodies have stimulated their turnover and deepened their impact on public awareness.[71] The increase of bank intermediation denominated in ECUs has been a necessary outgrowth of exchange market interventions operated by certain central banks as part of the daily border-crossing practice of the EMS.

[66] C. A. Ciampi, "The ECU: Its Development and its Future", *The World of Banking* (May-June 1987) pp. 4 *et seq.*

[67] BIS, 55th Annual Report (10 June 1985) p. 131.

[68] Ibid. 133.

[69] 39 *Monthly Report of the Deutsche Bundesbank*, 8 (August 1987) pp. 30, 32 *et seq.*

[70] Ciampi, "The ECU: Its Development and its Future", p. 6.

[71] *BIS, 55th Annual Report* (10 June 1985) p. 133.

The initiatives of the national authorities of some member countries with formerly volatile exchange rates such as Belgium, France and Italy have contributed to the expansion of private ECU turnover. Italy, for example, was one of the first countries to give the ECU foreign currency status by quoting it officially in the exchange market. The Italian treasury initiated the practice of fund raising in ECU when it issued ECU-denominated securities to be sold to both residents and non-residents.[72] From the outset, i.e., as early as 1979, Italian traders promoted the use of the ECU as a money of account in commercial operations and took initial steps to introduce the ECU as a money of payment as well. Italian initiatives to use the ECU in capital market operations have been less effective than the efforts of Belgian banks, although the Italian governmental planning authority expressly encouraged increasing the ECU share in international financing by designating it a privileged economic policy objective in 1985.[73] Altogether, the attitude of the Community and its member governments can be regarded as an official testimony for the ECU and has broadened market interest in its possibilities, particularly since 16 June 1987 when the *Bundesbank* changed its former restrictive authorization practice, thus permitting the private use of the ECU on the same scale as foreign currencies.[74]

Recourse to the ECU basket in private contracts provides a flexible device that can be adjusted to take account of any changes enacted under the EMS. This underscores the weight of Community and governmental support in promoting the use of the ECU in private transactions. An additional reason for the rapid expansion of the non-governmental ECU market is the introduction of new financial instruments and techniques in conjunction with progress in information technology. Therefore, it is not surprising that the use of the ECU has not been limited to Europe but has spread to other continents as well, notably to the U.S. and Japan.[75] In both countries the need to diversify portfolios has created new opportunities for the ECU. Thus it can be said that since its emergence the private ECU has been used as a means of payment and a denominator in capital market operations. Rather early, banks were obliged to develop techniques for transferring ECUs between financial institutions. The process was rather complicated at the beginning since any ECU denominated transfer implied the movement of the currencies in the ECU basket. In the mean time, however, the market-making banks for ECU operations have begun to act as clearing houses for groups of other banks which keep ECU denominated accounts with them. Thus ECU payments are effected between two sets of participants.[76]

To begin with, most banks got accustomed to using the ECU like any other currency. Their ECU holdings were kept on the books of one or more of the ECU market-making banks which would carry out the actual ECU transfers upon request. The transfers were either intramural or extramural. A large percentage of intramural transfers could be conducted by simple debt/credit book entries for transactions between deposit holders at the same banks, thus making it unnecessary to break the ECU down into its component currencies or, conversely, to transform those currencies into ECUs in proportion to the composition of the ECU basket.

---

[72] Ciampi, "The ECU: Its Development and its Future", pp. 4 *et seq.*
[73] *Ibid.*
[74] 39 *Monthly Report of the Deutsche Bundesbank*, pp. 30, 32 *et seq.*
[75] BIS, *55th Annual Report* (10 June 1985) pp. 132-133.
[76] "The Clearing and Payment System for the Private ECU", p. 1.

Only the market-making banks continued effecting extramural transfers in ECUs by conducting transactions with different financial agencies. This involved the creation of ECUs in cases of need but also their destruction if another means of payment had to be created - a very expensive procedure indeed.[77] Accordingly, the market-making banks made an effort sharply to reduce the creation or destruction of ECUs by setting up mutual lines of credit to forestall ECU transfers until certain limits were exceeded and furthermore by introducing new highly resourceful documentary transfer techniques. From there it was but a short step to the introduction of a multilateral clearing system operating between the market-making banks. As early as 1982, the EC Commission set up a working group comprising commercial banks and the EIB for the purpose of studying the possibility of initiating such a multilateral clearing system. This led to the creation of the ECU Banking Association (EBA) in September 1985. As one of the pillars of the ECU clearing system together with the BIS and the Society for Worldwide International Financial Telecommunication (SWIFT), the EBA replaced the original clearing system between the seven banks in the MESA Group (Mutual ECU Settlement Account).[78]

The structure and operation of the clearing system, which came into force on 1 October 1986, are based on the three institutions mentioned above. As the agent of the clearing banks, the BIS acts as a clearing and settlement centre. It receives deposits in ECUs from the clearing banks and settles the final clearing balances through their two current accounts, a clearing account which is cleared daily and a BIS account which must have a sufficient balance to cover daily clearing operations. The netting centre – the SWIFT – performs the technical aspects of the clearing operations. In practice, the clearing banks are linked directly to a central clearing computer. Operating through the agency of the SWIFT data transmission service, they receive uninterrupted information on ECU payments made between themselves.[79]

At 1:00 p.m. (Brussels time) the current day's operations stop with further transactions being recorded the next day. SWIFT then informs the clearing banks of their provisional balances which they attempt to cover by the usual market transactions - spot, deposit, swap. These, in turn, are channelled into the SWIFT system. SWIFT then calculates the provisional ECU debtor credit position of each clearing bank *vis-à-vis* the others and notifies the banks of their temporary position. At 2:30 p.m. the updated balances are transmitted to the BIS. If a clearing bank's account balance is insufficient, it will borrow the excess ECU balance of another bank on a short-term basis. Since the ECU clearing accounts with the BIS are without interest, this is an incentive for the clearing banks to lend to banks with insufficient accounts rather than hold their ECU balances idle. Such interbank trading of ECU balances on account with the BIS avoids frequent recourse to the component currencies and thus excessive and costly ECU balances with the BIS.[80]

[77] *Ibid.* 2.
[78] J. Siebelt, "Deutsches Devisenrecht 1914, 1958, 1989–Von der Zwangswirtschaft zur ordnungspolitischen Rahmenregelung" in Hahn (ed.) *Geldverfassung und Ordnungspolitik* (Baden-Baden 1989) p. 289.
[79] *Ibid.* 7.
[80] D. Rambure, "The ECU Clearing and Payment System" in R. M. Levich (ed.) *ECU* (London 1987) pp. 35-36.

At 3:00 p.m. the BIS completes account to account settlements, bringing the daily clearing to zero, provided the banks have confirmed the final balances produced by SWIFT and their BIS accounts have the necessary balance. Thus the clearing banks have a certain period of time within which they may settle their accounts by arranging ordinary money market transactions such as loans or arbitrage with the other clearing banks. In order to facilitate compliance with the system, two separate, successive phases of settlement may be noted. In the first phase, the BIS is advised of the final overall situation of each clearing bank after SWIFT has established their final debit or credit position *vis-à-vis* each other and notified them to that effect. In the second phase, final settlements may still be made between the clearing banks by book transfers between their BIS accounts without further intervention by SWIFT.[81]

It should also be noted that the BIS is not exposed to any kind of risk. A bank in default is withdrawn from the clearing before completion. Nor may a foreign exchange risk emerge due to a redefinition of the ECU as the counterparts in component currencies are adjusted accordingly. Moreover, the BIS does not even incur an interest rate exposure because the BIS deposits with the central bank and the bank deposits with the BIS are without interest.

The EBA's initial agreement with the BIS of 21 March 1986, effective since 30 April 1987, has been replaced by another agreement between the two parties.[82] The EBA, which could increase its membership to 30 banks as of 31 March 1988, was established with the general aim of facilitating operations in private ECUs and in particular for the purpose of implementing a clearing and settlement system which would allow every EEC member state to be represented by at least one of its banks. Membership in the association is open to banks which have their head office or a branch in one of the EEC countries and have shown interest in the development of ECU transactions. The clearing banks must satisfy a wide variety of rigorous criteria imposed by both the EBA and the BIS. The activities of the EBA range from studies and research work to representing members in dealings with national, community and international authorities. One of the members of the BEA is the EIB whose representative is a permanent member of the executive committee and one of the association's vice presidents. By the same token, the EIB is one of the clearing banks operating in the system and is currently the largest ECU borrower and lender.[83]

The clearing and payment system for private ECUs was introduced with the consent of EC central banks. Since the BIS was already an agent for the European Monetary Cooperation Fund (EMCF) within the framework of the EMS, the bank asked the EC Central Bank Committee of Governors whether it had any objections to it participating in the clearing system. The reply was affirmative provided the function of agent would not be binding on the BIS alone, the system would take due account of exchange control regulations in force and would not at any time run counter to the monetary objectives of the EEC member states. As a result, the central banks retain complete freedom of action and the clearing system may not function as lender of last resort or influence the money supply.[84]

[81] *BIS, 56th Annual Report* (9 June 1986) pp. 172-173.
[82] *BIS, 58th Annual Report* (13 June 1988) p. 198.
[83] "The Clearing and Payment System for the Private ECU", p. 3.
[84] Rambure, "The ECU Clearing and Payment System", pp. 35-36.

This explains certain techniques and particulars of the system, especially the operation of BIS accounts opened by clearing banks.

The system is meant to be closed. It is designed to have credit operations balance out debts, a scheme which depends on the clearing banks' readiness or ability to settle balances outstanding among themselves. Relevant decisions have to be made exclusively by the clearing banks once their final positions have been established by SWIFT. As was already mentioned, this occurs during the second phase of settlement. Since the BIS may not make any advances while the settlement process is in hand, the clearing banks must always have sufficient liquidity in ECUs to balance their BIS accounts, which may be used for clearing purposes only. All balances in BIS accounts have to be kept in ECUs.[85] The accounts are funded by transfers made by the clearing banks in the respective component currencies. These are drawn on a special account in the BIS's name at the central banks of the member states whose currencies belong to the ECU basket. Conversely, withdrawals from a BIS account are effected by debiting the special account in the BIS's name at the particular central bank and crediting it to the account specified by the clearing bank. Thus central banks will be in a position to guarantee that the money supply is in no way increased by the intermediary of the new system. ECUs are created only when the equivalent of each component currency is remitted to the central bank issuing the particular currency.[86]

IV. The ECU in the Federal Republic of Germany

Notice No. 1010/87 of 16 June 1987 on the assumption of liabilities denominated in ECUs by residents[87] marks a turn in the attitude of the Federal Republic's Central Bank regarding the private use of the ECU, which is now permitted on the same scale as foreign currency. In applying the Currency Act to the ECU, the *Bundesbank* is in effect treating it as a foreign currency. In particular, this means that residents may open ECU accounts at banks in Germany and take out certain ECU loans. Previously, it had been possible to purchase ECU claims against non-residents without restriction.[88] Under the 16 June 1987 regulations, nearly all ECU transactions can now be conducted from Germany as well. By changing its authorization practice, the *Bundesbank* recognized the progress made within the EC in liberalizing capital transactions and the rising importance of the ECU in money and capital transactions as well as in the foreign trade and payments of other EC states. By making the change, Germany emulated those EC members which had already put the ECU on equal footing with a foreign currency or were treating it as such although it lacks the essential characteristics of a currency.[89] In its publication of Notice No. 1010/87 the *Bundesbank* stressed that the enactment concerned the private use of the ECU, thus insisting on its strict distinction from the "official" ECU in the EMS. Moreover, the Federal Republic's Central Bank emphasized that the

[85] *Ibid.*
[86] Lefort, "Problémes juridiques", pp. 403 *et seq.*
[87] English translation in *Deutsche Bundesbank*, p. 37.
[88] "The Markets for Private ECUs", *ibid.* 30.
[89] Gramlich, "The European Currency Unit", 35 *Riv. dir. valutario e economia int.* (1988) pp. 305, 316.

special features of the Act also applied to private ECU purchases by EMS central banks which could not - and cannot - be channelled into official ECU circulation.[90]

The *Bundesbank*'s liberalization of the private use of ECU made it the last EC central bank to adopt that measure. The Community, in particular the Commission, had encouraged the opening of the German market for quite some time. Its initiatives had been supported by other EC member governments, notably Belgium, France and Italy, and the German Federal Government had repeatedly asked the *Bundesbank* to reconsider its strict attitude with a view to introducing a more lenient licensing practice to encourage further liberalization. The special constitutional privilege enjoyed by the Federal Republic's Institute of Issue prevented any direct interference in the rule-making process of the Central Bank Council, the decision-making body of the *Bundesbank*.[91]

Notice No. 1010/87 is the result of an assessment of the practice introduced in 1961 which permitted German resident banks and insurance companies to use foreign currencies in transactions and operations with resident clients.[92] This generous liberalization never threatened the Central Bank's monetary policy. The widespread fear that the German mark would be "crowded out" of the market by one or several foreign currencies proved unfounded, as did the analogous replacement of these currencies by the German mark. ECU operations as well as those of German credit institutions in foreign currencies remain subject to the Central Bank's monetary policy, in particular the requirement relating to minimum reserves and the banking supervision rules laid down and administered by the Federal Banking Supervisory Office (*Bundesaufsichtsamt für das Kreditwesen*).[93]

Powers of the *Bundesbank* to act in matters relating to the private use of ECUs were not derived from a statute on foreign exchange restrictions or controls as they were not deemed to serve the purpose of protecting German economic interests abroad. The only basis for the Central Bank's conduct and practice is a provision of monetary law, i.e., Section 3 of the Currency Act:

"Money obligations incurred in any other currency than Deutsche Mark will become binding only when approved by the office competent for the licensing of foreign exchange operations. The same holds true for debts whose amount expressed in Deutsche Mark is to be determined by the exchange rate of such other currency or the price or quantity of fine gold or of other goods or services."[94]

This provision was revised by Section 49 of the Foreign Commerce Statute which entered into force on 1 September 1961. The revision[95] restricts the scope of the first sentence of Section 3 of the Currency Act to transactions and operations between two or more West German residents. Moreover, Section 49 (2) relegated the power to authorize under the aforementioned clauses to the *Bundesbank*. Section 3 of the Currency Act, especially the first sentence, aimed at preventing the German mark from being replaced by foreign currencies at least in business transactions between

---

[90] "The Markets for Private ECUs", p. 30 n. 4.

[91] Gramlich, "The European Currency Unit", p. 306.

[92] Notice No. 1009/61 (24 August 1961); *Bundesanzeiger* No. 167 (31 August 1961).

[93] "The minimum reserve compensation for ECU liabilities to non-residents refers only to the foreign currency proportion", *Deutsche Bundesbank*, p. 30 n. 2.

[94] English translation in Gramlich, "The European Currency Unit", p. 307.

[95] *Ibid.* 307-308.

German residents, as was the case during the massive inflation of German currency after World War I from 1922 to 1924.[96] The second sentence of Section 3 is of interest today because it is meant to safeguard monetary nominalism often expressed by the equation "mark" equals "mark" which is still considered a fundamental rule of German monetary law and also of the Federal Republic's budget, economic and tax policies. When applying Section 3 (2) of the Currency Act, the *Bundesbank* has followed this doctrine by regarding the ECU first and foremost as an index for calculating the value of the currencies in the basket. With its notice No. 1010/87 of 16 June 1987 the *Bundesbank* did not alter its view that the ECU is such an index and that, as a value clause, it may serve as a potential anti-inflationary measure.[97] Accordingly, the liberalization of private ECU transactions led to a mere approximation of the treatment of foreign currencies. This also explains why the new authorization does not include the assumption of liabilities denominated in ECUs if the value of such liability is to be determined by the future exchange rate of a specific currency, by the future price of gold or by the future price or value of other goods or services. In short, the liberalization of private ECU transactions by the *Bundesbank* emphasizes a change in the authorization practice.[98] However, the cautious attitude of the German Central Bank towards the EMS unit remains intact. A different conclusion would presuppose the abolition of the Currency Act itself.[99]

V. The ECU and the SDR as a Means of Value Maintenance

Value clauses aim at protecting the parties to a transaction from the prevailing doctrine of nominalism which rejects automatic revalorization of the nominal amount to compensate for any reduction in the purchasing power of the particular currency between conclusion and maturity. As a result, the redemptive effect of a monetary disbursement is determined only by its nominal amount, i.e., the amount to be paid equals the originally agreed number of monetary units. With public international law and private law still recognizing extensive freedom of contract and an equally broad autonomy of the parties to determine the contents of their arrangements, protective and compensatory devices safeguarding monetary claims against depreciation due to currency erosion continue to be an obvious defence.[100]

Depending on the territorial scope of the agreement, two kinds of loss factors are involved in the depreciation of monetary claims. In national transactions between residents in the same monetary jurisdiction, the parties may agree or statutory provisions may require that only local currency be used as a standard of value and means of payment (legal tender). Accordingly, monetary liability is subject to a qualitative depreciation equal to the rate of inflation suffered by the particular currency so that the loss of the creditor corresponds to the inflationary gain of the debtor. Economically, this constitutes the purchasing power risk.[101]

[96] See numerous examples cited in Gramlich, *Kommentar*, 3 *Währungsgesetz*, Marginal Nos. 8-57, pp. 344-360.

[97] *Ibid.* Marginal No. 14, 346-347.

[98] *Ibid.* Marginal No. 15, 347-348.

[99] The introductory sentence of the *Deutsche Bundesbank's* Notice No. 1010/87 of 16 June 1987 refers to the Currency Act as its legal basis.

[100] Hahn, "Value Clauses and International Monetary Law", 22 *German Yb. Int'l. L.* (1979) 53-54.

[101] *Ibid.* 55.

Under both public international and private law, at least two currencies are involved in international transactions regardless of whether the standard of value and means of payment are identical or, as in numerous cases, the currency of account and of payment are different. This also holds true when the standard of value and the means of payment are governed by the same law, but the inflationary internal depreciation of that currency affects its exchange rate, for example, when a German claimant converts the amount paid to him in a depreciated foreign currency into German marks. Thus the actual value of a monetary claim is affected notably by the qualitative value of the national currency in the state of the claimant's residence but also by the economic impact of at least one other currency whose exchange rate fluctuates in accordance with the domestic rate of inflation. This is called the exchange rate risk.[102] Both types of monetary depreciation are included in the concept of currency value risk.[103]

One of the major means of allocating the disadvantages arising from risk has always been the inclusion of specific maintenance of value clauses whose usefulness, however, depends on their ability to protect parties to international transactions. Thus, prior to 15 August 1971 when gold was still the standard measurement of currencies and the system of fixed exchange rates was in force, gold was used as a term of reference in value clauses. Yet the undermining of gold as a standard of value and unit of account had begun in 1968 with the splitting of the price of gold in March 1968 when the single gold price was replaced by an official price and a market price. In 1971, the development continued when US dollars could no longer be converted into gold and a number of important national currencies switched to floating exchange rates in 1971 and 1973. The climax came in 1974 when the value of the SDR was no longer determined in terms of gold.[104]

The gradual elimination of the monetary functions of gold made the economic utility of gold value clauses increasingly doubtful even before the definitive discontinuation of the use of gold as a measurement of value under the unequivocal provisions of the Second Amendment to the IMF Articles of Agreement. Nevertheless, it is extremely difficult to specify the precise date on which the utility of gold value clauses had to be denied altogether on elementary grounds of risk avoidance. Similarly, the difficulty of determining the monetary value of gold has been confirmed by a number of recent judicial opinions. Before the official price of gold was legally abandoned, the courts were inclined to rely on it. Although it was no longer applied in practice, it had not been declared invalid. Thereafter, however, pegging the value of gold to its market price became questionable as the market price of gold is not at all stable but experiences considerable fluctuations. Thus, under the present monetary system, gold clauses can no longer be regarded as maintenance of value arrangements but have become speculative covenants.[105]

Before the breakdown of the par value system with its fixed exchange rates, there was a distinction between the concepts of revaluation and devaluation on the one hand, and appreciation and depreciation on the other. This was pointed out in the expert opinions presented during the Young Loan Arbitration as well as in its award

[102] See examples in D. Carreau, "Souveraineté monétaire et utilisation de la monnaie par les opérateurs privés" in Kahn, *Droit et monnaie*, pp. 399-407.
[103] F. Zehetner, *Geldwertklauseln im grenzüberschreitenden Wirtschaftsverkehr* (Tübingen 1976) pp. 1, 27.
[104] Hahn, "Value Clauses and International Monetary Law", pp. 66-67.
[105] *Ibid.* and n. at 67.

rendered on 16 May 1980 by the Arbitral Tribunal for the Agreement on German External Debts. Since the factual and legal situations assessed there occurred between 1961 and 1969,[106] the importance of value clauses was not so great in the then prevailing international context because they had to cope only with the relatively rare events of revaluation or devaluation. In the present situation, however, the need for value clauses is even greater than before. The reciprocal floating of various currencies, together with a general economic situation characterized by different inflation rates in various countries has given rise to frequent fluctuations in the relative values of the main currencies, thus increasing the risk of resorting to one national currency as the unit of account for international transactions.[107]

In particular, it seems important to distinguish between the effects of the exchange rate risk and those of the purchasing power risk of each currency in terms of goods and services. At this point it should be emphasized that a combination of currency clauses, in particular ECU and SDR clauses, are not "real value" clauses. Instead of eliminating the effects of the principle of nominalism by referring to non-monetary values, these clauses alleviate them by dividing the inherent risk among various currencies. Whereas these clauses reduce the risk arising from different inflation rates in various countries, they can do relatively little to alleviate the risk inherent in the general loss of purchasing power of various currencies as a result of the inflationary trend prevailing in the particular country. With these observations in mind, parties should resort to clauses which express the amounts due in monetary units consisting of a combination of currencies.[108] Of the various combinations of currency clauses, it seems most advisable to use those managed by established international institutions such as the SDR of the IMF and the ECU of the EC and EMS. Preference is given to units such as the SDR and the ECU for at least two reasons. First of all, they are widely known, and, furthermore, their value in terms of national currencies is calculated and published on a daily basis by the respective international organizations. The privileged position of official units of account can be attributed in particular to the fact that ECUs and SDRs are likely to produce an equitable allocation of inflationary losses between creditor and debtor as a result of their typical exchange rate maintenance effects. Moreover, the risk-scattering effect inherent in their structure should by and large exclude the possibility of a "windfall profit".[109]

The tendency to use SDR clauses in intergovernmental agreements, notably multilateral conventions such as the constitutive instruments of international organizations and their legal enactments continues to prevail. The IMF unit of account is used to a lesser extent in private law transactions of an international character. Like the SDR, the ECU was created under the aegis of the entity of which it is still the official denominator, i.e., the EC. Accordingly, the EC's budget and whatever financial operations are required for its administration as well as for agreements with states and enterprises which receive financial support from the

---

[106] "Arbitral Tribunal and Mixed Commission for the Agreement on German External Debts", *Reports of Decisions and Advisory Opinions* (Koblenz 1980) pp. 22-23.

[107] Hahn, "Value Clauses and International Monetary Law", p. 57.

[108] *Ibid.* 69-70.

[109] International Law Association, *Report of the 57th Conference, Madrid 1976*, Report by Committee on International Monetary Law, p. 69.

Community are denominated in ECUs. The number of ECU clauses in border-crossing private law transactions continues to rise and has probably surpassed the number of arrangements of that nature based on the SDR. If bank claims and liabilities in ECUs and ECU bonds are taken together, the percentage of ECU private law arrangements is sizable indeed and has to be recognized as an ever-present element in investments, as a borrowing medium and as a means of settling monetary obligations.[110]

When resorting to ECUs and SDRs, the parties should be aware of the possibility that these units of account could perhaps cease to exist some day. Whereas this is rather unlikely, the fact that the respective definitions of these units of account are subject to change by the institutions which manage them should not be overlooked. For example, various SDR clauses in international instruments take account of the possibility of changes in the definition of the SDR by making reference to "variable" or "frozen" SDRs or to such variants as the "modifiable SDR" or the "optional SDR". The most frequent practice is to use variable SDRs which acknowledge the amending powers of the IMF without restriction. The preference for these SDRs results from the organization's permanent control over the units, thus enabling parties to contact the Fund to determine the value of the SDR at any time in its existence.[111] Where parties place particular emphasis on maintaining the monetary value of the SDR at the time of the conclusion of the contract, they may prevent any changes that the Fund may introduce by "freezing" the composition in force on that particular date or at least by excluding specific modifications of basket structure or basket content. In due course SDRs outside the Fund's jurisdiction may represent another economic value than that of the variable SDRs after amendment of the law of the IMF. In such a case, the parties will no longer be in a position to refer to the calculations of the Fund but will have to establish the monetary value of the contractual unit of account themselves or entrust the task to another authority. This potential cost factor should be taken into account as an additional expenditure when negotiating the contract. Apart from such economic consequences, "frozen" units of account presuppose that the contract contains substantive or procedural safeguards which, in case of a deviation from the official basket formula, would guarantee that the actual value of the invariable unit could be established.[112]

Since the introduction of the private ECU, the EEC Commission has successfully encouraged the general use of what is known as the "open" ECU basket. As a result of this market practice, any changes made in the ECU definition at official level are automatically and directly reflected in private ECU agreements. Incentives to this effect have been provided by EC governments in countries where access to foreign currency assets and foreign currency loans is restricted by controls on capital movements. In the context of such controls, the ECU has at times enjoyed preferential treatment as an investment or borrowing medium since it is always defined at any given time at official level. This has led to an increase in the private use of ECUs. For instance, ECU bonds issued by European institutions in the French market were exempt from the foreign exchange control in securities transactions

---

[110] International Law Association, *Report of the 60th Conference, Montreal 1982*, Report by Committee on International Monetary Law, p. 239 *et seq.*

[111] Edwards, *International Monetary Collaboration*, pp. 174 *et seq.*, pp. 320 *et seq.*

[112] Reports by Committee on International Monetary Law (see *supra*, nn. 109 and 110).

(*devise titre system*) which was in force until May 1986.[113] Thus French investors could invest in foreign currencies at the official exchange rate by buying such bonds. Similarly, certain ECU bonds enjoyed preferential treatment under the Italian cash deposit requirement for foreign currency investment which was abolished in May 1987. With the increasing liberalization of capital transactions within the EEC, such special regulations have become obsolete. At the time, however, they made the ECU more attractive than it would have been under conditions of completely liberalized capital movements.[114]

This assessment of the SDR and the ECU as maintenance of value devices should encourage parties to use them as protective clauses in private law transactions and in bilateral and multilateral agreements subject to public international law. The related question of how the maintenance of value devices such as gold clauses has been adapted since the advent of the SDR and the ECU will be dealt with in another case study.

[113] Notice of the *Deutsche Bundesbank* (*supra* n.99) p. 32 n.6.
[114] *Ibid.* See tables (pp. 32-36).

2

Adapting Restructuring and Loan Agreements to New International Debt Management Strategies

Andre W. G. Newburg*

There has been a growing disenchantment, in debtor countries as well as on the part of bank lenders, with the debt restructuring strategy used in recent years in attempts to deal with the international debt crisis. Contrary to earlier expectations, credit flows to the debtor countries have not normalized; instead, the debtor countries' high interest burden has resulted in net capital outflows, the exportation of capital from countries that can ill afford them. In 1985, the year the "Baker plan" was proposed, the net flow of resources from debtors to creditors was $27 billion; in 1988 it was $30 billion.[1] Over the same period, economic austerity programmes reduced growth rates and purchasing power to politically dangerous levels.

The need for initiatives leading toward new debt management strategies has become evident, and some important steps in that direction have already been taken. Several major debtor countries have introduced various types of debt reduction measures. Recently, in a major shift of United States policy, U.S. Secretary of the Treasury Nicholas Brady proposed a new strategy, known as the "Brady Plan", aimed at voluntary debt reduction. The plan has the support of both the IMF and the World Bank.[2]

This Chapter will consider some of these developments and their effect on the legal relationships created by typical transnational debt restructuring and loan agreements. In particular, it will examine why Secretary Brady singled out certain provisions of such agreements, the so-called "sharing", "mandatory prepayment" and "negative pledge" clauses, as constituting substantial barriers to debt reduction,

*The author gratefully acknowledges the assistance of his colleagues, Lee C. Buchheit and Michael Glazer.
[1] "Of Debt and Democracy", *The Economist* (11 February 1989), p. 11.
[2] "IMF Debt Guidelines 'Focus on Burden Cuts'", *Financial Times* (26 May 1989), p. 3, col. 4; "World Bank Sets Rules for Role in Debt Strategy", *Wall Street Journal* (2 June 1989), p. A12, col. 6.

International Contracts and Payments (Šarčević, Volken, eds.; 1 85333 615 7; © Graham & Trotman, 1991; pub. Graham & Trotman; printed in Great Britain), pp. 25-32.

and will consider how restructuring agreements might be amended, and future loan agreements might be written, to take into account the need for eventual debt reduction measures.

I. Brief Historical Background

Students of the history of international lending have identified a series of boom-and-bust cycles since the beginning of the 19th century which indicate that periods of boom lending followed by default and restructuring have become a normal pattern.[3] However, while today most non-governmental creditors are commercial banks, in the past international development and balance of payments loans generally took the form of publicly issued bonds. The London financial market provided capital to developing countries (including the United States) to build railways and other major works and to balance government accounts. Merchant banks, primarily British, placed the bond issues and mediated between the large groups of bondholders (frequently represented by the British Council of Foreign Bondholders) and developing country borrowers.

When default threatened, the merchant bankers stepped in to provide bridge loans or to supervise workouts. The terms of the workouts sometimes involved significant reductions of the debt, or reduced interest rates, or both. In some cases, bondholders were assigned state revenues necessary to service the debts. In 1889, in one of the most extreme such cases, Peru in settlement of its external debt ceded the Peruvian state railways for 66 years, assigned a large share of its guano deposits, guaranteed a subsidy from customs revenues and granted five million acres of land.[4] Today, this kind of workout clearly would encounter understandable political difficulties.

II. Today's Debt Crisis

The economic circumstances that led to the current debt crisis are well known: the recycling of petrodollars in the mid- and late 1970s, cheap lending by commercial banks, the second oil shock of 1979, followed by recession, decline in oil prices and extremely high real interest rates in the early 1980s.[5] Financial innovation also played a role. The rapid growth in commercial bank lending of the 1970s was in large part facilitated by refinements in Euromarket lending practices, in particular the perfection of international loan syndication and the institution of floating interest rates, which reduced credit and market risks for individual banks. Syndicated lending made it possible for a large number of banks from different parts of the world to participate in a large loan negotiated by one or a few "lead

[3] It was on the basis of this historical record that a former president of the Bank of International Settlements is said to have remarked that "it was better to have loaned and lost than never to have loaned at all". See C. P. Kindleberger, "Debt Situation of the Developing Countries in Historical Perspective", Export-Import Bank Symposium, 21 April 1977.

[4] A. Fishlow, "Lessons from the Past: Capital Markets during the 19th Century and the Interwar Period", Int'l Organization (Summer 1985) pp. 36, 68.

[5] See e.g. K. B. Dillon, C. M. Watson, G. R. Kincaid, and C. Puckahtikom, "Recent Development in External Debt Restructuring", IMF Occasional Paper No. 40 (October 1985), pp. 5-9.

managers". Floating interest rates, based on the London Eurocurrency market, and the matching deposit technique, made it possible for banks to lend on a net "spread" basis, thereby avoiding interest rate risk.

The current debt crisis was unveiled in August of 1982 when Mexico announced that it could no longer service its external debts. During the fall of 1982, Argentina and Brazil also fell into arrears on principal payments. By the end of 1983, about 30 debtor countries were unable to pay their external debts and had initiated restructuring negotiations with bank creditors and official lenders.[6]

III. Debt Restructuring Procedures

One reason why the international debt problem has proved so intractable is that there are no settled international norms or procedures for dealing with state insolvency, the circumstance that arises when a state is unable to meet the foreign currency obligations that it and its public or private sector enterprises have incurred. In contrast to bankruptcy in municipal law, which provides procedures for arrangements and compositions with creditors and under which judicially approved creditor plans can be imposed on dissident creditors, country debt restructuring schemes with commercial bank syndicates require unanimity and cannot be imposed on dissenting creditors. Each round of debt restructuring for each debtor country has thus required difficult and protracted negotiations involving a wide array of lenders, including official creditors and virtually every bank in the world active in international financial markets, no matter how small its size or exposure.

Although each country's restructuring proceeded independently on a case-by-case basis, the negotiations between major debtor countries and their bank creditors initially produced generally similar solutions. The principal elements of these solutions were: (a) new IMF credits conditioned on meeting the economic performance criteria of an IMF stabilization and adjustment programme; (b) rescheduling of principal maturities, with interest payments to stay current; (c) trade and interbank credit lines to be maintained at fixed levels; and (d) limited amounts of new money from commercial bank creditors in order to maintain interest payments, thus preserving the appearance of continued debt service.

The initial reaction of commercial bank creditors was to demand higher "spreads" in order to compensate for what they viewed as an increased credit risk. This added to the debtors' burden, contrary to the usual practice in a domestic workout situation. More recently, some debtor countries have achieved lower margins, but this has had little effect on the amount of their interest payments.

IV. The Principle of Identical Treatment of Creditors

The documentary result of the restructuring of commercial bank debt has been voluminous agreements that in each case govern not only relations between the debtor country and its public (and, in some instances, private) sector enterprises, on the one hand, and a large number of commercial banks, on the other, but also

[6] Ibid.14.

relations among the bank creditors. In order to achieve unanimous bank participation, it was thought necessary to assure the banks that all similarly situated creditors would be treated substantially in the same manner. Most important, no bank was to be paid out, in whole or in part, before any other bank. Thus, loans of all banks were rescheduled over the same period, received the same interest, and were subject to new money calls *pro rata* to existing exposures.

The borrowers' assurances that each class of external creditors would be treated substantially identically was generally effective in dissuading individual banks from taking legal action to enforce their claims. By promising identical treatment, debtor governments were able to buy time to deal with a large and diverse number of creditors. As long as each bank was convinced that no other creditor would profit at its expense, it was willing to refrain from individual action.

Such self-restraint by individual creditors had the same practical effect as the "automatic stay" or "standstill" which in municipal law protects a debtor during a bankruptcy proceeding. In debt restructuring agreements, this result is sought to be ensured by various contractual provisions, in particular the "sharing", "mandatory prepayment" and "negative pledge" clauses.

V. Clauses Implementing the Identical Treatment Principle

The sharing clause is a provision in a loan agreement by which each bank agrees to share with all other banks that are parties to the same agreement any disproportionate payments that it may receive from the debtor. The principal objective is to avoid a situation in which one bank is preferred over another by being repaid in whole or in part while amounts owed other banks under the same agreement remain outstanding. One consequence of such a clause is that there is little advantage for a single creditor to take individual action to enforce its claim. The benefits of suing the debtor or exercising a right of setoff against the debtor's assets are largely diluted if any resulting recoveries are subject to sharing with the other lenders under the agreement.

A mandatory prepayment clause binds a debtor to make a ratable repayment of debt covered by a loan agreement if any portion of the debtor's outstanding debt, whether incurred under that agreement or not, is repaid prior to its scheduled maturity dates. This provision supplements the sharing clause, all by seeking to equalize the payment position of creditors under one agreement with all other lenders.

A negative pledge clause is intended to assure identical treatment of creditors by preventing the debtor from favouring certain creditors by granting them security interests in the debtor's property. The objective is to restrict the debtor from pledging its assets or revenues in a manner that would make them unavailable to satisfy claims of unsecured lenders. Such clauses typically provide that if any present or future debt is secured by assets or revenues of the debtor, the debt protected by the negative pledge clause must be similarly secured.

VI. Introduction of New Debt Reduction Techniques

In a corporate workout, one frequently sees the substitution of one type of debt for new, less burdensome debt with a lower interest rate or reduced principal amount, or for subordinated debt or equity, or a combination of new debt obligations and equity. Creditors accept such exchanges either as part of a judicially supervised proceeding or in implementation of an agreement with other creditors. Debtor countries have begun to use similar techniques to reduce outstanding bank debt: the cash buyback, debt/equity conversion and debt-for-debt exchange.

The new debt reduction techniques have been spawned by the realization that the original restructuring process has not worked. The rescheduling plus new money approach was thought to be a way of solving a "temporary liquidity crisis" and of fostering conditions that would enable debtors to return to voluntary capital markets. It has become evident that this approach has merely postponed the problem. As a result, both debtor nations and their creditors have recognized the need to return to the concept of burden sharing, with workouts analogous to those normally practiced in the private sector and to the international debt restructurings of the 19th century. It now appears likely that commercial bank creditors, like many bondholders in the 19th century, will be shouldering their part in the workout burden by voluntarily writing down their credits or exchanging them for new securities that reduce the debtor country's debt service burden.

The groundwork for various debt reduction techniques has been laid by the development of a secondary market in restructured credits, supplied by banks wishing to eliminate small participations, to rebalance portfolios or to dispose of written-down credits. Turnover in 1988 has been estimated to have amounted to as much as $40 billion, a sharp increase over the $15 to $20 billion estimated to have changed hands in 1987.[7]

This secondary market is not a trading market in the usual sense, as each transaction is separately negotiated, often through intermediaries. Trading volume differs significantly from credit to credit, and transactions in the obligations of some countries are rare. Nevertheless, for many countries, the secondary market has tended to establish "market" values reflecting the discount at which at least some banks are willing to sell their claims. During February of 1989, for example, Argentine debt sold at about 15 cents on the dollar, down from 65 cents in February of 1987, while Uruguayan debt sold at 59.5 cents, down from 71 cents in February 1987.[8]

All of the voluntary debt reduction techniques that have been used or proposed are designed to "capture", for the benefit of the debtor, at least a substantial portion of this discount by purchasing or exchanging outstanding debt for cash or new securities at a price approximating the "market" value of the outstanding debt.

VII. Current Debt Reduction Techniques

Debtor countries have used several techniques in the last few years to reduce their debt burden. One method a number of countries have adopted has been the conversion of external debt into local currency instruments which can be used to

---

[7] J. H. Fidler, "Busy Year for LDC Debt Trading", *Financial Times* (11 January 1989), p. 28, col. 5.

[8] U.S. Department of the Treasury, *Interim Report to the Congress concerning International Discussions on an International Debt Management Authority* (13 March 1989) (citing Salomon Brothers Inc. statistics); "Argentine Debt Falls to 15% of Face Value", *J. of Commerce* (16 May 1989), p. 70, col. 3.

make equity investments.[9] In a typical debt-for-equity exchange, a prospective investor buys a restructured credit in the secondary market at a discount, receives local currency in exchange from the central bank of the debtor country, and invests the local currency in a local business venture. In theory, everyone benefits: the foreign investor obtains the local currency at a favourable rate reflecting the discount at which he bought the loan; the local business receives an infusion of new equity capital; the original creditor receives cash for a loan that otherwise might not have been paid for many years; and the debtor country has reduced its aggregate stock of external debt, encouraged foreign investment in a domestic industry and removed a possibly troublesome member of the creditor group.

Debtor countries, as well as their private sector enterprises, have used cash purchases of their own debt as another method of reducing their debt burden. In the fall of 1988, for example, Chile purchased with foreign currency $291 million dollars of its restructured debt at a maximum price of 57.5%. In addition, several Chilean companies have conducted buyback programmes using local currency that have substantially reduced their external indebtedness. A buyback of debt for foreign currency permits a debtor nation to use current resources to reduce future debt service and to capture at least a portion of the market discount of its debt. Buybacks that use local currency have the further advantage of not requiring the expenditure of scarce foreign exchange reserves.

Debt for debt exchanges are a third debt reduction technique debtor countries have utilized. In 1988, Mexico offered to exchange, on a voluntary basis, government and public sector debt, which then traded for about 50 cents on the dollar, for a new issue of Mexican 20-year bonds bearing floating rate interest at a higher spread than was payable on the existing debts.[10] The principal amount of the bonds at maturity was collateralized by a special issue of U.S. Treasury zero coupon obligations, with a matching principal amount of maturity, purchased by Mexico with its foreign exchange reserves. Mexico's bank creditors were asked to make bids to exchange all or a portion of their existing debt, indicating the amount of discount they were willing to accept.

Through this debt for debt exchange, Mexico retired $3.6 billion of existing debt, obtaining a discount of about 30%. Mexico thereby not only decreased the face amount of its outstanding external debt, but also reduced its annual interest burden, even taking into account the foregone interest on the Mexican foreign exchange reserves used to buy the U.S. Treasury obligations and the higher rate of interest on the new bonds. For Mexico's bank creditors, the new bonds have the advantage, in addition to liquidity, of being excluded from new money calls and, as has become customary for publicly held obligations, from future restructuring.

These methods of sovereign debt reduction clearly do not in themselves suffice to resolve the debt crisis. The large-scale application of debt for equity exchanges would, for example, raise serious political problems in many Latin American countries which seek to limit the percentage of direct foreign investment. This concern has impeded debt-equity swap programs in Brazil and Mexico. Debt for equity exchanges can also present economic problems for the debtor country since

[9] Int'l Bank for Reconstruction and Development, *World Debt Tables* (Washington, DC, 1988), pp. xxi-xxii.

[10] Ibid. p. xxii.

the conversion of a government's foreign obligations into local currency may have an inflationary effect. Nevertheless, these techniques represent some of the best hopes for reducing in some measure the magnitude of the debt problem.

VIII. Obstacles to Voluntary Debt Reduction Techniques

An essential condition for voluntary debt reduction transactions is that each creditor be free to accept or reject (in the light of its circumstances) an offer to purchase or exchange the debt held by it. The principle of identical treatment of creditors imposed by certain clauses of restructuring agreements may not, however, permit such individual action.

The mandatory prepayment and sharing provisions were designed to prevent debtors from repurchasing their debt from some creditors and not others, or on terms that differ between creditors, in most cases even if the purchases are made without use of foreign exchange. The original restructuring agreements when drafted did not, for example, anticipate that an individual bank might be prepared to exchange its credits for payment in the debtor's currency or for a new security. The mandatory prepayment and sharing clauses of many agreements may apply to such exchanges or, at best, do not clearly exempt such transactions. Negative pledge clauses may also present a major obstacle since they ordinarily preclude collateralizing new debt, which may be the only way in which the debtor can structure a new debt instrument for which creditors will be willing to exchange outstanding debt.[11]

To make possible the implementation of voluntary debt reduction, contractual rules requiring identical treatment of creditors should be replaced by provisions that will permit debt reduction measures on condition that all creditors are given an equal opportunity to participate. In a number of instances this has already been done, either through case-by-case waivers or by amendment of restructuring agreements so as to permit certain categories of voluntary debt reduction transactions.

Before Mexico was able to effect the exchange of its debt for new collateralized bonds, it had to obtain from its creditors waivers of the negative pledge covenant contained in its restructuring agreements.[12] Amendments made in 1988 to the Chilean restructuring agreements excepted various types of debt reduction transactions, including certain debt repurchases and debt for debt exchanges, from mandatory prepayment and sharing. These amendments also modified the restructuring agreements' negative pledge clauses so as to permit exchanges of

---

[11] A relatively recent example of the invocation of a negative pledge to prevent a debtor from granting security to new lenders is *Citibank, N.A.* v. *Export-Import Bank of the U.S.*, No. 76 Civ. 3514 (S.D.N.Y. filed 9 Aug. 1976). In this case, which was settled before trial, Citibank brought suit when the Republic of Zaire proposed to deposit certain export proceeds in a special account for the benefit of new lenders.

[12] Negative pledge covenants are also contained in certain publicly held Mexican external bond issues, of which about $500 million was outstanding at the time of the debt for debt exchange. These have been excluded from restructuring and have continued to be serviced. Since it was impracticable to obtain waivers from the bondholders, Mexico complied with the "equal and ratable" security requirement of these negative pledge covenants by also securing the principal of the outstanding bonds by U.S. Treasury obligations.

restructured credits for secured debt, and the incurrence of certain types of new secured debt. Provisions designed to ensure that all affected creditors have the opportunity to participate in a debt reduction transaction were included and global ceilings were placed on the total amount of certain transactions.

Secretary Brady in effect proposed adoption of the equal opportunity principle when, as one element of his plan, he called on creditor banks to waive for a limited period the application of contractual provisions that may constitute barriers to debt reduction transactions. This waiver proposal would have been a useful first step in the implementation of the equal opportunity principle, but in view of the resistance of some creditors it now appears unlikely to be accepted. The fate of Secretary. Brady's proposal points up the difficulties that may be encountered whenever waivers from individual creditors are required. The waiver process not only is time consuming, but often can be blocked by a few recalcitrant creditors. To avoid such delay and uncertainty, restructuring agreements should be amended to establish more automatic processes based on the equal opportunity principle: sharing, mandatory prepayment and negative pledge provisions should not apply to specified types of debt reduction transactions offered on equal terms to all creditors.

As a policy matter, creditors should not in principle find these modifications objectionable. Such debt reduction transactions would allow creditors to invest in the debtor country at low cost, to reduce country risk or to trade up to more secure investments. In addition, reduction of a debtor country's external debt benefits creditors that elect not to participate in a debt reduction programme. Even if the transaction requires expenditure of foreign exchange reserves, it will reduce external debt service payments over the longer term and improve the debtor's financial condition, thereby enhancing the likelihood that the remaining creditors will be satisfied.

In general, both debtors and creditors should also consider incorporating the equality of opportunity principle in loan agreements. This has already been done in a number of "new money" and co-financing agreements documenting new loans made as part of the restructuring process. There may be merit in adopting such an approach even in loans to debtors that have no current debt servicing difficulties. By establishing in advance procedures by which debt reduction could be effected on an equitable basis, costly and possibly contentious negotiations could be avoided in case a restructuring eventually becomes necessary.

3

The Draft UNCITRAL Model Law on International Credit Transfers

Eric Bergsten*

The mandate given by the United Nations Commission on International Trade Law (UNCITRAL) in 1986 for its newest venture in the field of international payments was to prepare a set of Model Rules on Electronic Funds Transfers.[1] In 1988 the title of the project was changed by the Commission's Working Group on International Payments, to which the project had been assigned by the Commission, to the UNCITRAL Model Law on International Credit Transfers.[2] The change in title was the result of a greater understanding by the Working Group of the effect that the introduction of electronic techniques into the banking process is having on the appropriate legal rules governing interbank funds transfers.

I. The Banking Environment

There are only two fundamental means by which any interbank funds transfer can be initiated and processed. The first is that the transferor of the funds instructs his bank to debit his account and to credit, or to cause to be credited at another bank, the account of the transferee of the funds. In those countries where that procedure is the basic means of making funds transfers, it is commonly known as a *virement* or a *giro*. In the work of UNCITRAL it goes by the name of a credit transfer. The second possible means of making a funds transfer is that the transferee of the funds instructs his bank to credit his account and to debit, or to cause to be debited at another bank, the account of the transferor of the funds. That procedure, which is known in the work of UNCITRAL as a debit transfer, is the procedure followed when a cheque or a bill of exchange is collected.

---

*The views expressed in this article are those of the author and do not necessarily represent the views of the United Nations.

[1] Report of the United Nations Commission on International Trade Law on the Work of its Nineteenth Session, A/41/17, para. 230.

[2] A/CN.9/328, para. 19.

International Contracts and Payments (Šarčević, Volken, eds.; 1 85333 615 7; © Graham & Trotman, 1991; pub. Graham & Trotman; printed in Great Britain), pp. 33-50.

Those two fundamental means of making funds transfers permit, of a number of variations of greater or lesser importance, for the conduct of banking operations, for governmental monetary policy and for the development of appropriate legal rules. In the past the fact that there were a number of variations on the two fundamental means of making funds transfers has led to the development of separate sets of legal rules that seemed to reflect different economic and banking realities. However, the new electronic environment has led to a re-examination of the banking practices involved as well as the appropriate legal rules governing those practices. The result has been the recognition that all forms of funds transfer exhibit certain fundamental similarities, but that there are important differences between debit transfers and credit transfers that make it difficult to prepare a single legal text that regulates both in a comprehensive manner.

A funds transfer rests on the proposition that credit in an account with a bank has a monetary value equivalent to the same amount in the form of cash. The amount of value represented by the credit is increased by crediting the account and decreased by debiting it. Therefore, value can be shifted from one account to another by debiting the account from which value is to flow and crediting the account to which value is to flow. All of this is based on the elementary principles of bookkeeping.

The transferor and the transferee of the funds are usually thought of as being individual or commercial customers of a bank, and indeed they often are. However, the transferor or the transferee, or both, may just as well be a bank transferring or receiving funds for its own purposes. In either case, the transferor of the funds in the case of a credit transfer or the transferee of the funds in the case of a debit transfer must transmit an appropriate instruction to its bank. The instruction may be transmitted to the bank by the manual handing over of paper, magnetic tapes or other similar computer-readable data support, or by telex, on-line computer link or telephone.

When the accounts of the transferor of the funds and of the transferee of the funds are at the same bank, there is no intrinsic reason for the internal processes of the bank to differ whether the transfer is a debit transfer, because the transferee began the banking process, or a credit transfer, because the transferor began the banking process. In either case the final result is a debit and a credit to the same two accounts at the bank. Differences in procedure at a given bank between the two types of transfer would arise only because it was administratively convenient to batch process all the payment instructions of a given type at the same time. Similarly, while debit and credit transfers are subject to different legal rules even when the transfer is to be effected at one bank, there is little difference in the practical effect of those rules in a one-bank funds transfer.

When the accounts of the transferor and the transferee are at different banks, the banking processes are quite different for debit transfers and for credit transfers. In both cases an instruction must be sent from one bank to the next indicating which accounts are to be debited and credited and for what amount. There must also be a means for the bank transferring funds to pay the amount of the transfer to the receiving bank. In the case of a credit transfer, the information and the funds move in the same direction from the transferor's bank to the transferee's bank. In the case of a debit transfer, the information moves from the transferee's bank to the transferor's bank while the funds move from the transferor's bank to the transferee's bank. From that fundamental difference between debit transfers and credit transfers flow many consequences that explain why it has been so difficult to conceive of a set of legal rules that could encompass both.

It appears that until recently in every country the traditional domestic funds transfer system has concentrated on either credit transfers, under the name of *giro* or *virement*, or on debit transfers based on the collection of cheques. In only a few countries, such as France, were both systems in widespread use. Even in those countries it is striking to see the extent to which one or the other system was dominant. In particular, the law as taught and as written about in the standard texts usually treated the secondary method of making payments as being of comparatively little significance or interest. From the viewpoint of the typical student of the law of funds transfers, the secondary method usually might as well not have existed.

Nevertheless, in all countries there has been an awareness of both means of making funds transfers, because both methods have been in use internationally for a long time. Debit transfers have been common as international cheques and bills of exchange have been collected and a certain number of credit transfers have been made by written payment order, by telegram and by telex.

Some aspects of the law of debit transfers have been relatively uniform throughout large parts of the world. Since the use of bills of exchange originated as a result of the need to make international transfers, the law in all countries was originally relatively uniform and throughout the years it has retained much of that earlier uniformity. Furthermore, the law of negotiable instruments was one of the traditional fields for international unification efforts. Those efforts culminated in the civil law world in the Geneva Conventions of 1930 and 1931.[3] Similar efforts were not necessary in the common law world because substantial uniformity of the law existed as a result of the almost universal adoption of the English Bills of Exchange Act, 1882 in more or less pure form.[4] Worldwide unification of the law of negotiable instruments for international use is now possible with the adoption by the General Assembly of the United Nations in 1988 of the United Nations Convention on International Bills of Exchange and International Promissory Notes.[5]

However, unification of the law of negotiable instruments is not the same as unification of the law of debit transfers. The law of bills of exchange, promissory notes and cheques is the law governing the instrument, the rights and obligations of the parties to the instrument and the transfer of the instrument. It does not as such cover the collection of an instrument through the banking system. To be sure, the collection of an instrument through the banking system is affected by, and in turn affects, the law governing the transfer of the instrument. However, with the notable exception of Article 4 of the Uniform Commercial Code in the United States, relating to both clean and documentary collections, and of the Uniform Rules on

---

[3] Convention Providing a Uniform Law for Bills of Exchange and Promissory Notes (Geneva, 7 June 1930); Convention Providing a Uniform Law for Cheques (Geneva, 19 March 1931).

[4] The major exception is the United States. However, the Uniform Negotiable Instruments Law of 1896 was closely modelled on the Bills of Exchange Act. The NIL was replaced by Article 3 of the Uniform Commercial Code, which departed somewhat more from the Bills of Exchange Act in substance and considerably more in presentation.

[5] Adopted by resolution 43/166 of 9 December 1988. Canada signed the Convention on 7 December 1989, being the first to do so. The Convention was also prepared by UNITRAL. See E. Bergsten, *The United Nations Convention on International Bills of Exchange and International Promissory Notes*, p. xxx.

Collection prepared by the International Chamber of Commerce, relating only to documentary collections,[6] the law of the collection of negotiable instruments, i.e. the actual funds transfer process, is an uncodified and non-uniform law.

Similarly the law governing credit transfers is uncodified and far from uniform. While the particular mix of the sources of the law differs from one country to another, it consists of the application of the general principles of law, perhaps a few statutory provisions covering certain specific problems, contractual provisions, including general conditions of banks, and court decisions applying those different primary sources. As might be expected, it is difficult to learn, much less to understand, the precise nature of the legal rules in any country other than one's own. While that situation is far from unique to the law of credit transfers, it is of potentially greater importance in this field than in most others. International credit transfers by their nature are subject to the law of two or more states. Nevertheless, international as well as domestic credit transfers are expected to be processed with a minimum of individual attention so that the processing can be rapid and inexpensive. Any misunderstandings as to the relevant banking procedures and applicable legal rules will be a source of error, delay and expense.

II. Electronics and the New Funds Transfer Techniques

The use of electronics has no impact on the fundamental procedures by which funds transfers are made. An interbank funds transfer continues to be made by the entry of a debit to the account of the transferor of the funds and a credit to the account of the transferee of the funds. If the transferor's account and the transferee's account are in different banks, there must be a means to transfer the information and the funds between the two banks. The information and the funds continue to flow in the same direction in the case of a credit transfer and in opposite directions in the case of a debit transfer. Therefore, the accumulated heritage of legal rules governing both credit and debit transfers continues to be applicable and, more to the point, in many cases those rules continue to be appropriate. However, the use of electronics coupled with other developments in the banking system has made it necessary to reconsider the substance of the applicable legal rules and to consider the extent to which it may be necessary to unify internationally the rules governing at least the more important issues that arise.

The past forty years has seen a vast increase in the number and monetary value of both domestic and international funds transfers. That increase is the consequence of successful efforts by banks to encourage individuals to maintain current accounts, the growth in the world's economy, its international integration and the increase in the volume of financial flows as distinguished from transfers to pay commercial obligations. While most of those factors began to have their influence before electronics and computers were a significant factor in the banks, it was possible for them to reach their current magnitude only by the use of electronics and computers.

To greatly over-simplify for the purposes of analysis, banks use computers in the funds transfer process to achieve two different kinds of results. On the one hand, computers permit the processing of large volumes of transfers at a lower cost than the

---

[6] ICC Publication, No. 322.

processing of paper-based funds transfers. That use of computers is exemplified by the batch processing of transfers recorded on magnetic tape or on a similar device. It is of particular value when customers prepare the magnetic tapes themselves for such purposes as paying salaries or pensions directly to the bank accounts of the recipients. Batch transfers between banks may be made by the physical exchange of the tapes, either directly between the banks concerned or through a clearing house that receives tapes from multiple sources, sorts the transfers by destination and prepares new tapes for the receiving banks. Batch transfers may also be made by telecommunications, and such transfers are often made at night or other times of low utilization of the telecommunications facilities.

Since batch processing is done periodically rather than continuously, it is generally assumed that batch processed transfers are by their nature of small value and that they are not time sensitive. While that may describe the vast majority of such transfers, it cannot be said that it describes their nature. Transfers for the purpose of meeting a payroll may be highly time sensitive, and there is nothing to prevent large transfers from being made through batch systems. What is required to make them cost effective is planning the transfers in advance of the need to process them.

On the other hand, the linking of computers so as to permit data transfer by telecommunications permits the rapid transfer of funds transfer instructions.[7] That is of particular importance for time sensitive and high value funds transfers that cannot be planned in advance. At the simplest level, on-line data transfer is but an extension of telex. Individual free-form messages sent by data transfer must still be read by humans and they must be acted upon individually. The primary benefits of data transfer are realized when payment orders and other messages passing over the funds transfer telecommunications networks are standardized, thus permitting the automation of both the inputting of payment orders and the processing of payment orders received.[8] The result has been that the time and cost of sending and processing individual payment orders has been drastically reduced. The increase in the message handling capacity of the banks has led them to offer services to their customers, such as cash consolidation, that were unthinkable only a few years ago. Since the introduction of each new service in turn creates the need for additional

---

[7] The terminology to describe computer-to-computer messaging is constantly evolving. For commercial purposes generally, the currently accepted term is "electronic data interchange", or EDI. In this chapter the term "data transfer" will generally be used.

[8] The principal standardization of international payment orders has been achieved by SWIFT. Its formats have been used by the Banking and Related Financial Institutions Committee of the International Organization for Standardization (ISO) in preparation of standard telex payment orders, ISO 7746, and the draft standard payment orders by data transfer, DP 7982-2. Those standard messages have been developed within the industry-specific environment of banking. A concurrent effort has been undertaken within the Economic Commission for Europe of the United Nations to develop a format for non-industry-specific standard commercial messages of all types. That effort, which goes by the name of EDIFACT, has progressed to the point that a draft of messages for remittance advice, credit advice, extended credit advice, payment order and extended payment order have been prepared by the various EDIFACT Banking Message Development Groups. The draft payment orders are for customer-to-bank use. The draft messages were circulated to the members of the ISO committee's subcommittee on Information Exchange by letter of 5 December 1989 with a request that the draft messages be reviewed "to ensure that the financial industry's requirements have been considered to the fullest degree".

improvements in the services offered, developments in respect of funds transfers are in constant flux.

While batch processing of payment orders on magnetic tape and the individual sending and processing of payment orders by data transfer over telecommunications offer two different images of the impact of electronics on the funds transfer process, the two have had many common effects on the funds transfer process and on the legal rules that might appropriately be applied.

One of the most important of those effects is that the time it takes for a payment order to be processed and to pass between any two banks is more certain when electronic techniques are used than when the order is transmitted on paper. That increase in predictability of the time it will take for a payment order to be sent and processed is independent of whether the time involved is shorter, as in the case of on-line data transfer, or is longer, as is often the case when payment orders are transmitted by the exchange of magnetic tapes. This increase in predictability allows customers as well as banks to do more precise financial planning. It also puts more pressure on the banks to meet the target time periods for effectuating the transfers.

A second effect is that many legal rules on the time of completion of the credit transfer that were based on the procedures followed in a paper-based environment are no longer appropriate or, in some cases, easily applied. For example, it may not be thought to be appropriate for legal consequences to attach to the moment of crediting accounts if the accounts are no longer debited or credited on the basis of the time when a payment order is received or when a decision is made that it should be executed, as is the case in the many banks where debits and credits of certain types of payment orders are batch processed once a day.

A third concern is that the use of electronics does not leave the same type of audit trail as does the use of paper. That concern is at times overstated since a properly designed computer system can leave an audit trail that is at least as effective as a paper-based audit trail. In respect of the applicable legal rules, the greatest concern has been expressed as to the evidentiary value of the computer records of the bank.[9] Associated with that concern, but separate from it, has been the concern that electronic techniques lead to the possibility of error and types of fraud that are not possible with paper. The question has been raised whether the new sources of fraud and error lead to a need for different legal rules than those previously applied. Even if they do not, a change in the frequency of fraud or error or in the size of the resulting monetary loss and an increase in international transfers where it is more difficult to claim the resulting loss from foreign banks might lead to the conclusion that the losses should be distributed differently than they have been in the past.

An aspect of the concern over the distribution of the loss arising out of error or fraud that was less evident in respect of paper is the responsibility of telecommunications intermediaries. It has long been the general rule that the telecommunication carriers were not responsible for the losses that might occur because of the failure to deliver a message, its delay or the corruption of the message. Any loss resulting from a failure of the message to arrive, or from its delay or corruption was allocated by the general principles of civil law between the sender

---

[9] On the subject generally of the legal value of computer records, see A/CN.9/265 and the recommendation adopted by UNCITRAL in 1985, A/40/17, para. 260.

and receiver of the message, and usually on the sender.[10] Similarly, the question as to the responsibility of a clearing house that cleared cheques or of a courier service that carried cheques between banks for the losses that might be generated to the banks or to their customers because the clearing house or courier service caused delays in the collection of the cheques does not seem to have been of substantial concern. That is not true in regard to the value added networks like SWIFT or in regard to the clearing houses for electronic payment orders where the allocation of responsibility for potential loss is a major factor in the discussion of the appropriate legal rules.[11]

While the use of electronics has no effect on the fundamental nature of funds transfers, it has had a profound effect on the specific modalities by which funds transfers are made. Whereas paper-based debit transfers by means of the collection of cheques and bills of exchange are the normal means of making funds transfers in many countries, in most countries where debit transfers are made by electronic means, they are usually restricted to specific situations. Two of those situations are of particular importance. One of them is that a supplier of services to the public at large, such as electricity, gas or telephone, may be authorized to submit magnetic tapes containing an instruction to debit the accounts of its customers for the amounts of their bills and to credit its account for the total of its customers' bills. At present and for the foreseeable future, such debit transfers are limited to domestic transactions.

Of greater economic significance are the systems for the exchange of financial assets by delivery of securities against payment. In those systems a seller of securities sends the securities to the clearing agent, such as CEDEL or Euro-Clear, by the equivalent of a credit transfer while making claim against the clearing agent for the amount of money due. The clearing agent repeats the process by sending the securities to the buyer by the equivalent of a credit transfer while making claim against the buyer for the amount due. CEDEL and Euro-Clear are international systems; similar systems for delivery of securities against payment operate domestically in a number of countries.

It can be imagined that in the future trade payments against documents, including both collections and documentary credits, will be effectuated by electronic means.[12] However, that will be possible only when the claimant of the funds will be able to transmit by electronic means all the documents called for under the credit. At present such claims for payment are limited to the claim of a negotiating bank that has paid against the physical presentation of documents for reimbursement from the issuing bank of the credit, with a statement that the documents are to follow.

---

[10] e.g. United Nations Convention on Contracts for the International Sale of Goods, Article 27.

[11] H. Lingl, "Risk Allocation in International Interbank Electronic Funds Transfers: CHIPS & SWIFT", 22 *Harv. Int'l. LJ* (1981), p. 621.

[12] A "think tank" recommended to the Commission on Banking Technique and Practice of the International Chamber of Commerce that ICC should establish a subcommittee to consider the needs and possibilities in respect of the use of EDI with a view to developing an "EDI credit" parallel to the traditional documentary credit. ICC document No. 470/575. The recommendation was accepted by the Banking Commission at its meeting on 24 October 1989.

III. UNCITRAL Model Law

1. History of the Project

The history of the involvement of UNCITRAL in electronic funds transfers is in its own way a reflection of the evolution of thinking in this field during the past fifteen years. As early as 1975 the Commission requested the Secretariat "to obtain information regarding the impact, in the near future, of the increased use of telegraphic transfers and of the development of telecommunication systems between banks on the use of cheques for settling international payments" in order to determine the effect of such transfers on the draft Convention on International Bills of Exchange and International Promissory Notes and the draft Convention on International Cheques, which were then under preparation by the Commission.[13] By 1978 it appeared that the subject of electronic funds transfers might be of significance for the future, but the Secretariat's preliminary work found it difficult to distinguish between the legal problems that might arise as a result of the expected use of electronics for consumer purchases and the legal problems that might arise when SWIFT would come on line.[14]

The general perception at the time, especially among developing countries, was that electronic funds transfers was a subject of little immediate importance. The Commission's decision in 1978 was to put it on the priority list of subjects, though with a lower priority than some of the other subjects. That decision gave the Secretariat only a limited mandate.[15] Nevertheless, a decision was made to study the subject within the UNCITRAL Study Group on International Payments, an expert advisory group of banking and trade representatives who advised the Secretariat. As part of that study, in 1979 a questionnaire was sent to central banks around the world enquiring in part as to plans to create electronic funds transfer systems and in part as to the legal rules that would be applicable to the transfers.

As a means of gaining information on the legal issues the questionnaire was a failure; almost no one had any idea as to how to analyse the problems, much less how to answer them.[16] Nevertheless, the failure of the questionnaire suggested that UNCITRAL might profitably attempt to explore the issues with a view to reducing the general lack of knowledge about the subject. The Study Group decided to recommend to the Commission that the Secretariat be authorized to prepare a legal guide on electronic funds transfers that would be designed to provide guidance for legislators or lawyers preparing the rules governing particular systems for such transfers. That suggestion was accepted by the Commission in 1982.[17]

The basic approach taken in the UNCITRAL Legal Guide on Electronic Funds Transfers, which was prepared in collaboration with the Study Group, was to

---

[13] A/10017, para. 29. In 1984 the Commission decided to "postpone" any further work on the draft Convention on International Cheques, a decision that was understood to terminate any further work as a result of the decreasing use of cheques for international commercial payments. A/39/17, para. 88.

[14] A/CN.9/149/Add. 3.

[15] A/33/17, para. 67.

[16] A preliminary report was published in A/CN.9/199. The analysis of the full set of replies made for the Study Group was not published.

[17] A/37/17, para. 73.

explore the extent to which the introduction of the use of electronics in the funds transfer process affected the legal rules that might be appropriate for such transfers. No attempt was made in the Legal Guide to provide answers to the questions raised; it was thought to be too early for such an effort. While the Commission itself did not become involved in preparation or review of the Legal Guide, in 1986 the Commission authorized its publication in all six official languages of the United Nations as a product of the work of the Secretariat.[18]

At the same time the Commission authorized publication of the Legal Guide, it decided that an attempt should be made to build upon the work already undertaken so as to bring about a higher degree of international agreement on the appropriate legal rules to govern international electronic funds transfers. Because it was not clear at that time whether it would be possible to reach such a level of agreement that a single legislative text in the nature of a uniform law might be prepared, it was decided to prepare "model legal rules on electronic funds transfers" without specifying in any manner what the normative nature of those model legal rules might be.[19] The expectation was that it might be necessary in some cases to prepare alternative texts on particular points. Even that was expected, however, to contribute to a better understanding on the points in issue.

The task of preparing the model legal rules on electronic funds transfers was assigned to the Working Group on International Payments. The Working Group held its first meeting of two weeks' duration in November 1987, at which it discussed a number of legal issues that might be covered by the model rules. At the conclusion of the meeting the Working Group requested the Secretariat to prepare draft provisions for consideration at the next meeting. Since that time the Working Group has held an additional four meetings through December 1989 refining and considerably changing the draft provisions.[20] Current expectations are that the Working Group will complete its preparation of the text at either its meeting in July 1990 or at a meeting in November-December 1990. In either case the text, now renamed the draft Model Law on International Credit Transfers, is expected to be submitted to the Commission's session in June 1991 for a final three-week review followed by its adoption. Following the normal routine the General Assembly would then recommend to all states that they consider adoption of the Model Law.

2. Major Policy Questions

(a) Sphere of Application

While the sphere of application of a draft law is often thought of as among the least interesting questions to be considered, determination of the sphere of application is fundamental to the entire conception of the Model Law. The issue was first approached in an indirect manner in the UNCITRAL Legal Guide on Electronic Funds Transfers. The Legal Guide considered the extent to which the use of electronics affected the desirable legal rules governing debit transfers and credit transfers alike. While the intention was not so expressed, there was an underlying

---

[18] United Nations publication Sales No. E.87.V.9.

[19] n. 1, *supra*.

[20] The reports of the five meetings of the Working Group held to date are published in A/CN.9/297, 317, 318, 328 and 329.

assumption that it would be desirable to unify the legal rules governing such transfers in a single legal text. A conscious effort was made in the Legal Guide to use terminology that was equally applicable to all funds transfers. It seems fair to say that in the context of the Legal Guide that effort was successful.

A more ambitious effort to unify the legal rules governing all types of funds transfers was being made at the same time in the United States in the preparation of the proposed New Payments Code. Eventually that effort was abandoned. While many explanations could be given for its failure, one was certainly that in spite of the basic similarity between debit transfers and credit transfers in their ultimate effect, i.e. the entry of debits and credits to accounts at banks, the basic differences in the procedures that must be followed by the banks in processing and transmitting the payment messages led to the use of infelicitous terminology and the drafting of excessively complicated provisions. When the United States abandoned the preparation of the New Payments Code, it began the preparation of a new law designed for high-speed high-value credit transfers, the new Article 4A of the Uniform Commercial Code.

Following the experience in the preparation of the Legal Guide and that of the United States, which had already abandoned preparation of the New Payments Code, the UNCITRAL Working Group decided that its text would, at least for the time being, be restricted to credit transfers.[21] Credit transfers were thought to be both easier in their mechanics and more significant in international transfers than were debit transfers.[22]

On the other hand, after some debate the Working Group decided that the new text should not be limited to credit transfers made by electronic means, but should extend to paper-based credit transfers as well.[23] In part the decision was a reflection of the difficulty in defining an electronic credit transfer in the context of international transfers. While an electronic funds transfer subject to consumer protection legislation can be appropriately defined in terms of how the transfer is commenced, such a definition does not fit the prototype international transfers intended to be covered by the Model Law. A multi-million dollar transfer might as easily be initiated by a payment order from the originator on paper or by data transfer. Furthermore, most of the banking law rules to be included in the Model Law would be the same no matter what means were used to transmit the payment order from the originator to the originator's bank or between the banks. Where the use of electronics required the preparation of special rules, it was expected that they could be accommodated with ease within the Model Law. So far that judgment appears to have been correct.[24]

Again after long discussion it was decided that the Model Law should be limited to international transfers. That may seem to be a natural decision, since the function of UNCITRAL is to harmonize and unify the law governing international trade. However, one way to unify the law governing international trade is to unify the

---

[21] A/CN.9/318, para. 14.

[22] While that decision ignored the securities against payment form of debit transfer, it would be difficult to prepare a law for only the payment side of those transactions.

[23] *Ibid*. paras. 15-17.

[24] However, in the most recent meeting of the Working Group the United States delegation stated its great concern that the Model Law was not designed for high-speed on-line systems, as was Article 4A of the Uniform Commercial Code. A/CN.9/329, paras. 195-198.

domestic law on the subject in question. That was the highly successful technique used by the League of Nations in preparing the Geneva Conventions of 1930 and 1931 on negotiable instruments. Nevertheless, in the UNCITRAL Working Group it was felt that while there was a certain similarity to the problems faced by all countries in making international credit transfers, the problems faced by different countries and, therefore, the appropriate legal rules to govern domestic credit transfers, differed too widely to attempt to prepare a single Model Law to cover both.[25]

Having decided that the Model Law was to be restricted to international credit transfers, it was necessary to determine the criteria of internationality. That has been complicated by the fact that a credit transfer must be analysed in two radically different ways for different purposes. From one point of view it is a unified activity transferring funds from the originator to the beneficiary by the use of one or more banks. At the same time it is a series of individual transfers in which the originator and each sending bank in the chain leading to the beneficiary's bank issues a payment order and settles with its receiving bank for the order it issued. Both of those ways of analysing a credit transfer could be relevant to the determination whether a credit transfer is an international credit transfer, meaning that neither is self-evidently correct. In the former case an international credit transfer would be one in which the originator and the beneficiary were in different states. In the latter case an international credit transfer might be seen as comprising only that segment or those segments that involved the sending of a payment order from a bank in one state to a bank in a different state. While the exact wording for the scope of application of the Model Law is not yet agreed upon, the Working Group has taken an intermediate position and has decided that the Model Law should apply if the originator's bank and the beneficiary's bank are in different states or, if the originator is a bank, that bank and its receiving bank are in different states.[26]

When the Commission authorized the project, it directed that the new law should cover the rights and obligations of originators and beneficiaries as well as of banks. To implement that decision the Working Group has defined a credit transfer in Article 2(a) as "the series of operations, beginning with the originator's payment order, made for the purpose of placing funds at the disposal of a designated person". That means, however, that a credit transfer subject to the Model Law will include segments of the transfer in the country of the originator and of the beneficiary. Those segments may include a sending and receiving bank in that state. If the same banking channels are used for the domestic segments of international credit transfers and purely domestic credit transfers in those countries, there may well be two different laws governing what otherwise appear to be identical transactions. For that reason, states that consider adopting the Model Law for international credit transfers may decide that they will also apply it to purely domestic transfers.

---

[25] *Ibid.* para. 13.

[26] *Ibid.* para. 23. Article 1(1) as redrafted by the drafting group at the November-December 1989 session of the Working Group reads as follows: "This law applies to credit transfers where the originator's bank and the beneficiary's bank are in different States or, if the originator is a bank, that bank and the beneficiary's bank are in different States." At the time the report of the meeting was adopted, the Working Group "noted that the drafting group appeared not to have correctly implemented the idea expressed in paragraph 23, above". A/CN.9/329, para. 194. All references to articles of the Model Law refer to the text in A/CN.9/329, annex.

(b) Obligations of a Receiving Bank

Receiving banks of payment orders fall into three categories: the originator's bank, intermediary banks and the beneficiary's bank. Those three categories of banks form the credit transfer chain. Normally there is an explicit or implied contractual relationship between each link in the chain, i.e. between the originator and the originator's bank, between the originator's bank and any intermediary bank and between an intermediary bank and the beneficiary's bank, although banks often send payment orders to other banks with which they have no contractual relationship and on occasion even to banks with which they have had no prior dealings. On the contrary the originator seldom has a direct contractual relationship with any bank other than its own, although a contractual relationship between the originator and the subsequent banks can easily be implied by considering the choice of an intermediary bank by the originator's bank as having been made on behalf of the originator.

The traditional rule has been that a receiving bank has no obligation as a matter of law to execute a payment order unless the bank had undertaken the obligation in respect of the specific payment order, whether or not there was a pre-existing contractual relationship between the sender and the receiving bank. That traditional position is not completely satisfactory in modern society where banks play a fundamental role in making possible the transfer of funds between distant parties. Their position in regard to funds transfers might be assimilated to that of a common carrier of persons, goods or telecommunications. If such an assimilation is made, a bank would be obligated to act upon a payment order received, subject to its right to protect its own economic interests by assuring itself that it would be reimbursed for the amount of the transfer, plus its fees for undertaking the service.

The Working Group has attempted to reconcile those two opposed positions. The draft Model Law starts from the traditional proposition that no receiving bank is as a matter of law obligated to act upon the instructions contained in a payment order it receives until it undertakes those obligations by a volitional act in regard to the specific payment order after the order has been received. In the schema of the Model Law that result is achieved by providing that the receiving bank is bound on a payment order when it has "accepted" the order.[27]

The Model Law sets out two major exceptions to the general principle that the receiving bank is not bound to act unless it has undertaken obligations by a volitional act in respect of a specific payment order. The first arises out of the recognition that the sender of a payment order normally has every right to expect that the receiving bank will execute the order it has received. If the receiving bank is not going to execute the order, good banking practice calls for it to notify the sender that it will not do so. The Model Law raises that element of good banking practice to a legal obligation.[28] However, the receiving bank is not required to give its reasons for its rejection of the payment order.

The receiving bank's obligation to notify the sender that it will not execute the payment order received is sanctioned by the rule that a receiving bank that fails to give the required notice of rejection accepts the order.[29] The only exception is that a

[27] Articles 6(2) and 8(1).
[28] Articles 5(3) and 7(2).
[29] Articles 5(2)(a) and 7(1)(a).

receiving bank does not accept the payment order by virtue of its failure to give notice of rejection if the reason it failed to execute the order was that it had not received payment from the sender of the order.[30] The sanction for its failure to give notice in that case is left to the provisions on damages.

The Model Law contains other obligations of notification by the receiving bank that are also intended to assure the proper functioning of the international credit transfer system. In essence, whenever the receiving bank receives a payment order that is ambiguous or cannot be executed, e.g., the order is to pay francs without it being clear whether Belgian, French or Swiss francs are meant or the amount is expressed twice and the two expressions of the amount do not agree or the order has been sent to the wrong bank, the receiving bank is obligated to notify its sender of the ambiguity or the inability to execute the order.[31] However, a failure by the receiving bank to send one of those required notices does not lead to acceptance of the order; the sanction for failure to give such a required notice is left to the provisions on damages.

The second exception to the general principle that a receiving bank is not obligated on a payment order until it has undertaken the obligation by a volitional act in respect of the specific order lies in a rule, first introduced at the July 1989 session and refined at the November-December 1989 session of the Working Group, that a receiving bank that has agreed with a sender that it will execute payment orders upon receipt accepts the payment order when the order is received. Such an agreement implies, and may even state, that the receiving bank will not reject the payment order for insufficient funds. Contractual agreements of that nature exist under the CHAPS rules and in many bilateral agreements between banks. Those agreements are intended to assure senders, as well as their instructing parties, that the credit transfer will be carried out as intended. As a result they increase the efficiency of the credit transfer system by eliminating any reason for the receiving bank to delay executing the order for reasons other than those that go to the inadequacy of the data on the payment order itself.

While the conceptual basis for acceptance of a payment order by all banks is the same, there are naturally some differences in the volitional acts that different categories of banks might take to accept the order. In the case of a receiving bank that is not the beneficiary's bank, the primary volitional act would be to issue to the beneficiary's bank or to an appropriate intermediary bank a payment order of its own that was intended to carry out the credit transfer.[32] In the case of the beneficiary's bank, the primary volitional acts that the bank might take to accept the order would be to credit the beneficiary's account, give him notice that the funds were available or otherwise place the funds at his disposal.[33]

The primary volitional acts that a receiving bank might take to accept a payment order are essentially the same acts that it would take to implement the order, i.e. in the case of a receiving bank that is not the beneficiary's bank, the sending of its own payment order that is intended to implement the order received and in the case of the beneficiary's bank, placing the funds at the disposal of the beneficiary. That does not

[30] *Ibid.*
[31] Articles 6(3)-(5) and 8(2)-(5).
[32] Article 5(2)(d).
[33] Article 7(1)(d)-(g).

mean that the concept of acceptance has no value. As has already been noted, a receiving bank might accept a payment order by virtue of having failed to give notice that it was rejecting the order or because it had agreed with the sender that it would execute the sender's orders upon receipt. Moreover, the payment order sent by the bank might contain errors that cause the credit transfer to be delayed. In such a case the receiving bank would have accepted the order by issuing its own order but would have failed in the obligations that arose as a result of the acceptance.

(c) Obligations of the Beneficiary's Bank and Completion of the Credit Transfer

The obligation of the beneficiary's bank is ultimately to place the funds at the disposal of the beneficiary. Placing the funds at the disposal of the beneficiary may involve crediting the account, giving notice to the beneficiary of the credit and making the funds available for withdrawal in cash or for transfer to other accounts. The Working Group has been uncertain whether the Model Law should impose those obligations on a beneficiary's bank that has accepted the payment order or whether those matters should be left to the law applicable to the account relationship between the beneficiary and the bank.

One view which has been expressed and is reflected in the current draft of the Model Law is that the credit transfer should be considered to have been completed by the acceptance of the payment order by the beneficiary's bank.[34] That view has its most important effect when acceptance occurs on receipt of the payment order because of an agreement between the sender and the bank to that effect. In such a case the payment order is accepted before the beneficiary's account is credited. The rationale behind that view is that it is the beneficiary who chooses the beneficiary's bank and he should bear the risk of the bank's errors or delays. Moreover, the beneficiary and his bank may have an agreement as to the time when the account will be credited, whether and when notice of the credit will be given and when the funds will be available to the beneficiary.[35] Finally, such a substantive policy decision would make it possible to avoid including in the Model Law any statement as to what obligations the beneficiary's bank should have towards the beneficiary.[36]

A different view which has been expressed is that the purpose of a credit transfer is to make the funds available to the beneficiary. Therefore, the credit transfer should be considered to be completed only when the beneficiary's bank performs an act that

---

[34] The definition of "credit transfer" in Article 2(a) currently so provides, and Articles 7, 8, 10, 11, and 14 implement that view. However, at its most recent session the Working Group placed the relevant words in square brackets "to indicate that neither the substance of a rule as to when a credit transfer was completed nor the location of such a rule was being decided . . .", A/CN.9/329, para. 33.

[35] In "The Chikuma", *Lloyd's Rep.* 1 (1981) p. 371 (H.L.), an originator was found not to have made a monthly payment on a charter party on time even though the beneficiary's account had been credited on the day the payment was due because the credit was value dated two banking days later. Although the practice of value dating credits two days after the day of receipt is widely practised in some countries, it appears to be legally based upon a contractual agreement between the beneficiary and the bank, an agreement that may be unknown to the originator.

[36] The current text of article 8(1) provides that "the beneficiary's bank is, upon acceptance of a payment order received, obligated to place the funds at the disposal of the beneficiary in accordance with the payment order and the applicable law governing the relationship between the bank and the beneficiary".

is both volitional and relevant to placing the funds at the disposal of the beneficiary.[37] Under that view the Model Law would state the obligations of the beneficiary's bank, but they may be obligations owing to the sender and not to the beneficiary.[38]

While the principal discussion on this issue in the Working Group to date has been in the context of deciding what obligations the Model Law should place upon the beneficiary's bank,[39] it is widely understood that the decision as to the time of completion of the credit transfer will have important effects on other aspects of the Model Law. The sooner the credit transfer is considered to be completed, the sooner the beneficiary begins to bear the risk that the beneficiary's bank will become insolvent. Before that time, either the originator or one of the banks in the credit transfer chain bears that risk.

An additional concern that has been discussed on several occasions, but not yet decided, is the extent to which the Model Law should provide a rule as to the time when an obligation is discharged by virtue of a credit transfer.[40] There seems to be rather general agreement that the time of discharge should be closely linked to the time when the credit transfer is completed, and that at least in most situations those points of time should be the same. As a result the drafts of the Model Law prepared by the Secretariat have included a provision that an obligation would be discharged upon acceptance of a payment order by the beneficiary's bank that was intended to discharge the obligation.[41] There has been a certain amount of support for the inclusion of such a provision in the Model Law on the grounds that differences in the law as to the time of discharge of obligations pose one of the more serious problems associated with international credit transfers. The criticism of the Secretariat's draft has been more substantial. The majority in the Working Group seem to be in agreement that it would be inappropriate to include the provision in a Model Law on the banking process of credit transfers.[42] On the other hand it seems likely that the Working Group will adopt a provision specifying when the beneficiary's bank owes the beneficiary and the transfer of funds from the originator to the beneficiary has been completed. It can then be expected that the law governing the underlying obligation will consider that to be the time when the underlying obligation is discharged.

(d) Liability, Damages and Allocation of Risk

The most significant of the unresolved problems in the Model Law involves the remedies available to the banks and their customers when the credit transfer is not completed when and how expected. In effect, decisions on the imposition of liability are decisions on the allocation of risk.

One risk which must be anticipated is that the credit transfer is never completed. That may occur because of an error on the part of one of the parties, particularly that the identification of the beneficiary or of the beneficiary's bank is incorrect or there is

[37] A/CN.9/329, para. 152.
[38] *Ibid.* para. 165.
[39] *Ibid.* paras. 151-159.
[40] A/CN.9/317, paras. 158-162; a/CN.9/328, paras. 37-43; A/CN.9/329, paras. 189-192.
[41] Article 14(2).
[42] A/CN.9/329, para. 191.

such incompleteness or ambiguity in a payment order that the credit transfer cannot be carried out. Normally, such an error can be repaired. The receiving bank that finds it cannot execute a payment order is required to give notice of the problem to its sender[43] and the sender is required to assist in seeing that a proper payment order is issued to the beneficiary's bank.[44] As a result, the credit transfer may be completed late, with whatever consequences that may entail, but it may also not be completed.

The credit transfer may fail to be completed for other more dramatic reasons, i.e. one of the banks in the credit transfer chain may become insolvent after having received the payment order and the funds to pay for it but before the bank has executed the order or the outbreak of war, imposition of currency controls or other external factors may intervene (all of these situations will be referred to hereafter as involving an insolvent bank). In such a case the funds may be lost in whole or in part or the period of eventual realization may be measured in years. From a current point of view, the two situations are the same. It is clear that such a risk of loss is greater in international funds transfers than it is in domestic funds transfers, and that there are fewer institutional or regulatory means to eliminate it.

The loss might be allocated to the originator on the grounds that the transfer is being carried out at its request, to the originator's bank on the grounds that the originator's bank undertakes an obligation to see to the completion of the credit transfer, or to the bank that sent the payment order to the insolvent bank. A variation on the last possibility is that the loss would fall on the party that designated use of the insolvent bank. While that would often be the insolvent bank's sending bank, it could be any party to the credit transfer, including the originator or even the beneficiary.

The current draft of Article 11 of the Model Law provides in the pertinent part that

"a receiving bank other than the beneficiary's bank that accepts a payment order is obligated under that order: . . . (b) where a payment order consistent with the contents of the payment order issued by the originator and containing instructions necessary to implement the credit transfer in an appropriate manner is not issued to or accepted by the beneficiary's bank—to refund to its sender any funds received from its sender, and the receiving bank is entitled to the return of any funds it has paid to its receiving bank."

Under that provision the originator has a right to recover from the originator's bank and that bank from its receiving bank. It is the insolvent bank's sending bank that ultimately bears the risk of loss. Since the originator's right to the refund from the originator's bank is not based on a prior refund to that bank from its receiving bank, another way of describing the allocation of risk is that the originator's bank is responsible to the originator for the successful completion of the credit transfer. Although it has a right of reimbursement from its receiving bank, it bears the risk that it will not be able to recover the reimbursement.

While the refund to the originator of the principal amount of an unsuccessful transfer is not considered under the Model Law to be a matter of damages, the same question of responsibility arises in respect of damages, i.e. whether the originator's bank should be responsible to the originator for any damages resulting from delay or failure to perform the credit transfer at banks subsequent to the originator's bank.

---

[43] Articles 6(3)-(5) and 8(2)-(5).
[44] Article 11(a).

The argument in favour of such responsibility is that an originator that is not itself a bank has little opportunity to find out where any delay or error occurred in the credit transfer, especially when it may have occurred at a bank in a foreign country. Furthermore, the originator has few means to persuade a foreign bank with which it has no continuing relationship to reimburse it for any losses it may have suffered as a result of the bank's failures. In case of litigation, the originator would normally have to proceed in a foreign country, at a distance, perhaps in a foreign language and subject to foreign substantive and procedural rules. It is much easier for the originator's bank to claim against its receiving bank for reimbursement for the damages it has had to pay to the originator.

While those arguments have been accepted so far in regard to the refund of the principal amount, and the current draft in respect of damages generally reflects such a rule,[45] they have been strongly contested in the latter context.[46] In that context the counter-argument has been raised that a bank should be responsible only for its own failures. That is often said to be of particular importance in an international transfer where the standards of performance of banks in a foreign country may not be the same as in that of the originator's bank. Of course, one type of failure by the originator's bank could be to choose an inappropriate intermediary bank. However, it would be rare when the choice of a particular intermediary bank could be shown to have been negligence.

At an early stage in the preparation of the Model Law the question appeared to be important,[47] but in the light of other decisions that have been made, it may currently have greater symbolic than practical significance. As noted the principal sum is to be returned to the originator by the originator's bank if the credit transfer is not successful. There has been general agreement that a bank will be liable for consequential damages only under restricted conditions, if at all.[48] There is also rather general agreement that a bank should pay interest for any delay in executing a payment order that it has received, whether or not the bank was at fault, and that the beneficiary should have a direct right to claim that interest even though it would seldom have any contractual relationship with the bank where the delay occurred.[49] On the other hand there is no agreement as yet as to whether a loss arising out of a change in exchange rates during a period in which the credit transfer was delayed should be compensated in damages.[50]

That suggests that there may be relatively few items of damage of economic significance arising out of the failure of a subsequent bank for which an originator might wish to claim against the originator's bank. Nevertheless, the issue may turn out to be fiercely contested because of its symbolic importance as to whether the banking system, through the originator's bank, is responsible to the originator for the proper execution of the credit transfer or whether each bank is responsible only for its own actions.

---

[45] Article 12(2).

[46] A/CN.9/328, paras. 66-74 and 144; A/CN.9/329, paras. 187 and 188.

[47] A/CN.9/297, paras. 55-60; A/CN.9/318, paras. 146-150.

[48] Article 12(5)(d). See A/CN.9/317, paras. 115-117 and A/CN.9/328, paras. 140-143.

[49] A/CN.9/328, paras. 121-132; A/CN.9/329, para. 188. Although generally agreed upon, the agreement is not as yet reflected in the text of the Model Law.

[50] A/CN.9/328, paras. 133-136; A/CN.9/329, para. 188.

IV. Conclusions

The preparation of the draft Model Law on International Credit Transfers is far from completed. There are a number of important policy questions yet to be settled. The text needs further polishing for consistency, presentation and agreement of all six language versions.[51] Nevertheless, the Working Group has made notable progress in its five sessions. The basic structure of the Model Law is agreed upon and many issues that seemed to be intractable have been settled. It can be expected that in 1991 UNCITRAL will present the Model Law to the international community for its evaluation and, one can hope, its widespread adoption.

[51] At the session of the Working Group in November-December 1989 a drafting group was created that undertook the first review of Articles 1-9.

4

The Law of International Documentary Credits: Principles, Liabilities and Responsibilities

Ljudevit Rosenberg

I. Introductory Remarks

This Chapter deals with the law of international documentary credits, the scope of which is broader than that of the legal and technical provisions of the *Uniform Customs and Practice for Documentary Credits*, as revised by the International Chamber of Commerce in Paris (hereinafter: 1983 revision or UCP).[1] This is quite under-standable as the institution of documentary credits cannot be separated from the municipal law of which it is a part. The municipal law governing a given case is determined by the choice-of-law rules on documentary credits. Accordingly, the ICC notes: "It still has to be appreciated . . . that UPC are not and cannot be intended to give precise answers to each and every problem arising in practice."[2] In addition, it should be noted that the instruments, institutions and entire mechanism of the law of international payments, including the field of documentary credits, are developing extremely quickly. As a result, the law of documentary credits has its own special features, its own doctrine, case law and business practices, thus requiring an appropriate methodological approach to the subject-matter.

Bearing this in mind, I shall first attempt to present the basic principles of the law of documentary credits, dealing thereafter with the liabilities and responsibilities of banks as well as with the possibility of banks to invoke the exemption clauses contained in the 1983 revision of the UCP. Documents are not the subject-matter of this Chapter and thus will be mentioned only briefly, as will other problems outside the scope of this Chapter such as stand-by and deferred payment credits, combined transport documents, etc.

---

[1] *UCP Revision 1983*, ICC Publication No. 400.
[2] *UCP 1974/1983 Revisions Compared and Explained–Documentary Credits*, ICC Publication No. 411, p. 7.

International Contracts and Payments (Šarčević, Volken, eds.; 1 85333 615 7; © Graham & Trotman, 1991; pub. Graham & Trotman; printed in Great Britain), pp. 51-67.

II. Basic Principles

The revised UCP of 1983 are based on the principles set forth in the revisions of 1962 and 1974. As already mentioned elsewhere,[3] the 1974 revision recognized the three basic principles of the 1962 revision: (1) banks deal in documents, not in goods, (2) documentary credits are independent of commercial contracts, and (3) the relationships created in documentary credits are separate and independent. The fourth principle concerning the examination of documents was also incorporated into the 1983 UCP and revised by adding the following sentence to Article 7: "Documents which appear on their face to be inconsistent with one another will be considered as not appearing on their face to be in accordance with the terms and conditions of the credit."

Stricter criteria were adopted in the 1974 revision requiring the banks to examine all documents submitted by potential credit beneficiaries in order to determine: (1) whether they are in accordance with the terms and conditions specified in the letter of credit and (2) whether the data contained therein is consistent. Only after such ascertainment can the documents be held on their face to be in accordance with the terms and conditions of the letter of credit and thus be recognized as operative credit instruments. If this is not the case, the bank must refuse to honour the documents and return them to the applicant. In this context it should be pointed out that the relationships involved in such matters concern only the bank authorized to perform the credit obligation and the credit beneficiary. As such they do not affect the examination of credit documents in interbank matters, for example, in relationships between the issuing bank and the bank authorized to confirm, accept, negotiate or advise the credit. This aspect will be discussed later in connection with interbank relationships under the 1983 rules.

1. The Principle of Incorporation

According to the principle of incorporation in Article 1 of the 1983 UCP, the provisions of the UCP are to be binding on all parties unless otherwise expressly agreed. Consequently, it follows that the provisions of the 1983 revision shall be binding on all parties to documentary credit transactions which have not expressly agreed that any other or all other provisions shall apply. Furthermore, the text of all letters of credit issued, confirmed, accepted, negotiated or advised must contain the following clause: "This credit is issued subject to Uniform Customs and Practice for Documentary Credits, 1983 revision ICC Publication No. 400." If the parties have stipulated any provisions other than those formulated in the UCP, only those provisions of the UCP shall apply which have not been stipulated otherwise.

It is true that the above clause was incorporated into letters of credit prior to the 1983 revision; however, its incorporation is now expressly prescribed by a special provision (Article 1) of the UCP rules. This was not the case in para. a of the General Provisions and Definitions of the 1974 revision which reads as follows:

"These provisions and definitions and the following Articles apply to all documentary credits and are binding upon all parties unless otherwise expressly agreed."

---

[3] L. Rosenberg, *Pravo medjunarodnih plaćanja u poslovnim transakcijama* [*Law of International Payments in Business Transactions*], vol. II (Zagreb 1975) pp. 51 *et seq.*

Moreover, it should be noted that application of Article 1 of the 1983 revision has also been extended to stand-by documentary credits and deferred payment credits as well as to credits advised in the sense of Article 12(c) UCP. This also includes cases where the issuing bank instructs a bank (advising bank) by any teletransmission to advise a credit or an amendment to a credit and intends that the mail confirmation, the operative amendment or the teletransmission be the operative credit instrument. In the last case, Article 12(c) of the 1983 revision provides that "a teletransmission intended by the issuing bank to be the operative credit instrument should clearly indicate that the credit is issued subject to Uniform Customs and Practice for Documentary Credits, 1983 revision, ICC Publication No. 400". Article 12(a) refers to cases where a mail confirmation is to be considered the operative credit document. Analogue to Article 12(c), such mail confirmations of operative credit documents must also contain the clause specified in Article 1.

It should be noted that the provisions on standard forms for opening documentary credits[4] which have been applied since 1 January 1979 do not conform to the 1983 revision, especially to Articles 1 and 12(c). Since these rules correspond to the 1974 revision, it is quite natural that they are no longer adequate for modern banking methods involving documentary credits and must be revised to ensure proper application of the 1983 UCP rules, in particular to guarantee incorporation of the clause on application of the provisions of the 1983 UCP in all operative credit instruments, including stand-by letters of credit, credits with deferred payment, and credits advised in the sense of Article 12(c).

2. Separation of Documentary Credits and Commercial Contracts

This principle was already incorporated in the 1974 revision in para. c of the General Provisions and Definitions. One of the most important principles of documentary credits, it postulates that documentary credits are by their nature independent of and separate from sales or other contracts. Accordingly, banks which are parties to documentary credit transactions are in no way concerned with or bound by such contracts. This means that the obligation of the issuing bank to pay, accept or negotiate credits is fully independent of the obligation to pay amounts specified in sales or other commercial contracts. The text of Article 3 of the 1983 revision has been amended to include the following phrase: "even if any reference whatsoever to such contract(s) is included in the credit".[5]

It appears that the above phrase was added in response to the inclusion of stand-by credits in the definition of documentary credits in Article 2 UCP of 1983. As a rule, the non-performance of the debtor's or principal debtor's obligation arising from a commercial contract is one of the conditions for the performance of stand-by credit obligations, as is normally the case in respect of bank guarantees, the texts of which usually refer to commercial contracts. Extending the definition of documentary credits to include stand-by credits has made it difficult to ensure the

---

[4] *Standard Forms for Issuing Documentary Credits*, ICC Publication No. 323.

[5] Article 3 of the 1983 revision reads as follows: "Credits, by their nature, are separate transactions from the sales or other contract(s) on which they may be based and banks are in no way concerned with or bound by such contract(s), even if any reference whatsoever to such contract(s) is included in the credit."

"sacrosanctity" of the legal nature of monetary obligations of issuing banks arising from letters of credit as opposed to the monetary obligations of debtors based on commercial contracts. Thus it seems that the drafters of the 1983 revision added the above phrase in order to guarantee the separation of documentary credits and commercial contracts in cases involving stand-by credits. This, however, has not solved the problem. The fact that letters of guarantee normally refer to commercial contracts means that they necessarily assume an accessory character. This cannot be prevented, not even by the addition of the above phrase. This is the case in respect of stand-by credits as well as the bank guarantees specified by the ICC in the Uniform Customs for Contract Guarantees.

3. Banks Deal in Documents, not in Goods

In the 1983 revision, this principle is regulated in a separate provision (Article 4) which has been expanded to include the performance of engineering works, other projects, etc.[6] Article 4 reads as follows:

"In credit operations all parties concerned deal in documents and not in goods, services and/or other performances to which the documents may relate."

The principle that banks deal in documents and not in goods was expanded to include transactions involving services and other performances, thus broadening its application to stand-by credits which are used primarily for non-title transactions, i.e., when the transport documents are not documents of title but, as the case may be, are issued by the beneficiaries, experts or other persons. These documents confirm that the debtor specified in a given commercial contract, i.e., the applicant for the stand-by credit, has not performed his obligation. In this way the 1983 revision made a concession favouring the legal rules of countries which forbid or restrict the issuance of bank guarantees containing abstract obligations relating to obligations arising from commercial contracts.

Although the 1983 revision extended UCP application to stand-by credits, such application of UCP is obviously unusual in international commodity transactions and is not practiced in the business world. In view of the fact that credit documents can now be used for non-title transactions as well as for title transactions, it can be said that the inclusion of stand-by credits in the 1983 revisions has weakened the significance of credit documents just as much as it has proved useful. On the other hand, one must admit that by expanding the application of UCP to stand-by credits, the drafters of the 1983 revision took account not only of the increasing use of stand-by credits but also of the difficulty of issuing bank guarantees in some countries and of the cold reception which this principle received by some businessmen in connection with performance-guarantees as defined in the Uniform Rules for Contract Guarantees (ICC Publication No. 325).

In order to illustrate the differences between documents used for stand-by credits and those used for ordinary documentary credits, I shall describe the manner in which payment was effected in an arbitral dispute in Switzerland between an American firm (as plaintiff) and a Yugoslav enterprise (as defendant) in which I

---

[6] Rosenberg, *Pravo medjunarodnih plaćanja*, p. 25. The text of Article 8(a) of the 1974 revision did not contain the words "services and/or other performances to which the documents may relate".

took part. After several years of litigation the parties reached a settlement, according to which the American plaintiff undertook to pay the Yugoslav defendant the sum of $570,000 within six months from the date the settlement was reached. In addition, the defendant received an irrevocable guarantee by a first-rate bank for the payment of $570,000 to be used if the plaintiff should fail to pay the agreed sum before or on the final day of the six-month term. Having informed the defendant that American law barred the issuance of such a guarantee, the plaintiff's counsel proposed that a stand-by letter of credit be issued instead. The stand-by credit issued was collectible upon fulfilment of the following conditions: (1) before expiry of the six-month term the defendant/beneficiary was to present the issuing bank a written statement saying that the plaintiff had not paid the amount stipulated in the stand-by credit, and (2) another written statement was to be presented by the defendant/beneficiary to the bank containing proof that the signature on the first statement had been authorized by a competent Yugoslav court or administrative authority, that the signer was authorized to sign for the defendant firm and that his signature on the written statement corresponded to the one registered to act in behalf of the defendant firm. Upon due submission of both documents to the bank which had issued the stand-by letter of credit, the bank paid the amount to the defendant.

This example shows that the defendant was able to collect the amount designated in the stand-by credit by presenting documents to the bank which in fact were *scriptura propria* drawn up by himself. In this case, these were neither transport nor commodity documents having the character of documents of title as this was a non-title transaction without documents of title.

4. Independence and Separation of Contractual Relationships in Credit Transactions

This principle is contained in Article 6 of the 1983 revision which, apart from an apparently minor matter, does not differ from the text of para. f of the General Provisions and Definitions of the 1974 revision. The minor change is the addition of the word *the* so that the new text now reads: "relationships existing between the banks". This emphasizes that the provisions apply to contractual transactions existing between banks participating in credit transactions in *concreto*, and not generally. Article 6 reads as follows:

"A beneficiary can in no case avail himself of the contractual relationships existing between the banks or between the applicant for the credit and the issuing bank."

Thus it follows that each contractual relationship in a credit transaction is fully independent of the other contractual relationships in that transaction. Furthermore, no non-bank agent can avail itself of the contractual relationships existing between the banks participating in a given transaction. This is significant because it means that the applicant for a particular credit cannot avail himself of or interfere in the contractual relationship between the issuing bank and the bank which it has instructed to negotiate or advise the credit. This applies even to a greater extent to the credit beneficiary. Both parties are mutually isolated in their contractual relationships: the applicant for credit in his relationship to the issuing bank and the credit beneficiary in his relationship to the bank which has issued or confirmed the credit. In no case may the parties become involved in the credit relationships between the banks themselves. This also includes any relationships with other banks which may have been authorized to examine the documents or to pay, accept and negotiate them but without assuming any obligations towards the credit beneficiary. Accordingly, there are no legal grounds on which a credit beneficiary could take action against such banks. Similarly, the applicant for credit could not take court action against these banks unless they had confirmed the particular credit, in which case they would be confirming and not advising banks, as is usually the case. According to Article 6 of the 1983 revision, advising banks or any other authorized banks not bound by contractual relations in the particular credit transaction may not interfere with or avail themselves of contractual relationships existing between other banks. Although these interbank relationships are of utmost importance, neither the applicant for credit nor the credit beneficiary may interfere with and even less avail themselves of such relationships despite the fact that they are parties to the basic transactions out of which the other relationships arose and that the entire modern documentary credit mechanism has been created to serve them. This raises the question of whether the provision of Article 6 of the 1983 revision has upset the principle of equality of interests of the parties to documentary credit transactions to the advantage of the banks and the disadvantage of the so-called "business partners".

This issue is even more important when one takes into account Article 11(c) of the 1983 revision which states:

"Unless the nominated bank is the issuing bank or the confirming bank, its nomination by the issuing bank does not constitute any undertaking by the nominating bank to pay, to accept or to negotiate."

The emphasis here is on "its nomination . . . does not constitute any undertaking by the nominating bank to pay, to accept, or to negotiate".

Articles 16(e) and 20(a) and (b) of the 1983 revision should also be taken into account in this context. Article 16 governs interbank relationships, mutual liabilities, obligations and responsibilities, in short, the most important area reserved for the banks. Although more will be said about interbank relationships later, at this point we are interested in the effects of this provision on one of the basic principles of the law of documentary credits. Article 16 reads as follows:

"If the issuing bank fails to act in accordance with the provisions of paragraphs (c) and (d) of this Article and/or fails to hold the documents at the disposal of, or to return them to, the presentor, the issuing bank shall be precluded from claiming that the documents are not in accordance with the terms and conditions of the credit."

Furthermore, Article 20(a) provides that "banks utilising the services of another bank or other banks for the purpose of giving effect to the instructions of the applicant for the credit do so for the account and at the risk of such applicant". The risk of the applicant is such that the "banks assume no liability or responsibility should the instructions they transmit not be carried out, even if they have themselves taken the initiative in the choice of such other bank(s)" (Article 20(b)).

Again the question arises: What options are left to the applicant for credit if the "other" banks fail to carry out the instructions of the issuing bank? And to the credit beneficiary? As we saw in Article 6, the beneficiary cannot avail himself of the contractual relationships between the banks, thus making it impossible for him or the applicant for credit to take action against any of the "other" banks involved in the credit transaction. Moreover, Article 20 excludes the issuing bank from any liability for possible omissions of its "correspondents" even when the bank itself has taken the initiative in choosing such banks. Accordingly, the principle *culpa in eligendo* is not recognized although it is quite normal that banks should be more aware of the standing of their correspondents than credit applicants and beneficiaries.

Bearing this in mind, especially the fact that the issuing bank acts for the account and at the risk of the applicant for credit, we are of the opinion that this problem should be discussed by all parties to documentary credit transactions. In this context, the principle of independence and separation of relationships in a credit transaction is a matter in which the courts should be empowered to ensure the equality of interests of all participants in business practices of such importance as documentary credits.

5. Examination of Documents and the Standard of Strict Compliance

The examination of documents and the standard of strict compliance is found in Article 15 of the 1983 revision, which is identical to Article 7 of the 1974 revision. The views of the drafters of the UCP expressed therein are understandable and correct. In view of the new provisions of the 1983 revision, especially Articles 11 (d), 15 and 16 (a)-(f), it can be concluded that the 1983 revision emphasizes and confirms even more strongly that banks taking part in documentary credit transactions are bound:

- to examine the documents presented with reasonable care;
- on the basis of such examination, to ascertain that they appear on their face to be in accordance with the terms and conditions of the credit;
- to ascertain whether the documents presented are on their face consistent with one another (interdocumentary consistency);
- if interdocumentary inconsistency is detected, to determine that the documents are considered as not appearing on their face to be in accordance with the terms and conditions of the credit.

On the basis thereof, the banks are bound to decide whether to accept the documents and perform their credit obligations or to refuse the documents and return them to the presentor.

Problems arise when the credit beneficiary and the examining bank disagree on whether the documents appear on their face to be in accordance with the terms and conditions of the credit or when the credit beneficiary is of the opinion that the examining bank did not perform its duty with reasonable care. The problem is even greater when the issuing bank instructs a bank to examine the documents and then disagrees with its decision. For example, it could occur that the authorized bank determines that the documents appear on their face to be in accordance with the terms and conditions of the credit and thus effects payment, accepts the obligation for a deferred payment credit, accepts bills of exchange drawn on it or negotiates bills of exchange drawn on the applicant for credit or on it, whereupon the issuing bank ascertains that the documents are not consistent on their face with the terms and conditions of the credit. Another conflicting situation could occur between the applicant for credit and the bank which honoured the credit if this bank is not the issuing bank. Under Article 6 of the 1983 revision, the applicant for credit cannot avail himself of the contractual relationship between the issuing bank and the paying bank. Similarly, in accordance with Article 20(a) and (b) the issuing bank is excluded from all liability for the actions of the remitting bank.

Another problem which arises concerns establishing objective criteria to determine whether a bank has proceeded with reasonable care. I am of the opinion that this problem cannot be solved by establishing general criteria but rather that such a decision will have to be made on a case-to-case basis. The courts should also play a decisive role, especially when it comes to applying the standard of strict compliance and/or of reasonable and more flexible ascertainment as laid down in Articles 24 and 41(c) of the 1983 revision. Thus, for example, Article 24 states:

"Unless otherwise stipulated in the credit, banks will accept a document bearing a date of issuance prior to that of the credit, subject to such document being presented within the time limits set out in the credit and in these Articles."

If no such time limit is designated, the time limit specified in Article 47 shall apply.

Similarly, Article 41(c) provides that "the description of the goods in the commercial invoice must correspond with the description in the credit. In all other documents, the goods may be described in general terms not inconsistent with the description of the goods in the credit". This provision provides a more flexible criterion for examining documents and thus will certainly have a positive effect on business practices. The former criterion of strict formal compliance was the cause of numerous disputes arising as a result of errors in the description of goods. Although the above-mentioned flexibility concerns the description of goods in commercial invoices and other documents, Article 41(c) nevertheless sets a limit to this flexibility by providing that inconsistencies should not be such so as to make the general description of the goods in other documents inconsistent with the description of the goods in the credit (and not with the description of the goods in the commercial invoice).

The introduction of a more flexible criterion for the examination of documents was, among other things, the result of the inclusion of stand-by credits in the UCP. As was already mentioned, documents which are not documents of title, i.e., "other documents" are used for stand-by credits. In respect of non-title transactions, Article 23 of the 1983 revision provides a more flexible criterion for the examination of documents when documents other than transport documents, insurance documents and commercial invoices are used. In such cases the credit should stipulate by whom such documents are to be issued and their wording or data content. If the credit fails to do so, the banks will accept such documents as presented, provided it is clear that the goods and/or services described therein are those referred to in the commercial invoice(s). Although the approval of documents depends on the judgement and conscientious appraisal of the examining bank, one should not forget that the so-called "legalized" discretionary right of banks is involved in this method of examining documents, thus entailing a certain risk which may jeopardize legal security, the most sensitive condition in international documentary credit transactions.

In regard to the so-called standard of strict compliance, we refer to the case law for a survey of problems arising in the practice.[7] Here we will mention only two cases,

---

[7] See B. Kozolchyk, *Letter of Credit* (Tübingen 1979) p. 77 and the literature and case law cited there in support of standard of strict compliance. In particular, the author emphasizes judgment J.C.P. 1967 II. 14956 of the *Cour de Paris* of 31 May 1966, in which Stoufflet remarked: "The bank may not pay unless the documents are not only individually in accordance with the credit but also mutually consistent." At pp. 82 *et seq.* judgments of English, French, Italian and German courts are mentioned which contain exceptions to the standard of strict compliance.

the first of which concerns a German firm that bought chemicals from a Spanish firm in Madrid (12 U 144/1982, judgment of the *Oberlandesgericht* of Hamburg of 24 May 1983).[8] Payment of the price was to be effected by an irrevocable letter of credit through a Madrid correspondent bank. In accordance with the contract, the German buyer ordered the issuing bank in Germany to open a credit in favour of the Spanish supplier and to authorize Banco Exterior de España in Madrid to confirm the credit, to accept and honour the credit documents and to return them to the issuing bank. Having confirmed the credit, Banco Exterior de España of Madrid notified the beneficiary (the Spanish supplier) who presented his documents for examination. Although Banco Exterior de España ascertained documentary consistency, the forwarder's confirmation of taking delivery of the goods presented by the beneficiary contained the clause "ex warehouse Bilbao" instead of "FAS–Bilbao" as stipulated in the credit. Upon receipt of the honoured documents from Banco Exterior de España, the German issuing bank did not notice the inconsistency and transferred the money to the confirming bank in Madrid. The documents were then sent to the applicant for credit (the buyer) who noticed the inconsistency, refused to accept the documents and demanded that the amount paid be reimbursed. When the issuing bank made no reimbursement, the applicant sued the German bank for reimbursement plus damages.

The court held that the confirming Spanish bank had honoured documents which on their face were inconsistent with the credit documents, thus violating its obligation to examine the documents with reasonable care. This, however, did not relieve the issuing bank of its obligations to the applicant for credit because the confirming bank had acted merely in a complementary capacity without replacing the issuing bank. The most important argument supporting the plaintiff's claim that the issuing bank had not fulfilled its obligation was the fact that it had accepted inconsistent documents from the Spanish confirming bank without objection and without immediate notification that it was refusing the documents and returning them. Maintaining that the defendant bank had failed to comply with the requirements specified in Article 8(e) of the 1974 revision (which corresponds to Article 16(e) of the 1983 revision), the court ruled that it thereby lost its right to object to the confirming bank because it had accepted documents which on their face were not consistent with the terms and conditions of the credit and consequently were not operative credit instruments.

It is interesting to note that the court did not discuss the question of the extent to which the issuing bank was liable to the applicant for credit for the omissions of its correspondent, Banco Exterior de España, in the sense of Article 12(a) of the 1974 revision, which corresponds to Article 20(a) of the 1983 revision. This certainly would have been useful. As it is, however, one can see that the principle of strict compliance has its *raison d'être* and that the new flexible approach to the examination of documents is a source of potential risks, especially when the issuing bank accepts inconsistent credit instruments from its correspondent as in the case above.

In *The Commercial Banking Co. of Sydney Ltd.* v. *Jalsard Pty Ltd.*,[9] which deals with the question of gross negligence by banks in examining and honouring documents, the buyer (Jalsard Pty Ltd.) brought action against the defendant bank, claiming that it had accepted documents which on their face were inconsistent with the terms and

---

[8] Published in *RIW*, 5 (1984), pp. 392 *et seq.*

[9] Published in *Ll.Rep.* (1972), p. 529.

conditions of the credit. Among other things, a certificate of inspection had to be presented. Although the credit beneficiary did present a certificate of inspection, it indicated that only the packaging had been inspected and not the goods, which were substantially damaged. Whereas an organoleptic inspection had been carried out, the particular defects could be detected only by a special electrical technique.

In its ruling the Supreme Court of New South Wales ordered the bank to pay damages, maintaining that it had accepted documents which did not correspond to the conditions of the credit. The bank appealed the judgment which was then revised by the Privy Council on the following grounds:

- In the court's opinion, as far as the usual interpretation of the words *certificate of inspection* is concerned, the minimum requirements had been satisfied. If the parties considered it necessary to use special inspection methods, this should have been explicitly stated in the credit.
- In regard to the credit, the bank had not made a mistake by accepting a document which showed that the inspection had been carried out.
- The document presented by the beneficiary was a certificate of inspection which the bank was obliged to accept. Consequently, the bank had not acted with gross negligence and thus the appeal was founded.

Among other things, this case is instructive in respect of the analysis of the meaning of the term *on its face*. The court found the certificate of inspection to be consistent *on its face* with the conditions specified in the credit.

III. Liabilities and Responsibilities

The provisions on the liabilities and responsibilities of banks participating in credit transactions are among the most important clauses of the UCP and constitute the framework of the law of international documentary credits. The relevant provisions are formulated much more clearly in the 1983 revision, especially those regulating the liabilities and responsibilities of issuing banks *vis-à-vis* the banks they authorize to pay, accept or negotiate credits, or incur a deferred payment undertaking. Although these interbank relationships are now clarified, some matters concerning the responsibilities of issuing banks towards their applicants for credit are still unresolved. The provisions on the exemption of banks from liability or responsibility in Articles 17, 18 and 20 and those on Acts of God were simply copied word-for-word from the 1974 revision. The obligation of banks to examine documents with reasonable care set forth in Article 15 has already been discussed in detail and will not be repeated here.

1. The Right to Reimbursement

Article 16 governs the relationship between the issuing bank and the bank authorized and nominated to effect payment. If upon receipt of the documents the issuing bank ascertains that the remitting bank has effected payment on the basis of documents which appear on their face to be in accordance with the terms and conditions of the credit, it is obliged to reimburse the amount paid. In essence, the subject-matter of a documentary credit transaction is the purchase of documents, their price being the amount indicated in the credit. Accordingly, the effect of an irrevocable credit is to substitute the issuing banker for the buyer as the person who undertakes to "buy" the shipping documents. This is an undertaking which is absolute in the sense that so long as the documents of title to the goods which the seller tenders to the banker are in order, in the sense of being those prescribed in the credit, the bank must accept them regardless of any controversy between the seller and the buyer as to whether the contract of sale has been performed.[10]

On the other hand, if the issuing bank determines that the accepted documents are not in accordance with the terms and conditions of the credit, it must notify the remitting bank thereof without delay, i.e., by the fastest means of telecommunication (including telephone) but not by teletransmission which is used when advising credits (Article 12). Most likely, the drafters of the 1983 revision intentionally made this distinction since authenticated telephone conversations are most frequently used in practice for the notification of objections to documents. In such cases, the issuing bank will either hold the documents at the disposal of the remitting bank or return them to the beneficiary if it has received them directly from him. It is important to note that the issuing bank must state its reasons for refusing the documents, i.e., point out the discrepancies in the documents. Should it fail to do so, its objections shall be deemed unfounded and it will be precluded from making further objections.

An issuing bank which has acted in the above manner is entitled to claim from the remitting bank refund of any reimbursement which may have been made to that bank (Article 16(d)). If, however, the issuing bank fails to act in this manner, and/or fails to hold the documents at the disposal of, or to return them to the presentor, it shall be precluded from claiming that the documents are not in accordance with the terms and conditions of the credit.

If the remitting bank draws the attention of the issuing bank to any discrepancies in the documents or advises the issuing bank that it has paid, incurred a deferred payment undertaking, accepted or negotiated under reserve or against an indemnity in respect of such discrepancies, the issuing bank shall not thereby be relieved of any of its obligations under any provisions of Article 16. Furthermore, such reserve or indemnity concerns only the relations between the remitting bank and the party towards whom the reserve was made, or from whom, or on whose behalf, the indemnity was obtained (Article 16(f)). Accordingly, such agreement on indemnity has no effect on the credit obligation undertaken by the issuing bank.

Article 16(f) uses the term *indemnity* instead of *guarantee*, thus increasing the means of compensating a bank which agreed to accept documents with discrepancies or, even worse, honoured a credit without any documents. In any case, such banking practices are undesirable and it is quite correct that the consequences should be borne by the banks agreeing to such practices. Disputes concerning the bank's right to reimbursement can be settled only on the basis of the relations between the banks honouring such credits and those providing the indemnity. Neither the relations between the issuing bank and the applicant for credit nor those between the issuing bank and other banks are involved.

In this regard, a distinction should be made between cases where documents have been honoured on the basis of a reserve or indemnity given to the bank by the credit

---

[10] H. C. Gutteridge and M. Megrah, *The Law of Banker's Commercial Credits*, 5th ed. (London 1976) p. 1958.

beneficiary and those where a carrier delivered the goods to the beneficiary without a transport document. In the first case, the question of the bank's right to reimbursement concerns the bank which honoured the documents and the beneficiary who offered the indemnity, without relieving the issuing bank of any of its obligations towards the applicant for credit. Whereas such cases fall under Article 16(f), another case which is common in practice does not, i.e., when the cargo reaches the port of destination before the buyer has received the documents. In such cases it is common for the shipmaster to deliver the goods without the bill of lading on the basis of a receipt presented by the "alleged" buyer. Here the shipowner is fully liable if it is found that the cargo was delivered to an unauthorized person, i.e., not to the person who subsequently proves to the *bona fide* holder of the bill of lading. In view of the fact that a bill of lading is a document of title and that the shipowner is not only authorized but also obliged to deliver the goods only to the person in possession of the bill of lading, any departure from this rule qualifies as a civil offence for which the shipowner is fully liable.

Although attention has been drawn to such cases, they occur again and again and are often planned with scientific precision well in advance. Goods which have been sold in a documentary credit transaction reach the port of destination (unloading) much earlier than the documents. The shipmaster delivers the goods to the alleged buyer against a bank guarantee or an indemnity receipt. After taking possession of the goods, the buyer usually sells them abroad and then declares bankruptcy. Since the guarantee or receipt presented to the shipmaster is invalid, the seller cannot collect his money.

In a similar case before the *Bundesgericht* of the German Federal Republic,[11] the Court recognized the fact that it has become common international practice for goods to be handed over at the port of destination against an indemnity receipt if the bill of lading has not yet arrived. Although this practice is based on the good will of all parties to avoid unnecessary expenses, the Court warned that it places the shipowner at considerable risk that the person taking possession of the goods may not be authorized to do so. In conclusion the Court maintained that, in order to avoid possible damages, the holder of the bill of lading or authorized person is required, if possible, to take the necessary steps to prevent delivery of the goods to an unauthorized person, thus acting in accordance with the principle of good faith.

Returning to cases where the issuing bank has failed to substantiate discrepancies detected in the documents or to detect such discrepancies at all, thus forfeiting its right to object to the remitting bank, the question arises as to its liability towards an applicant who is of the opinion that the documents do not correspond to the terms and conditions of the credit and thus has refused to accept the documents or has informed the bank that he is holding them at its disposal. Since the provisions of Article 16 offer no answer to this delicate question which concerns the essence of the liabilities of banks, we turn to Article 20 of the 1983 revision on the exemption of banks from liability, the text of which was taken from Article of the 1974 revision with minor language improvements.

---

[11] 36 *BGHZ* (1962) p. 329, cited at J. Zahn, *Zahlung und Zahlungssicherung im Aussenhandel*, 5th ed. (Berlin New York, 1976), p. 209 d.

2. The Exemption of Banks from Liability and Responsibility

Article 20(a), which was cited above, exempts the issuing banks from liability for actions undertaken by other banks for the purpose of giving effect to the applicant's instructions. It is quite understandable that the issuing bank utilizes the services of other banks "for the account" of the applicant; however, it is questionable whether the applicant should bear the risk for the actions of a foreign bank with which he is unfamiliar and has no connection or legal relationship, especially when he has not chosen the bank himself and has no means (*de facto* and *de jure*) of controlling or influencing its actions. Therefore, it would perhaps be helpful to add the words "on the order" to the text, which would then read as follows:

"Banks utilising the services of another bank or other banks for the purpose of giving effect to the instructions of the applicant for the credit do so for the account, at the risk and on order of such applicant."

If the banks hold it reasonable for them to exempt themselves from all liability for the actions undertaken by their correspondent banks in the realization of their credit obligations towards the applicant for credit, the question arises as to why it is deemed reasonable to shift this risk to the applicant who is not involved in the relationship between the issuing bank and the correspondent bank.

Furthermore, Article 20(b) provides that the banks assume no liability or responsibility if the instructions they transmitted to other banks are not carried out. In my opinion, this provision conforms in principle neither with the basic rules of the law of contract nor with those of commercial law in general nor with the basic principles of the law of documentary credits. If the issuing bank and the applicant for credit conclude a contract in which the bank agrees to issue and effect a credit in accordance with the applicant's instructions, this means that the two parties have created an independent contractual relationship with mutual rights and obligations for both parties, including the bank.

In accordance with the applicant's instruction, the issuing bank is obliged to open a letter of credit with all the features constituting an instrument for financing various transactions (commodity and service) as defined in Article 2 of the 1983 revision. According to this article, the expression *documentary credit* means:

"any arrangement, however named or described, whereby a bank (the issuing bank) acting at the request and on the instructions of a customer (the applicant for credit) is to make a payment to or to the order of a third party (the beneficiary), to pay or accept bills of exchange (drafts) drawn by the beneficiary, or to authorize another bank to effect such payment or to pay . . . against stipulated documents . . .".

From this definition it is clear that banks operate and act "at the request and on the instructions" of their customers; however, it is not stated that they act "at the risk" of their customers as well. Furthermore, the issuing bank is obliged to make payments, accept or pay bills of exchange, or to authorize other banks to carry out such operations. In this connection Article 11 of the 1983 revision provides that the issuing bank shall nominate other banks and authorize them to pay, accept or negotiate against documents which appear on their face to be in accordance with the terms and conditions of the credit. If another bank has been nominated to perform the credit obligations of the issuing bank towards the applicant for credit, the other bank is an accessory to the issuing bank for the purpose of fulfilling its obligations towards the applicant for credit.

In other words, the bank enters a second contractual relationship with the other bank which it has chosen, nominated and authorized to fulfil its obligations towards the applicant for credit in the first contractual relationship. Shifting the risk of the second relationship to the applicant for credit although he is not a party to this relationship is difficult to justify legally, especially in light of the fact that his relationship with the issuing bank is separate and independent of the second relationship. Consequently, I am of the opinion that the question of non-performance of instructions transmitted to the other bank primarily concerns the issuing bank because it has a direct contractual relationship with this bank and thus it alone can resolve any dispute arising as a result of an omission on the part of the other bank. Therefore, it is difficult to defend the provision which exempts the issuing bank from the liabilities and responsibilities emanating from the other relationship.

It should, however, be pointed out that Article 20(b) is relevant only in cases in which the other bank is not willing to carry out the instructions of the issuing bank ("Banks assume no liability or responsibility should the instructions they transmit not be carried out . . ."). Therefore, if the other bank acts contrary to the instructions received from the issuing bank, I believe that in such a case the issuing bank cannot be exempted from liability or that such a clause would have no legal effect.

This view was confirmed by a judgment of the Supreme Commercial Court in Belgrade (Sl. 49/1964).[12] In the grounds of the judgment the Court upheld the stand taken in the contested judgment that the defendant bank–the issuing bank–could not be exempted from liability by invoking Article 14(2) of the UCP of the Lisbon Revision of 1951 because its liability was founded by virtue of the fact that it had violated Articles 9 and 10 of the UCP. Under these provisions (which correspond to Articles 15, 16 and 20 of the 1983 revision), the defendant bank was obliged to examine carefully the documents accepted by its correspondent bank in Cairo and, after having established that they did not comply with the terms of the credit, to notify the correspondent bank of its objection by telegraph or other means, including the statement that it was holding the documents at its disposal or was returning them to it. Moreover, it should have insisted that the correspondent bank request that the coverage be refunded, if necessary by going to court at the expense of the plaintiff whose interests it would be protecting. This view on the above-mentioned issues was taken and substantiated by the same Court in its earlier ruling Sl. 192/1963.

In the doctrine the view is held that numerous aspects of the interpretation of the exemption clause will depend on the stand of the municipal laws involved, thus making these problems attractive for a comparative analysis.[13]

Furthermore, it should be mentioned that the wording of Article 20(b) of the 1983 revision is not clear and that this fact alone can be the source of numerous misunderstandings. If the method of grammatical interpretation is applied, one may conclude that the issuing bank is exempted from liability for the actions of its correspondent bank only in the event that the latter has "not at all" followed the instructions of the first bank, i.e., if the correspondent bank did not respond to the instructions of the issuing bank. Although questionable, such a view would

---

[12] Rosenberg, *Pravo medjunarodnih plaćanja*, p. 105.

[13] F. Eisemann and R. Eberth, *Das Dokumenten Akkreditiv im Internationalen Handelsverkehr*, 2nd ed. (Heidelberg 1979) pp. 127 *et seq.*

nevertheless be less rigorous; this, however, would depend on the consequences. On the other hand, if the issuing bank were exempted from liability for actions of the other bank which were contrary to the instructions it had transmitted to it, in my opinion the above criticism would be justifiable.

Finally, a few words should be said in connection with Article 20(c), according to which "the applicant for the credit shall be bound by and liable to indemnify the banks against all obligations and responsibilities imposed by foreign laws and usages". This provision is unclear and no explanation has been offered by the ICC Commission for Banking Techniques and Practice. In this respect Ventris commented in his book:

"A would-be plaintiff might experience a little on a defendant in imposing liability in an English court on a defendant under this paragraph. It could be argued that it is void for lack of clarity."[14]

3. Other Liability Exemption Clauses

The liability exemption clause contained in Article 17 of the 1983 revision, which is identical to Article 9 of the 1974 revision, is without effect if liability is exempted for actions for which banks are responsible such as checking the formal requirements, accuracy, validity, authenticity of documents, etc. Article 17 shall apply only if the circumstances are such that they could not be established by the bank within its general obligation to examine the documents with reasonable care. On the other hand, if the bank knew at the moment the documents were presented that some of them were falsified and/or that certain data therein was falsified (e.g., in the bill of lading), the bank may not be exempted from liability. On the contrary, if it fails to refuse such documents, its liability for damages is unlimited.

In connection with the liability exemption clause in Article 17, the ICC Commission for Banking Techniques and Practice mentions several cases in which this clause would not apply.[15] For example, if the bank involved is the party which committed the fraud or falsified the documents or if it knew or in any way could have known about the fraud before such documents were presented to it, it shall be liable for damages. Furthermore, the exemption clause in Article 17 shall not apply if it was evident on the face of the documents that fraud had been committed and if the bank in question violated its basic obligation to examine all the documents with reasonable care.

In this context the ICC Commission for Banking Techniques and Practice refers to the judgment of the House of Lords in *United City Merchant (International) Ltd. and others* v. *Royal Bank of Canada and others*[16] which confirms the ability of English courts to recognize circumstances in which banks have failed to comply with their credit obligations in cases which turned out to involve fraud or the fraud was self-evident and could or ought to have been noticed during examination of the documents. This stand has also been taken in various judgments by German, Swiss, Austrian, Italian, Dutch and American courts.[17]

[14] F. M. Ventris, *Banker's Documentary Credits*, (London 1980) pp. 23 *et seq.*
[15] ICC Publication No. 411, *supra*, n. 2, at p. 34.
[16] *Ll.Rep.* 2 (1982), p. 1.
[17] Rosenberg, *Suvremeni pravni problemi bankarske prakse* [*Contemporary Legal Problems of Banking Practices*] (Zagreb 1980) pp. 44 *et seq.*

In their judgments English courts have expressed their views on the use of court injunctions requested by the applicant for credit for the purpose of preventing the issuing or other bank from honouring documents. According to the English courts, the relationship between the confirming bank and the credit beneficiary is based on a banking obligation which is abstract in character and thus the confirming bank is obliged to honour credit documents presented by the beneficiary, provided such documents comply with the terms and conditions prescribed in the operative credit instrument. Insisting that courts should not interfere in the law of documentary credits in a way which could lead to abuse and legal uncertainty, English courts have taken the view that such court injunctions are inadmissible and contrary to the nature of irrevocable documentary credits. This includes court injunctions which prevent the credit beneficiary from realizing his rights in disputes involving the issuing or confirming bank.

For example, in *Hamzeh Malas and Sons* v. *British Imex Industries Ltd.*[18] successive delivery of the iron bars purchased from the British firm was stipulated, with the payment for each partial delivery to be effected by an irrevocable documentary credit. The Jordanian buyer opened such a credit in favour of the English seller; however, upon receipt of the first partial delivery, he objected to the quality of the goods and requested that an injunction be issued to freeze the credit which had already been opened for the second delivery. In both instances, however, the buyer's request was rejected. Citing the grounds for his judgment, Lord Justice Jenkins of the Court of Appeal stated that it is certain that nobody will prevent the seller from receiving the purchase price if it has been agreed that payment be effected on the basis of an irrevocable and confirmed letter of credit. In cases where the seller has purchased the goods from a third person for this purpose, the seller would be able to use the irrevocable credit opened in his favour to pay the persons from whom he has purchased the goods. This system of financing would be impossible if the applicant were permitted to freeze the credit should a dispute arise between himself and the credit beneficiary.

In *Discount Records Ltd.* v. *Barclays Bank Ltd. and Another*[19] the buyer requested a court injunction, claiming that the credit beneficiary planned to collect the agreed amount in a fraudulent manner; however, the buyer had no reliable means of proving the alleged fraud. The Chancery Division rejected the buyer's request for the injunction, citing Judge Megarry as follows:

"I would be slow to interfere with banker's irrevocable credits, and not least in the sphere of international banking, unless a sufficiently grave cause is shown for interventions by the court that are too ready or too frequent might gravely impair the reliance which, quite properly, is placed on such credits."

In conclusion it can be said that English courts issue injunctions for documentary credits only in extreme cases where there is proof of abuse of law and fraud. The party requesting such an injunction is required to present valid proof together with his request. Alleged fraud is insufficient.

---

[18] Judgment of the Court of Appeal (London) of 10 December 1957; published in *Weekly LR* (1958) p. 100.

[19] Judgment (1974) D. No 1992, Chancery Division; published in *Ll.Rep.* (1975) p. 444. For more information, see P. Holden, "Irrevocable Credit: No Injunction to Stop Payment", *J.Inst. of Bankers (1975)* pp. 298 *et seq.*

As regards the liability exemption clauses in Articles 18 and 19 of the 1983 revision, I refer to my book as there have been no changes since its publication.[20]

4. Liability for Reimbursement and the Introduction of Reimbursing Banks

Article 21 of the 1983 revision deals with the obligation of reimbursement, specifying the conditions for reimbursement of the amounts paid by the banks which were authorized and nominated to honour documents in accordance with the instructions of the issuing bank and the terms and conditions of the particular credit (remitting banks). The novelty in this provision is the introduction of so-called reimbursing banks for the purpose of reimbursing the remitting banks. It should be noted that the payments of reimbursing banks are regarded as *clean payments*, provided that the particular bank is authorized to reimburse the remitting bank on the basis of its confirmation that if accepted, the documents complied with the terms and conditions of the credit.

Finally, the issuing bank is now obliged to compensate the paying, accepting or negotiating bank for any loss of interest if reimbursement is not provided upon the first request made to the reimbursing bank or as otherwise specified in the credit or agreed upon by both parties.

---

[20] Rosenberg, *Pravo medjunarodnih plaćanja*, p. 103 n. 9. See also F. Eisemann and R. Eberth, *Das Dokumenten Akkreditiv im Internationalen Handelsverkehr*, p. 148 n. 2.

5

Contract Guarantees

Lars A. E. Hjerner

I. Introduction

This article analyses the work of the International Chamber of Commerce (ICC) in the field of *contract guarantees*. Although such guarantees are also issued by institutions other than banks, they are sometimes referred to as *bank guarantees*. In English business circles, they are often called bonds. In 1978 the ICC approved and published (Publication 325) its *Uniform Rules for Contract Guarantees* (hereinafter: Uniform Rules or 325 Rules). This was followed in 1982 by another publication (No. 406) *Model Forms for Issuing Contract Guarantees* (hereinafter: Model Forms). Although the 325 Rules are currently being revised, they are still in force and it is uncertain when the revisions will be completed and approved. In order to understand the specific nature of contract guarantees and the problems which arise in practice, it is necessary to examine both the 325 Rules and the new Draft rules.

II. The Need for Uniform Rules for Contract Guarantees

There are three different types of contract guarantees: tender guarantees (or bonds), performance guarantees and repayment guarantees.

A *tender guarantee* often has to be submitted by a tenderer who makes a tender for a contract for the delivery of goods or for the construction of civil engineering works such as plants, bridges or roads. If the tenderer fails to sign the contract awarded to him or provide a performance guarantee (which may have been a condition for his obtaining the contract), the buyer, i.e., the beneficiary under the guarantee, shall be entitled to collect payment against the guarantee as a cover for the damages suffered or to be suffered as a result of the tenderer's failure to sign and proceed with the contract.

International Contracts and Payments (Šarčević, Volken, eds.; 1 85333 615 7; © Graham & Trotman, 1991; pub. Graham & Trotman; printed in Great Britain), pp. 69–86.

A *performance guarantee* is given to cover loss and damages a buyer may suffer if the seller or supplier does not perform the contract according to the terms and conditions stipulated therein.

Finally, a *repayment guarantee* is issued to guarantee reimbursement of an advanced payment made by the buyer in cases where the contract stipulates that advance payment made shall be repaid in certain circumstances.

In each type of guarantee there are at least three parties involved: the guarantor, the principal and the beneficiary. In international contracts there is also an intermediary bank, the so-called instructing party. The guarantor, the party issuing the guarantee, is often a bank; however, guarantees can also be issued by insurance companies and other institutions. Sometimes a parent company issues a guarantee in favour of a subsidiary. Such guarantees, however, usually do not follow the 325 Rules. The party requesting the guarantee is the principal. This is the seller or supplier of the goods and services or other contractor. The person in whose favour the guarantee is issued is called the beneficiary. This is the buyer, i.e., the party inviting the tender or awarding the contract. If the beneficiary has his place of business in the same country as the principal, the principal approaches the guarantor directly and instructs him how to issue the guarantee. On the other hand, if the beneficiary's place of business is abroad, the principal usually contacts a bank in his own country which then instructs a bank in the beneficiary's country to issue the guarantee. In such cases the intermediary bank in the principal's country is the instructing party.

The interests of the beneficiary, principal and guarantor always differ. For his part, the beneficiary wants to receive a compensatory sum of money if the principal fails to meet his obligations arising from submission of the tender or has been awarded the contract and fails to perform it in accordance with the terms. Similarly, the beneficiary wants to secure repayment of any payments or advances he has made if the principal fails to perform the contract. In other words, he wants to be sure that he will receive such amounts as may be due to him, even if the principal fails to pay such amounts, whether by reason of unwillingness or inability to pay.

As for the principal, i.e., the tenderer or the party to whom the contract has been awarded, he does not want to be forced to pay against the guarantee if he has met his obligations arising from submission of the tender or if he has been awarded the contract and performed it in accordance with its terms.

Regardless of whether the guarantor is a bank, insurance company or other institution, it wants to fulfil its obligations in the terms of the guarantee without becoming involved in possible disputes between the beneficiary and principal. This applies particularly to disputes on whether or not the principal has properly performed his obligations arising from submission of the tender or from the contract awarded.

In view of these different interests, a contract guarantee has the difficult task of: (1) balancing the interests of the three parties so as to create a fair equilibrium and (2) defining the rights and obligations of the parties with sufficient precision so as to avoid disputes. In the past this has not always been possible. Sometimes lack of experience or abuse by the party with greater bargaining power led to inequitable situations resulting in distrust and dispute.

Thus it became evident that a set of rules was needed which would establish a uniform practice guaranteeing an equitable balance of the interests of the parties concerned while observing the commercial purpose of the contract guarantee, i.e., to ensure the availability of funds from an independent third party if the beneficiary should have a justified claim against the principal.

To this end, the ICC convened a Working Party whose members represented different interest groups in both the industrialized and developing countries. In close co-operation with interested intergovernmental and international commercial organizations–particularly the United Nations Commission on International Trade Law (UNCITRAL)–the Working Party drafted the Uniform Rules. As rapporteur and member of the ICC Working Party, I made the first draft of the Uniform Rules in 1968. Thereafter, the Working Party met several times a year and reported on its progress to the Banking and the Commercial Practice Commissions of the ICC. After the Uniform Rules were finally accepted and published in 1978, it took another four years before the Model Forms were finalized and published.

III. The 325 Rules

1. Scope of Appplication

In drafting the Uniform Rules care was taken to allow maximum flexibility yet achieve the goals mentioned above. As a result, application of the Rules is entirely voluntary. In this sense, Article 1(1) of the Rules provides that the Rules shall apply if the guarantee *itself* provides for the application of the Rules. In such cases, the Rules are binding on all parties to the guarantee "unless otherwise is expressly stated in the guarantee or any amendment thereto". Thus it follows that the parties may agree on partial application of the Rules.

This is particularly important in connection with so-called on-demand guarantees, i.e., guarantees payable on first or on simple demand. It is true that all guarantees are payable only on demand; however, the term *on-demand guarantee* usually signifies that the only condition stipulated for payment is simple demand on the part of the beneficiary. Therefore, guarantees of this type are sometimes called *unconditional guarantees*. This term, however, is not always adequate as there may be some restrictive conditions. For example, payment may be effected only if the claim is submitted before the expiry date of the guarantee.

As we shall later see, the most disputed issue concerns the extent to which the payment of a guarantee should be made subject to certain conditions. The 325 Rules attempt to strike a balance in this respect by making tender guarantees payable under less stringent conditions than performance and repayment guarantees. Nevertheless, influential interest groups now strongly support revisions which would make the payment of guarantees less conditional than under the 325 Rules. Those against such revisions argue that, in accordance with the principle of party autonomy, parties wishing to use the 325 Rules but less conditional guarantees may do so by contracting out of Article 9 of the Rules.

Although party autonomy is the leading principle of the Rules, it may happen that in some countries there are mandatory regulations in the field of guarantees. For example, mandatory rules of national law may require that claims under the guarantee be made within the limitation period prescribed by national law, regardless of other limitation periods stipulated in the Rules or in the guarantee itself. In this respect, Article 1(2) of the Rules provides that the mandatory provision shall prevail. In such cases, the guarantee is not entirely null and void but is valid as revised. Similarly, Article 1(2) may also come into play when a provision is invoked such as § 242 BGB or § 36 of the Scandinavian Law on Contracts, according to which a condition in a contract may be modified if it proves to be manifestly unfair.

As mentioned above, the Rules shall apply if reference is made to them in the guarantee. In this context the question arises as to whether the Rules may be applied in cases where the guarantee contains no reference to the Rules but the parties have referred to them in their correspondence or otherwise. This question would have to be solved according to the general principles of interpretation and of contract law, not by the Uniform Rules. Furthermore, if the parties have made no reference to the Rules at all, can they be applied on the ground that certain trade practices prescribed therein belong to customary law? Certainly the Rules cannot be said to be customary law in their entirety; however, this does not exclude the fact that some provisions prescribe trade practices which can be regarded as belonging to customary law. It is easy to cite provisions where this would *not* be the case. For example, the provisions stipulating the limitation period for filing a claim in Article 4 and the expiry of a guarantee in Article 5 would certainly not apply unless the Rules as such are applicable. Perhaps it could be argued that the provision in Article 8(2) requiring the guarantor to notify the principal or the instructing party upon receipt of a claim reflects trade practice and customary law; however, I am not prepared to state any definite opinion on that point in either direction.

2. Definitions and Liability

Article 2 of the Rules defines various terms already mentioned above: tender, performance guarantee, repayment guarantee, principal, instructing party, the guarantor and beneficiary under a guarantee. On the other hand, it does not attempt to define the nature of the guarantee. In this respect, it does not specify whether the guarantee is a primary and independent obligation or a secondary and accessory one, nor does it indicate the legal consequences of such characterization. It should be noted that the *link* between the performance of the guarantor's undertaking and default by the principal is established in the definitions.

The liability of the guarantor to the beneficiary is dealt with in Article 3. From this Article it follows that the terms and conditions under which the guarantor is liable should be defined in the guarantee itself or stipulated in the Rules. Giving proper legal effect to what is commercially intended requires that the guarantee be drafted with clarity and precision. It is obviously essential that the guarantee indicate precisely the amount to be paid by the guarantor and the conditions for payment. The guarantor should not be placed in the situation of an arbitrator who has to decide on fairly loose grounds whether the principal has defaulted. If this situation nevertheless occurs, the provisions in Article 9 on documentation to support a claim should prevail. The evidence required to prove that the principal has defaulted should be specified in detail as this gives the beneficiary the right of claim under the guarantee. In the same token, the amount of the claim should be indicated in the guarantee.

Article 3(2) provides that the amount of liability stated in the guarantee shall not be reduced by reason of any partial performance of the underlying contract. Should this not be the intention of the parties, as might be the case in respect of some performance bonds, this must be expressly stated in the guarantee. Thus Article 3(2) emphasizes the independent character of the guarantee vis-à-vis the underlying contract. This is in keeping with Article 2(2) which provides that the guarantor may rely *only* on those defenses permitted by the Rules or by the terms and conditions specified in the guarantee. Although there may be a link between the default of the principal and the undertaking of the guarantor, the guarantor may not refer to the underlying contract unless such reference is permitted in the guarantee.

3. Last Date for Claim and Expiry of Guarantee

The unconditional condition of Article 4 of the Rules has already been mentioned, i.e., the last date on which a claim can be made which must be observed even in unconditional guarantees (on-demand guarantees). Of course, it is best to designate the last date for a claim in the guarantee itself by referring either to a specific date or event. Sometimes, however, this is not possible or may have been overlooked. Depending on the type of guarantee, the expiry date may also have to be defined differently.

Overprotection should be avoided particularly in the case of tender guarantees as the costs or conditions therein may influence the readiness of contractors to submit tenders. The expiry date of a tender guarantee should be set as close as possible to the date on which the contract is to be awarded to one of the tenderers. It would not be in the interest of either the beneficiary or the principal to insist on a tender guarantee being outstanding for a long time if such is unnecessary.

In respect of tender guarantees, Article 4 provides an expiry date of six months from the date of issue of the guarantee. This, however, may not be long enough. On the other hand, a tender guarantee may expire prior to the date specified in the guarantee. In this sense Article 5(2) provides that a tender guarantee offered by the party awarded the contract will expire when that party has signed the contract or, if a performance guarantee is required according to the contract or the invitation to tender, when that performance guarantee has also been provided by the successful tenderer.

As for tenderers whose tenders are *not* accepted, their tender guarantees cease to be valid when the contract has been awarded to another tenderer, regardless of whether that award results in a final contract between the parties. Consequently, it should not be possible for the party inviting the tenders to keep the other tenders and their tenderers "in reserve" while waiting to see if the negotiations with the successful tenderer will result in a final contract.

In the case of performance guarantees, the expiry period is also six months. Here, however, the time commences to run from another date, i.e., the date specified in the contract for delivery or for completion of the contract. If the parties "agree" upon an extension of the delivery period, the expiry of the guarantee is automatically postponed. On the other hand, if the delay in delivery is *not* agreed upon but represents a breach of contract, the Rules do not provide for automatic extension of the guarantee. Accordingly, the beneficiary must make claim against the guarantor within six months from the day the delay started.

In cases where there is a maintenance or guarantee period after delivery of the goods, the Rules provide that it should be indicated in the performance guarantee that such maintenance or guarantee period is to be "expressly covered" by the guarantee. This basic requirement may be easily overlooked by the beneficiary upon receipt of what he believes to be an effective guarantee for the full performance of the contract by the supplier. If delivery is made *before* the expiry of the delivery period, it may be doubtful as to whether the guarantee covers not only delay in performance but also *defective* performance. Therefore it is necessary to be very precise in this respect when drafting the guarantee. The Model form for performance guarantees in ICC Publication 406 does not expressly cover the maintenance period.

In regard to repayment guarantees, the 325 Rules merely state that the last date for a claim of repayment is six months from the date of delivery or completion as specified in the contract.

Article 5 on the expiry of the guarantee is more or less self-evident. If no claim has been received by the guarantor on or before the expiry date or if any claim arising under the guarantee has been settled in full satisfaction of all the rights of the beneficiary thereunder, the guarantee ceases to be valid. For the principal it is important that the date of expiry of the guarantee be defined; after that day he can no longer be charged by the guarantor for having provided the guarantee.

Sometimes the mere holding of the document containing the guarantee is incorrectly regarded in certain circles as substantiating the rights under the guarantee. Article 6 of the Rules attempts to clarify this matter by emphasizing that retention of the document containing the guarantee does not in itself confer any right upon the beneficiary. Consequently, the documents should be returned to the guarantor without delay. Even if this is not done, failure to do so has no influence on the rights and obligations of the parties under the guarantee.

4. Amendments to Contracts and Guarantees

A contract or guarantee may sometimes have to be amended. In simple situations where the *guarantor* wishes to amend the terms or conditions of the guarantee, Article 7(3) provides that to be effective against the beneficiary, any amendment has to be agreed to by the beneficiary. The same applies in regard to the principal if amendments are to be effective against him. Particularly in the case of on-demand guarantees, it may occur that the beneficiary abuses his rights under the guarantee by requesting the guarantor to pay or "prolong". In such cases, the guarantor cannot pay unless the conditions for payment are satisfied. If he does pay, he may not have any means of recourse against the principal. Similarly, the guarantor may lose his right of recourse against the principal if he prolongs the guarantee. Thus, any change in the terms or conditions of the guarantee should be agreed upon by the principal and the beneficiary in order to be effective. This reduces the risk that a guarantee could be used by the beneficiary as a means of pressuring the principal into renegotiating the terms of the contract.

The situation is more complicated when changes are made in the underlying contract. In regard to tender guarantees, it is quite normal for some terms of the tender to be changed before the contract is finalized. In the same token, it is not unusual to have some conditions of a large contract amended during its performance. In cases where the underlying contract is amended, the question arises as to whether the guarantee is still valid and effective. In this respect, the Rules make a distinction between tender guarantees and performance guarantees.

As concerns tender guarantees, the Rules stipulate that such guarantee is valid only in respect of the *original* tender submitted by the principal and that it is not effective in the event that any amendment has been made thereto. Furthermore, it is not valid beyond the expiry date specified in the guarantee *unless* the *guarantor* has given notice in writing or used a similar means of communication to acknowledge that the guarantee applies to the amended contract or that the expiry date has been extended. In such cases, the guarantee is valid and effective between the guarantor and the beneficiary; however, the guarantor loses his right of recourse against the principal unless the principal has also agreed to such extension (Article 7(3)). Although this solution does not entirely exclude the possibility that the beneficiary could use the tender guarantee as a means of forcing amendments of the tender in his favour, it at least makes it more difficult for him to do so.

As for performance guarantees, it is natural for an amendment between the contracting parties to be agreed upon during the period of performance of the contract. Therefore, the main rule provides that–without further stipulation–the performance guarantee is valid not only in respect of the principal's obligations set forth in the original contract but also in respect of any amendment thereto. A natural restriction of the main rule provides that the guarantee shall not be valid in excess of the original amount or extend beyond the original expiry date.

At the same time, however, the Rules also provide that a performance guarantee may stipulate that it shall *not* be valid in respect of any amendment to the original contract, or that the guarantor shall be notified of any such amendment for his approval and, failing such approval, the guarantee will not be valid in respect of a contract which has been amended after the guarantee has been issued. This alternative is provided as a safeguard for the guarantor. Since an amendment of the contract or an extension of the delivery period could increase his risks to the point of jeopardizing his chances for successful recourse against the principal, it is only reasonable that this express approval should be a requirement for validity in such cases.

5. Submission of Claim

The rules provided in Article 8 on submission of the claim have more or less the character of recommendations and thus are not operative in the real sense. Under para. 1 the claim should be made in writing and received by the guarantor no later than the day of expiry. Upon receipt of the claim the guarantor should notify the principal or the instructing party, as the case may be, not only of the claim itself but also of any documentation received. Problems may arise in connection with the requirement that documentation–preferably an arbitral award, court decision or approval of the principal–be presented by the beneficiary when making claim. Since it may be difficult for the beneficiary to provide adequate documentation at the time of the claim or even before the expiry date of the guarantee, Article 8(3)(c) provides that such documentation may be presented after receipt of the claim within the time limit specified in the guarantee or, failing such specification, as soon as practicable. If an arbitral award or a court decision is required, this can obviously take a long time; however, if the claim has been made, this apparently excludes the guarantee from expiring before the necessary documentation can be presented. Only in cases where the beneficiary must provide the necessary documentation himself, for example, an expert affidavit, a fixed time limit of six months is stipulated.

It should be noted that the wording of Article 8(3) is ambiguous in that it stipulates that in any event a claim shall not be honoured if the guarantee "has ceased to be valid in accordance with its own terms or with the provisions in the Rules". This implies that a claim would not be honoured if the necessary documentation–an arbitral award or court decision–cannot be presented before the expiry date of the guarantee. It appears that the Rules intended to make a distinction between *the last day for a claim* and the *date on which the guarantee ceases to be valid* but fail to do so. In practice, if the claim is made in time, the guarantee does not cease to be valid because the case has not been settled before the expiry date.

6. Documentation to Support Claim

The most disputed article of the 325 Rules is Article 9 specifying the documentation to support the claim. Referring to party autonomy, the first part of Article 9 leaves it to the parties to determine which type of documentation shall be required. Failing such specification, the beneficiary is required to submit the documents set forth in subparagraphs a and b. In a somewhat confusing manner, Article 9 also refers to on-demand guarantees (those requiring "only a statement of claim by the beneficiary") and stipulates that documentation must also be submitted to support claims for such guarantees unless provided otherwise. This means that, if the Rules apply to an on-demand guarantee, in order to be effective "on demand" the guarantee must explicitly exclude Article 9 or state that the requirements for documentation under subparagraphs a and b do not apply. It does not suffice to state that, although subject to the Rules, the guarantee is payable on first and simple demand. By including on-demand guarantees in Article 9, the draftsmen of the 325 Rules deliberately hoped to discourage their use. In this respect they may have gone too far.

As for performance guarantees and repayment guarantees, subpara. b provides that the claim shall be supported by a court decision or an arbitral award justifying the claim, or the approval of the principal in writing to the claim and the amount to be paid. Although this rule is less complicated than that in subpara. a, it may nevertheless lead to complications. There is no indication as to whether the court decision should be final, i.e., no longer subject to appeal; however, even to obtain a decision in first instance may take considerable time. In the meantime, the guarantee is of no use to the beneficiary although he had probably thought that, by using a bank guarantee, he would quickly receive the money as compensation for his loss suffered by the alleged breach of contract by the principal. The situation may even be worse for the beneficiary if disputes between him and the principal have to be settled by arbitration. It is well known that even "speedy" arbitration procedures last longer than one year and frequently two or more years. Such solution is obviously unsatisfactory if the purpose of the guarantee was to make the money available to the beneficiary easily and quickly. This, however, has to be balanced against the risk that money has been paid and in the end the claim cannot be justified.

Proceeding to tender guarantees, we see that *no* decision of a court or arbitral tribunal is required in support of the claim. This is not surprising as at that stage no contract has been concluded between the beneficiary and the principal. Thus a bona fide statement by the beneficiary suffices in which he acknowledges that the principal's tender was accepted but thereafter the principal failed to sign the contract or to provide the performance guarantee as designated in the tender. In addition to such statement, the beneficiary must offer to have any dispute arising between himself and the principal regarding repayment of the sum paid under the tender guarantee settled by arbitration.

7. Final Provisions

The final provisions of the 325 Rules contain clauses on the applicable law (Article 10) and the settlement of disputes (Article 11). As throughout the Rules, party autonomy also prevails in regard to the choice of law. Failing an agreement on the applicable law, the guarantee will be governed by the law of the guarantor's place of business. Accordingly, if the instructing bank uses a local bank in the country of the beneficiary to issue the guarantee, the law of that country—including its mandatory rules—will govern the guarantee. Although this may not seem attractive to the principal, beneficiaries often require that the guarantee be issued by a local bank. Moreover, the result could turn out to be the same even if the principal and the instructing party succeeded in introducing a choice-of-law clause into the guarantee according to which the law of their country would be applicable. In such cases, the mandatory rules in the country of the local bank would nevertheless prevail in accordance with Article 1(2), as indicated earlier. Furthermore, if the mandatory rules in the country of the local bank are characterized as public policy, they would apply irrespective of any choice of law made by the parties. Therefore, there can be no guarantee that a choice-of-law clause inserted by the principal and the instructing party would be effective. If the issuing bank has more than one place of business, the law of the place of the *branch* which issued the guarantee would apply.

The rules on the settlement of disputes are rather drawn out. First of all, by way of a recommendation rather than a binding rule, the parties are reminded that they may agree upon arbitration either in accordance with the ICC Rules or the UNCITRAL Arbitration Rules. This is followed by the operative part: in case the beneficiary and the guarantor have agreed upon arbitration, the principal or the instructing party, as the case may be, shall have the right to intervene in the arbitral proceedings. On the other hand, if the guarantor and the beneficiary have *not* agreed to arbitration or to the jurisdiction of any specific court, any dispute between them shall be settled exclusively by the competent court of the country of the guarantor's main place of business or, at the option of the beneficiary, by the competent court of the country of the branch which issued the guarantee. In other words, if the parties have not agreed to arbitration or to the jurisdiction of any specific court, any disputes between them relating to the guarantee are to be settled by the competent courts of the guarantor's country.

8. Experience in Practice

Having been in force for more than 10 years, the 325 Rules have been used by parties with varying success. The main criticism has been directed against Article 9 and the fact that the Rules cannot be easily applied to on-demand guarantees. It has been said—and probably rightly—that on-demand guarantees are the most common form of guarantee requested by certain groups of beneficiaries. By requiring documentation to support the claim, Article 9 directly negates the very character of on-demand guarantees which are intended to assure the availability of the money on demand. It appears that the strongest criticism comes from certain continental bank circles. On the other hand, other business circles confirm that the 325 Rules have been accepted in guarantees even with developing countries where governmental agencies often require submission to local rules and the use of on-demand guarantees. Despite their limited success, it seems that dissatisfaction prevails.

IV. New Draft Rules For Contract Guarantees

In view of the dissatisfaction with the 325 Uniform Rules, in 1985 the Committee of London and Scottish Bankers submitted a draft Code of Practice for Contract Guarantees or Bonds to the ICC for consideration. This was followed in 1987 by a new edition of the Draft. In the mean time, the ICC convened a new joint working party consisting of members from the Banking and the Commercial Practice Commissions. Conflicting views have been expressed and defended by the members of the ICC Working Party. In particular, some banking circles favour on-demand guarantees which, in their opinion, are easier to handle. On the other hand, spokesmen for the industry–supported to some extent by a number of bankers– favour conditional guarantees and a system similar to the 325 Rules. Furthermore, it has been suggested that the rules for guarantees should be as similar as possible to the rules for letters of credits (ICC Publication 400: *Uniform Customs and Practice for Documentary Credits*). In this respect it is argued that stand-by letters of credits are used as an alternative to bank guarantees.

By now the ICC Working Party has produced several drafts. In particular, UNCITRAL and its Working Group on International Contract Practices has showed increasing interest in the project. At its session in November 1988 the UNCITRAL Working Group studied the ICC draft rules of 1988 and delivered a report with its comments (A/CN 9/316). After taking into account the views of the UNCITRAL Working Group as well as comments by National Committees and other interested circles, the ICC Working Party presented a revised draft in February 1989 (460/470–Int. 35). In all probability the February draft (Draft rules) will not be the final one. Nevertheless, it is useful to comment on these rules as they differ considerably from the 325 Rules in several important aspects.

1. Scope of Application

The scope of application of the Draft rules is identical to that of the 325 Rules. It should be noted, however, that the Draft Rules make no distinction between the various types of guarantees: tender guarantees, performance guarantees and repayment guarantees. As we will see, this may cause some problems when it comes to applying the revised rules to guarantees other than performance guarantees.

Whereas Article 1(1) of the Draft rules is the same as its counterpart in the 325 Rules, the Draft rules have no provision favouring mandatory rules as in Article 1(2) of the 325 Rules. This is surprising because it is generally accepted that mandatory rules of the applicable law apply irrespective of the will of the parties. Moreover, mandatory rules of the *lex fori* may also apply as a matter of public policy. Sometimes parties attempt to exclude any and every national legal system by referring to *lex mercatoria* or to general principles of law or trade law. Although this method is also used to evade mandatory rules of law, it is doubtful whether a court would accept such arguments. In the same token, it is difficult to believe that the Draft rules intend to set up a different system. In my opinion, a reference to mandatory rules would be useful.

The Draft Rules introduce the term *counter-guarantee* which is defined as the written undertaking of the instructing party by which payment is promised to the guarantor on receipt of his notification that he has been called upon to effect payment under the guarantee. Since no subsequent reference is made to the counter-guarantee, it is unclear how such guarantee is to be dealt with. Obviously the instructing party and the guarantor may agree that the counter-guarantee is subject to the Draft rules in one way or another; however, failing such agreement, the rules will not apply. It does not suffice that the main guarantee is subject to the rules.

2. Relation to the Underlying Contract

Article 2(b) of the Draft rules emphasizes the independence of guarantees by specifying that they are "independent" of any underlying transaction. Furthermore, it is stated that the terms of any underlying transaction shall in no way affect the guarantor's rights and obligations under a guarantee even if reference is made thereto in the guarantee. According to the Draft rules, a guarantor's obligation of performance under any guarantee is to pay the sum or sums specified therein, provided the terms and conditions of the guarantee are complied with.

In my opinion, it is questionable whether such frankness will help. Later the Draft rules stipulate that all guarantees should expressly identify the underlying transaction for which the guarantee was issued (Article 3(d)). Similarly, Article 20 provides that the bona fide statement accompanying a demand for payment shall specify the breach of contract in respect of the underlying transaction. Apparently, it is believed that in the exceptional case that the principal were able to prove that the contract in the underlying transaction had not been breached, he would be able to obtain a court injunction to stop payment under the guarantee regardless of the provision in Article 2(b). Furthermore, reference to the underlying contract is inevitable in guarantees in which the amount of liability depends on the progress made in the performance of the underlying construction contract. The Draft rules take this into account when they provide that a guarantee may contain express provisions for reduction by a specified amount on a specific date or upon presentation to the guarantor of documents specified for this purpose in the guarantee. Such document could be an affidavit of an engineer or an approval of the beneficiary of part performance under the underlying contract. This is also possible under the 325 Rules, the wording of which is even clearer. There Article 3(2) provides that the amount of liability stated in the guarantee shall not be reduced by reason of any partial performance, *unless so specified* in the guarantee.

3. Payment in Money Only

Under the Draft rules no alternative forms of payment are permitted. From Article 2(b) it follows that payment can be made only in *money*. On the contrary, the 325 Rules can also be used for alternative forms of payment such as the engagement of another contractor. It should be noted that such types of guarantees are rarely used in practice and are not issued by banks.

4. Instructions for Drafting and Issuing Guarantees

Article 3 of the Draft rules contains instructions on how a guarantee should be drafted and issued. They are in the form of recommendations and thus it seems that their non-observance would not have any legal consequences. For example, it is recommended that all instructions for the issue of a guarantee and any amendments thereto be clear, precise and avoid excessive details.

5. Validity of Guarantees

Unfortunately, the Draft rules give no guidance on how to deal with amendments to either the guarantee or the contract. Thus the question could arise as to whether the guarantee is valid in respect of any amendments made to the guarantee itself or to the underlying contract. As to amendments to the guarantee, it can be argued that the rule in Article 7(3) of the 325 Rules could still apply. In this case, any amendment to the guarantee has to be approved by the beneficiary or the principal in order to be effective against that party. The situation is more difficult when it comes to amendments made to the underlying contract after the guarantee has been issued. Since the Draft rules are silent on this matter, it seems that payment under the guarantee–as originally defined–would not be justified (cf. Article 7(1) 325 Rules).

Article 5 of the Draft rules provides that all guarantees are *irrevocable*. This provision has obviously been introduced under the influence of the UCP (*Uniform Customs and Practice for Documentary Credits*, ICC Publication No 400) which make a point of emphasizing that documentary credits may be either revocable or irrevocable (Article 7 UCP). In the case of guarantees, however, it seems to me that it is unnecessary to state that they are irrevocable as this is self-evident. Similarly, it can be argued that Article 6 of the Draft rules is superfluous. Under the influence of Article 10 UCP, Article 6 provides that a guarantee enters into effect as from the date of its issue, unless its terms expressly provide that such entering into effect is subject to conditions verifiable by the guarantor. Even without such provision it goes without saying that a guarantee will enter into effect on the date of issue unless provided otherwise.

6. Inability of Guarantor to Issue Guarantee

Article 7 of the Draft rules deals with situations where the guarantor has received instructions to issue a guarantee but by reason of national law is unable to fulfil the terms and conditions of the guarantee according to such instructions. In such cases, the guarantor shall immediately inform the principal or the instructing party, as the case may be, that he is unable to issue the guarantee as instructed and is therefore requesting appropriate instructions. Such situations are not frequent; however, it may occur, for example, that the guarantor is instructed to issue a guarantee in US dollars but cannot do so because national regulations require that guarantees be issued in local currency only. Or national law may provide that the period of validity of a guarantee cannot be shortened.

In the 325 Rules this problem would fall under Article 1(2) on the application of mandatory rules which, as mentioned above, has been omitted from the Draft rules. There, however, no reference is made to specific situations such as the one in Article 7 of the Draft rules. On the other hand, in the commentary to the 325 Rules, it is stated in a more general way that good faith and fair dealing require that a party, whether principal, instructing party, guarantor or beneficiary, who is aware of the effect of any mandatory rules in his national law preventing the instruction to be carried out, shall advise the others thereof at the time of the issue of the guarantee.

7. Liabilities and Responsibilities

The provisions of the Draft rules on the liability of the guarantor to the beneficiary take on an air of verbosity when compared with the corresponding provisions in the 325 Rules. For example, Article 3(1) of the 325 Rules provides *that* the guarantor is liable to the beneficiary only in accordance with the terms and conditions specified in the guarantee and the 325 Rules, *and that* the guarantee may rely only on those defences which are based on the terms and conditions specified in the guarantee or in the rules. In contrast, the Draft rules are modelled on the UCP and thus go into detail on matters which are sometimes not absolutely necessary in the field of contract guarantees.

This is the case in Article 8 of the Draft rules which provides that all documents presented under a guarantee must be examined with reasonable care to ascertain whether or not they appear on their face to conform with the terms and conditions for the guarantee or if they appear to be inconsistent with one another, and if not, they shall be rejected (cf. Article 15 UCP). Although this provision may not do any harm, it is worth noting that, as a rule, an arbitral award or a court decision is the only document presented for the payment of a guarantee. Contrary to bills of lading and other transport documents presented under a letter of credit, such documents do not need to be examined to determine whether they appear on their face to be consistent with the requirements under the guarantee.

Similarly, it is questionable whether the provision in Article 9 of the Draft rules is necessary. Modelled on Article 16 UCP, Article 9 provides that a guarantor shall have reasonable time to examine a claim and to determine whether to pay or reject it. If the guarantor decides to reject the claim, he is obliged to inform the beneficiary without delay and return the documents.

In Articles 10-14 of the Draft Rules a number of grounds for exemption from liability are introduced which can be found in Articles 17-20 UCP. For example, Article 10 exempts guarantors and instructing parties from liability for the form, sufficiency, accuracy, genuineness, falsification or legal effect of any document presented to them under a guarantee. In the same token, they are not liable for the general and/or particular statements made therein or for the good faith or acts or omissions of any person. Such exemption from liability may be important in respect of test certificates of goods presented under a letter of credit; however, they are of limited relevance for the documents presented under a guarantee.

Article 11 of the Draft rules, which reproduces Article 19 UCP word for word, seems to be more important for guarantors. Under Article 11 guarantors and instructing parties assume no liability or responsibility for the consequences arising out of delay and/or loss in transit of any message, letters, claims or documents or for delay, mutilation or other errors arising in the transmission of any telecommunication. Moreover, guarantors and instructing parties assume no liability for errors in the translation or interpretation of technical terms and reserve the right to transmit guarantee texts or any parts thereof without translating them. Generally speaking, this provision has greater effect in respect of letters of credit as a delay in the transmission of a guarantee text, for example, can do little harm to the principal under a guarantee.

Article 12 contains the same traditional *force majeure* clause as Article 19 of the UCP. Although the UNCITRAL Working Group objected to the wording of the clause, the ICC Working Party chose to retain it. The main intention of a *force majeure* clause is to exempt the party invoking *force majeure* from *liability for damages* to the other party. It goes without saying that performance cannot be made or requested as long as the *force majeure* prevails. In this respect, Article 12 is acceptable. What happens, however, when *force majeure* is no longer at hand? Is the guarantor obliged to perform under the guarantee or have the circumstances changed to such an extent that he is permanently relieved of his obligation? Furthermore, will the guarantor be obliged to perform under the guarantee if *force majeure* prevents him from making payment and then the guarantee expires or is no longer payable under the original terms and conditions after the state of *force majeure* has ceased?

Whereas the Draft rules provide no explicit answers to these questions, the UCP do not require the bank to incur a deferred payment or effect payment under credits which expired during such interruption of their business, unless specifically authorized to do so (see Article 19, second sentence UCP). Arguing that the *force majeure* clause should be two-sided in the sense that it should also cover the beneficiaries, the UNCITRAL Working Group proposed that the payment period be prolonged when *force majeure* prevents the beneficiary from presenting his claim. This proposal was not accepted.

Following Article 20 UCP, Article 13 of the Draft rules goes even further in exempting the guarantor and/or the instructing party from liability. First of all, Article 13 provides that, when using the services of some other party for the purpose of giving effect to the instructions of a principal, the guarantor and the instructing party do so for the account of and at the risk of the principal, even if the guarantor or the instructing party has chosen the collaborating party. Accordingly, if the instructing party uses a local bank in the country of the beneficiary to make payment under the guarantee and the local bank fails to comply with the instructions from the instructing party as properly understood, the principal has no recourse against the instructing party. This puts the principal in a rather precarious position. Without the support of the instructing party, it will be difficult for him to make the local bank liable for the error.

Moreover, Article 13 makes the principal liable to indemnify the guarantor or the instructing party, as the case may be, against all obligations and responsibilities imposed by foreign laws and usages. This means that the guarantor or the instructing party will have recourse against the principal if, under foreign law or foreign public policy, a restriction or limitation in the contract terms, expiry date or presentation of the documents is ineffective or set aside by a court in the foreign country.

Although the exemptions specified in Articles 10, 11 and 13 are mitigated to some extent by Article 14 which states that guarantors and instructing parties may not rely on the terms of the above articles for their own "grossly negligent or willful acts", the question arises as to what exactly is meant by the term *"grossly negligent or willful acts"*. Some acts of a guarantor or instructing party can always be considered wilful, even if they are not performed for the purpose of damaging the principal. Therefore, it has been suggested that the rules should instead refer to a standard such as that in the UN Convention on International Bills of Exchange and Promissory Notes (Articles 25 and 26) or in the ICC Uniform Rules for Collections which states that banks must act in good faith and exercise reasonable care.

8. Right to Claim and Submission of Claim

Article 4 of the Draft rules introduces a new rule which provides that the right to claim under a guarantee cannot be assigned. In other words, the beneficiary himself must appear as claimant under the guarantee, i.e., he cannot transfer his right to a financier, bank or other party. This provision is modelled on Articles 54(b) and 55 UCP.

Article 16 provides merely that in the event of a claim the guarantor shall, without delay, inform the principal or its instructing party of the claim. In my opinion, the most important factors have been omitted from this provision. If the duty of notification is to serve a useful purpose, notice should be given *before* payment is made under the guarantee and in *good time* so as to enable the principal to take action and if necessary stop payment, e.g., by securing a court injunction. Similarly, the notification of claim should include copies of the *documents* received, thus enabling the principal to determine whether the claim is justified or not. Although such amendments were proposed in both the UNCITRAL Working Group and the ICC Working Party, they were opposed particularly by banks. In practice, guarantees referring to 325 Rules sometimes add that payment shall be made upon demand plus a bona fide statement–unless the principal within 30 days starts a court action or an arbitration procedure, in which case payment is postponed until a decision in the dispute is made by the court or arbitral tribunal. In my opinion, this results in a more equitable balance between principal and beneficiary than allowing payment to be made before the principal is able to take any counter-action.

Under Article 19 all documents specified in the guarantee must be presented to the guarantor on or before expiry of the guarantee, otherwise the claim will be rejected. This provision more or less follows the UCP Rules (Article 46(b)). In doing so, however, it overlooks the fact that the documents stipulated in a letter of credit represent the goods and thus have a different function than those required under a guarantee. If a document is required under a guarantee (except a bona fide statement), it will be an arbitral award or a court decision. As already mentioned, it may take a long time to produce such award or judgment and in the meantime the guarantee may expire. In view of this, the present wording of Article 19 is probably a mistake. What may be intended is that the *claim be made* before expiry of the guarantee. An arbitral award or court decision cannot be presented until the proceedings have been closed; in the meantime the guarantee must remain valid.

9. Conditions for Making Payment

This brings us to Article 20, the key provision of the whole project as it specifies the requirements for securing payment. Article 20 contains three alternatives which provide that payment shall be made to the beneficiary:

(1) on simple demand, i.e., by merely submitting the claim; (2) by submission of claim and a bona fide statement; or (3) by submission of claim, a bona fide statement, and any other document specified in the guarantee.

This provision is still disputed and it is uncertain which alternative will prevail. On the one hand, the critics of on-demand guarantees argue that such a simple condition for payment may invite abuse as it strengthens the bargaining position of the beneficiary considerably. The draftsmen of the present Draft rules have attempted to pacify the critics of on-demand guarantees by stating in the *Introduction* to the Rules that the ICC strongly opposes and intends to discourage the use of on-demand guarantees. Furthermore, the ICC hopes that the present Draft rules will help convince beneficiaries that such guarantees are unnecessary. It is doubtful, however, whether this will satisfy the critics of on-demand guarantees. It should not be forgotten that, in accordance with the principle of party autonomy, any other condition stipulated by the parties shall prevail over the Rules.

If a bona fide statement is required in support of the claim, such statement should indicate that the principal has failed to perform his obligations and state expressly which obligations have been breached. It was proposed that the bona fide statement should also confirm that the beneficiary had suffered damages up to the amount claimed and that the amount claimed had been paid neither directly nor indirectly. This proposal, however, was rejected.

In regard to the third alternative, it is unfortunate that the text does not mention which other documents may be specified in the guarantee. In the Model Forms three documents are mentioned: a decision of a court in *first* instance, an arbitral award justifying the claim, or the approval of the principal in writing. Opponents of this alternative argue that the presentation of such documentation is too unfavourable for the beneficiary. Since the purpose of contract guarantees is not only to provide security for the beneficiary's claim but also to give him satisfaction within a reasonably short time and, if possible, to shift the burden of being claimant in court or arbitral proceedings to the principal, such requirements are unacceptable.

Therefore, a more flexible approach would be to make a claim supported by a bona fide statement payable, unless the principal has initiated court action or arbitral proceedings within–say–30 days from the date of submission of the claim.

There is another solution which may be worth mentioning. Since the Draft rules make no distinction between tender guarantees, performance guarantees and repayment guarantees, the special situation of the tender guarantee has been overlooked, i.e., there is still no underlying contract. Therefore, as in the 325 Rules and the Model Forms, it might be advisable to include the following possibility: If payment is made, the beneficiary automatically acknowledges that any claim from the principal for repayment of the amount paid under the guarantee is submitted to arbitration or to the jurisdiction of a specific court.

After payment of a claim, the guarantor must submit, without delay, the claim documents to the principal or the instructing party.

10. Expiry of Guarantee

As a rule, a guarantee stipulates an expiry date, either a fixed day or a date after six months or any other period of time after the issue of the guarantee. Under both the 325 Rules and the Draft rules, the expiry date is the final day on which a claim can be made; otherwise it will be rejected because the guarantee has ceased to be valid. Sometimes the expiry is fixed by linking it to a certain event, the so-called expiry event. Such event could also be the starting point for calculating a period after the elapse of which the guarantee expires. For example, the expiry event may be the day of issue of a take-over certificate or the date of a bill of lading. Whereas the 325 Rules describe various possible expiry events for the three types of guarantees, no such examples are presented in the Draft rules. Instead, the Draft rules merely clarify the situation where a guarantee mentions both an expiry date and an expiry event. In such cases, the guarantee expires on whichever of these two alternatives occurs first.

Under Article 23 of the Draft rules, the guarantee expires if it is returned to the guarantor. Otherwise, the possession of the guarantee does not give the beneficiary any specific rights. In this respect, the provisions of Articles 23 and 24 are the same as those in the 325 Rules.

The guarantor is obliged to inform the instructing party or the principal when the guarantee has terminated for one or another reason or has been reduced (Article 25). Whereas this presents no problem, it may occur that the guarantor is faced with a request to pay or prolong the guarantee. This is particularly important in the case of on-demand guarantees. Of course, the conditions for payment under the guarantee must be fulfilled. In the case of an on-demand guarantee, a bona fide statement may or may not be required. However, even if these conditions are satisfied, the Draft rules provide that the guarantor shall not make payment immediately but inform the principal or the instructing party and suspend payment for such time as the guarantor shall consider reasonable to permit the principal and the beneficiary to reach agreement on an extension of the guarantee and arrange the same. It is also expressly stated that the guarantor shall incur no liability–in terms of interest or otherwise–for any delay in payment which may result from such procedure. It goes without saying that it does not suffice for the principal and the beneficiary to agree. The instructing party and the guarantor must also agree to such extension in order for it to be operative.

11. Final Provisions

As in the 325 Rules, the applicable law will be that of the guarantor's place of business. In regard to the settlement of disputes, the relevant provisions are shorter and less complicated than those of the 325 Rules. No reference is made to arbitration, neither to the ICC Rules nor to the UNCITRAL Rules. Instead, disputes arising out of the guarantee are to be settled by the competent court of the country of the guarantor's place of business.

V. Concluding Remarks

In conclusion it can be said that neither the 325 Rules nor the Draft rules seem quite sufficient. The Draft rules have not only failed to win the support of all groups but have also been strongly opposed by some. As a result, the February draft of 1989 will be replaced by a new June draft with minor revisions. At present, nobody can predict what the final outcome will be. In all probability it will take time. In comparison with the 325 Rules, which took some 10 years to finalize, the work on the revisions has been going on only four years.

6

Bills of Exchange in International Trade

Reinhard Welter

I. Historical Aspects

The history of international trade is closely linked with bills of exchange. In the twelfth century, bills of exchange were used by money changers in Northern Italy who exchanged money into foreign currency for their clients, i.e., importers who purchased goods abroad. Exposed to the risk of robbery and other perils when taking the currency to fairs,[1] they were grateful when some money changers offered to perform the transport service: The client would pay the desired amount in local currency and obtain a receipt promising that the equivalent amount would be refunded in foreign currency[2] abroad. Although there may have been earlier forms of such transactions in the Arab world of finance, these receipts are commonly regarded as the first promissory notes.[3]

The next step was to avoid the risk of physical transport altogether. Instead of taking the money to the place of designation, the money changer had a foreign colleague pay the respective amount in his local currency.[4] This order was contained in a letter[5] given to the client together with the receipt. Upon presentation of the two documents, the client would receive the stipulated sum in foreign currency from the money changer abroad. It was not long before the receipt and letter were combined in one document which already contained the basic features of a bill of exchange: the liability of the drawer (domestic money changer) was documented as well as his order that the drawee (money changer abroad) pay a certain sum. The client's position substantially improved when the drawee began to sign the bill, thus accepting the obligation as his own (acceptance).[6] Another step forward was

[1] Cf. M. Rowe, *Letters of Credit* (London 1985) p. 85.
[2] Cf. G. Ripert and R. Roblot, *Traité Elémentaire de Droit Commercial*, vol. 2, 10th ed., ed. R. Roblot (Paris 1986) at n. 1916.
[3] *Ibid.* nn. 1915 *et seq.*
[4] *Ibid.* n. 1916.
[5] Cf. the French term for bill of exchange *lettre de change*.
[6] Cf. Ripert and R. Roblot, *Traité Elémentaire de Droit Commercial*, at n. 1917.

International Contracts and Payments (Šarčević, Volken, eds.; 1 85333 615 7; © Graham & Trotman, 1991; pub. Graham & Trotman; printed in Great Britain), pp. 87-107.

achieved when the rights under the documents could be passed to a third person free from defects in the title (concept of negotiability).[7] The client (payee and transferor) placed an order on the back of the bill,[8] called an "indorsement",[9] and delivered the bill to the transferee. As between indorser and indorsee, the indorser was also liable for the amount of the bill. Like the drawer, he would have to pay if the drawee failed to do so.

Thus medieval trade developed an instrument which was virtually identical to our present day bill of exchange. Centuries of practice have added to its commercial and legal sophistication; however, the basic features have remained unchanged. As to the impact of codification, it is fair to say that it reflects international commercial customs to a large extent.[10] Therefore, it is not surprising that there is hardly any other field in which worldwide uniformity has been reached to a similar extent. The Conference at Geneva in 1930, held under the auspices of the League of Nations, achieved a considerable degree of harmonization in the civil law world.[11] More than 40 states have either adopted[12] or closely follow the Geneva Uniform Laws on Bills of Exchange and Promissory Notes.[13] Other states follow the principles of the English common law. The gap between the two systems is supposed to be filled by the UNCITRAL Convention on International Bills of Exchange and International Promissory Notes.[14]

II. Present Day Use of Bills of Exchange in International Trade

The importance of bills of exchange is due to the fact that this instrument serves two outstanding interests of the parties to international trade transactions. Whereas the seller is interested in securing payment, the seller and buyer are often both interested in finding the most favourable way of financing the proceeds of the sale. There are

---

[7] Cf. its recognition in English Law in B. Crawford and J. D. Falconbridge, *Banking and Bills of Exchange*, vol. 2, 8th ed., ed. B. Crawford (Toronto 1986) p. 1171, with further references.

[8] "Pay A.B.".

[9] *Dorso*, i.e. "back" in Italian.

[10] On the history of codification, cf. Ripert and Roblot, *Traité Elémentaire de Droit Commercial*, at nn. 1915, 1921 *et seq.*

[11] Cf. *ibid.* at nn. 1922 *et seq.*

[12] See *League of Nations Treaty Series*, vol. CXLIII (1933-1934) pp. 257, 317, 355 and 407; for the present situation, cf. Crawford and Falconbridge, *Banking and Bills of Exchange*, p. 1182 where 21 member states are cited: Austria, Belgium, Brazil, Denmark, Finland, France, Greece, Italy, Japan, Monaco, The Netherlands, Norway, Poland, Portugal, Sweden, Switzerland, USSR, German Democratic Republic, Federal Republic of Germany, Hungary and Luxemburg. About as many states are considered to be quasi-Convention States (e.g., Argentina, Czechoslovakia, Spain and Yugoslavia, cf. Ripert and Roblot, *Traité Elémentaire de Droit Commercial*, at n. 1924).

[13] League of Nations Convention No. 3313; cf. *League of Nations Treaty Series*, vol. 143, p. 259 (Uniform Law relating to bills of exchange and promissory notes, dated 7 June 1930).

[14] See E. Bergsten's article in this book; M. Rowe, "Bills of Exchange in International Trade", in N. Horn (ed.), *The Law of International Trade Finance* (Deventer 1989) p. 245; E. Schinnerer, *Zu den Konventionsentwürfen von UNCITRAL für ein internationales Wechselrecht und ein internationales Scheckrecht* (Vienna 1983) and Crawford and Falconbridge, *Banking and Bills of Exchange*, p. 1183; for more details on the process of unification, see W. Vis, "Unification of International Trade Law" (with special reference to negotiable instruments and commercial arbitration), in *World Trade and Trade Finance, Proceedings of the Southern Methodist University Institute on International Finance* (Albany 1985) pp. 6-7.

numerous ways of satisfying these needs in international practice, and bills of exchange definitely play an important part in such procedures.

1. Bills of Exchange in Connection with Documentary Collection and Letters of Credit

Transactions to be paid by "open account" or "cash with order" normally do not meet the requirements of international trade.[15] As a rule, documentary collection provides the lowest level of security accepted by parties to international transactions.

(a) Documentary Collection

After shipping the goods, the exporter submits the transport documents to his bank (remitting bank),[16] which transfers them to the collection bank. Upon payment, the buyer obtains the shipping documents which transfer the title and grant him access to the goods (e.g., a bill of lading). On the way from the exporter to importer, the documents are accompanied by a payment instrument.[17] The exporter (drawer) draws the bill of exchange on the importer (drawee) who pays against presentation of the documents and the bill.

The purpose of such a bill of exchange should not be overestimated as in this context it only represents the creditor's order to pay. After payment it may serve as a receipt in the hands of the importer.[18] In countries where considerable stamp duties are levied on bills of exchange,[19] banks try to find a less costly way of documenting the payment. To avoid these duties, collecting banks often keep the bill in their files and issue a receipt to the importer instead.

(b) Letters of Credit

Letters of credit provide the exporter greater security because the bank guarantees payment against presentation of the documents,[20] thus avoiding the risk that the importer may refuse to pay. The bank issues an irrevocable letter of credit which is often confirmed by a bank in the importer's country.[21] Again the documents are usually accompanied by a bill of exchange which serves as a payment instrument.[22] The exporter who is beneficiary of the letter of credit draws a bill on the buyer or bank where payment is available.[23] If the bill is payable at sight, it only represents the exporter's order to pay against presentation of the documents.

On the other hand, if the bill is a term bill and the bank issuing or confirming the letter of credit guarantees to honour the bill by acceptance (Article 10(a)(iii)

[15] Cf. P. Melly, *Introduction*, in C. J. Gmür (ed.), *Trade Financing*, 2nd ed. (London 1986) pp. 3.

[16] Ibid. 5; P. O'Hanlon, "Documentary Collection", *ibid.* 9 *et seq.*

[17] Cf. Melly, *ibid.* 5; O'Hanlon, *ibid.* 10; R. P. Lawrence, "Bills of Exchange", *ibid.* 45.

[18] J. C. D. Zahn, E. Eberding and E. Ehrlich, *Zahlung und Zahlungssicherung im Aussenhandel*, 6th ed. (Berlin and New York 1986) p. 307.

[19] e.g. Germany.

[20] P. O'Hanlon, "Letter of Credit", Gmür (ed.), *Trade Financing*, p. 21; M. Rowe, *Guarantees, Standby Letters of Credit and Other Securities* (London 1987) pp. 8, 9.

[21] Cf. Melly, *Introduction*, p. 6; O'Hanlon, "Letter of Credit", p. 21.

[22] Lawrence, "Bills of Exchange", p. 46; Rowe, *Guarantees, Standby Letters of Credit and Other Securities*, p. 15.

[23] O'Hanlon, "Letter of Credit", p. 22; Lawrence, "Bills of Exchange", p. 46.

Uniform Customs and Practice for Documentary Credits),[24] the accepted draft can be used to finance the proceeds of the sale. The seller may offer the bill to his bank as security for advances. Since this is self-liquidating and non-risk financing,[25] the customer may expect favourable terms. Furthermore, the seller may cash the proceeds at once by requesting his bank to discount the bill, thereby taking advantage of favourable terms on the discount market.

(c) Negotiation of Drafts under Letters of Credit

It often occurs that the beneficiary of a letter of credit prefers to present the documents to a bank other than the paying bank, particularly if the paying bank is located in the country of the currency of account of the transaction. If the letter of credit is made negotiable, the beneficiary may present the documents to the specifically nominated bank or, if it is freely negotiable, to any bank.[26] According to the Uniform Customs and Practice for Documentary Credits (UCP), the issuing bank pays without recourse to drawers and/or bona fide holders, drafts drawn by the beneficiary, at sight or at a tenor, on the applicant for the credit or on any other drawee stipulated in the credit (Article 10(a)(iv) UCP).

As a rule, the draft is drawn on the applicant (buyer). If it is payable at sight, the negotiating bank pays the draft (i.e. its nominal value less negotiation fees). The negotiating bank then presents the draft and documents to the issuing bank for reimbursement (Article 11(d) UCP). If reimbursement cannot be obtained,[27] the negotiating bank may take recourse to the drawer (seller and beneficiary of the letter of credit). Such recourse, however, is not admitted if the negotiating bank has confirmed the credit.[28] The same operation applies in the case of drafts not payable at sight with the exception that the negotiating bank does not obtain reimbursement until maturity. Therefore, the negotiating bank pays only a discounted value of the draft, not the nominal value. Again the draft represents an order to pay and thus determines the maturity of reimbursement. Economically speaking, the negotiating bank finances the proceeds of the letter of credit until maturity.

A similar procedure applies in the case of so-called drawing authorizations. The buyer's bank authorizes a bank in the seller's country to buy drafts. These are drawn by the seller either on the buyer (authority to purchase) or the authorized bank itself (authority to negotiate). In the latter case, the acceptance will be discounted by that or by any other bank.[29] As a banker's acceptance, it guarantees favourable financing of the proceeds.

[24] UCP, 1983 revision, International Chamber of Commerce Publication no. 400; cf. O'Hanlon, "Letter of Credit", pp. 22, 23, 34.

[25] Lawrence, "Bills of Exchange", p. 46.

[26] O'Hanlon, "Letter of Credit", p. 22.

[27] For example, if the documents do not comply with the letter of credit; cf. P. Ellinger, "The Law of Letters of Credit", in N. Horn (ed.), *The Law of International Trade Finance* (Deventer 1989) p. 213.

[28] *Ibid.* 212; O'Hanlon, "Letter of Credit", p. 22; Lawrence, "Bills of Exchange", pp. 46, 49; Rowe, *Letters of Credit*, p. 87.

[29] Cf. Zahn, Eberding and Ehrlich, *Zahlung und Zahlungssicherung im Aussenhandel*, p. 340.

2. Forfaiting

Rarely able to finance the transactions by themselves, exporters who grant trade credit to buyers usually have to rely on financing from a third party, e.g., their bank. There are various ways of financing accounts receivable.[30] From a legal point of view, it is essential to guarantee that the seller's claims against his customers serve as collateral or security. Bills of exchange are involved in forfaiting transactions, which are particularly suited to the needs of international trade.

Economically speaking, forfaiting enables exporters who have agreed to deferred payment to sell their accounts receivable without recourse.[31] Forfaiting therefore goes beyond mere discounting in that the risks of collection are shifted to a certain extent to the purchaser, i.e., the government-related risks. The techniques are based on the use of bills of exchange and thus the features of this instrument are significant for the operation.

At this point some legal details of negotiable instruments should be examined as well as important differences in the legal situation of civil law and common law states under the Geneva Convention.[32]

(a) Requirements for Standard Non-recourse Purchase of Accounts Receivable

Technically speaking, the purchase of accounts receivable without recourse generally requires:

- that the operation not be based on book debts as this would demand cumbersome documentation of each single transaction;
- that the purchaser (forfaiter) not get involved in disputes concerning the underlying contract due, for example, to alleged bad performance. This provides another argument against the purchase of book debts which would have to be assigned[33] as the legal validity of such assignments is often questioned in international context;[34]
- that the forfaiter not bear the risk of insolvency on the part of the individual buyer.[35] On the other hand, assessing and taking on the country risk may prove to be very useful to exporters. This can be achieved by rendering a third party in the importer's country liable who does not represent an individual risk, e.g., a bank.[36] Guaranteeing third party liability in a formally simple and safe procedure would obviously help standardize the transaction.

[30] L. B. Bjornstad and S. S. Klingenberg, "Accounts Receivable Financing", in Gmür (ed.), *Trade Financing*, pp. 81 *et seq.*

[31] Gmür, "Forfaiting", in id. (ed.), *Trade Financing*, p. 109; H. U. Jäger, "Export Factoring and Forfaiting", in N. Horn (ed.), *The Law of International Trade Finance*, p. 283.

[32] As to possible legal complications in the context of international forfaiting, see Rowe, *Guarantees, Standby Letters of Credit and Other Securities*, p. 35.

[33] Without regard to the applicable law, the debtor's position would not be infringed upon by the assignment of book debts; cf. Gmür, "Forfaiting", p. 114.

[34] Cf. Bjornstad and Klingenberg, "Accounts Receivable Financing", p. 83.

[35] This would be non-recourse international factoring which involves severe problems of individual risk assessment in foreign countries; cf. *ibid.* 81.

[36] R. Davies and A. Grabiner, "Legal Issues in Trade Financing", in Gmür (ed.), *Trade Financing*, p. 217.

(b) Useful Features of Bills of Exchange

It appears that the bill of exchange may offer a solution which meets these requirements to a large extent.

(i) Documentation and handling of accounts receivable

The debts are recorded on bills of exchange which can be sold as such. The individual purchase can be easily documented as it is based on the bill itself.

(ii) Cutting off defences

Roughly speaking, bills of exchange may also help cut off defences. For example, a forfaiter who holds the buyer (acceptor) liable under the bill will not get involved in disputes arising as a result of bad performance of the underlying contract. The situation, however, is far more complex, especially from the point of view of international law.

Immediate and remote parties

First of all, it should be noted that defences are not cut off between immediate parties to the instrument (seller as drawer/payee and buyer as acceptor). Whereas international unification and harmonization does not touch upon this matter, it can generally be said that the respective national laws regard the participation of parties to a bill as an additional[37] obligation. Nevertheless, the defences of the underlying contract can generally[38] be invoked by the liable party. In most cases, the effects of a bill of exchange are limited to a shifting of the burden of proof. This, however, is only a rule of thumb. For more details, the law governing the performance of the underlying contract should be consulted.[39]

The picture changes when one examines the position of subsequent parties to the bill, for example, a third-party payee in addition to the drawer and acceptor or indorsees. Now the rules of law relative to bills of exchange have to be applied. In order to present a global survey of these rules, the two different existing systems have to be taken into account.

Geneva Convention

Under the Geneva Convention, the rights of third parties are determined on two levels. First of all, the holder must be lawful in order to be entitled under the bill of

---

[37] Not necessarily separate and independent from the underlying transaction (*abstract*); cf. Ripert and Roblot, *Traité Elémentaire de Droit Commercial*, nn. 1928, 1929, 2045.

[38] Cf. E. P. Ellinger, *Modern Banking Law* (Oxford 1987) p. 509. For example, an immediate party is entitled to plead *partial failure* of consideration if the holder has not fulfilled his obligations arising out of the underlying contract. It is, however, necessary that the holder's breach entitles the acceptor to a *quantified or liquidated* amount. This will not be the case if the goods turn out to be of inferior quality, whereupon the buyer becomes entitled to recover an amount of damages to be *determined by the court*. There is no evidence that a similar distinction should be applied on the Continent; cf. recent developments in German law which, as Ripert rightly points out (in Ripert and Roblot, *Traité Elémentaire de Droit Commercial*, nn. 1929, 2045), has *traditionally* emphasized the abstract nature of liability under a bill of exchange, BGH *WM* (1986), 415 = *WuB* I D 4.-3.86 Emmerich = *NJW* (1986), 1872 and W. Flume, "Die Wandlungseinrede des Käufers bei Wechsel- oder Scheckhingabe" *NJW* (1986), p. 2482.

[39] As to French law, cf. Ripert and Roblot, *Traité Elémentaire de Droit Commercial*, nn. 1929, 2045.

exchange.[40] If there are any defects in acquiring the title in the bill, a holder who has acquired the instrument in good faith as to the status of the previous holder (no gross negligence) hereby becomes lawful holder.[41] A stolen instrument may thus entitle the holder to all claims incorporated therein.

Personal defences in a narrower sense are dealt with in Article 17 which provides that persons sued on a bill of exchange cannot set up against the holder defences founded on their personal relations with the drawer or with previous holders. The holder, however, is not protected when, in acquiring the bill, he has knowingly acted to the detriment of the debtor. This rule, however, does not cover all defences which have to be taken into account. If, for example, the issuance of the instrument is invalid for reasons of minority or has been effected unwillingly,[42] the general theory of liability under a bill of exchange comes into play.[43]

Common law states
In the common law system no distinction is made between the title of an instrument and cutting off defences against liability on the instrument. The protection is based on the quality of the holder: mere holder, holder for value and holder in due course.[44] A holder in due course holds the bill free from any defect of title of prior parties as well as from mere personal defences available to prior parties among themselves (Section 38 Bills of Exchange Act = BEA). In order to be considered holder in due course, the holder must have taken the bill, complete and regular on the face of it, under certain conditions. For example, he must have taken the bill in good faith and for value, and at the time the bill was negotiated to him, he must not have had notice of any defect in the title of the person who negotiated it (Section 29 BEA). Thus it follows that the payee cannot be holder in due course under Section 29 BEA.[45]

Section 29(2) BEA specifies to what extent defences are cut off in favour of a holder in due course. This section refers to defects such as fraud, duress, force and fear, other unlawful means, illegal consideration or when the bill is negotiated in breach of faith, or under circumstances which can be qualified as fraud. This might lead to the conclusion that neither personal defences nor any defects of title can be held against a holder in due course. On the contrary, most authors agree that there is a category of defences available even against a holder in due course.[46] These so-called real or absolute defences[47] include:

(1) complete incapacity to incur contractual liability by virtue of a signature on the instrument;

---

[40] Anyone who in fact possesses the instrument and establishes his title through an uninterrupted series of indorsements is presumed to be the lawful holder (Art. 16(1) of the Geneva Convention).

[41] Art. 16(2) of the Geneva Convention.

[42] e.g. theft of a signed but not yet issued bill.

[43] e.g. in German law the *Lehre vom zurechenbaren Rechtsschein*; cf. A. Baumbach and W. Hefermehl, *Wechselgesetz und Scheckgesetz*, 16th ed., ed. W. Hefermehl (Munich 1988) Art. 17 WG nn. 9 *et seq.*; on French law see Ripert and Roblot, *Traité Elémentaire de Droit Commercial*, nn. 1932 *et seq.*

[44] Cf. Ellinger, *Modern Banking Law*, pp. 504; M. Megrah and F. R. Ryder, *Byles on Bills of Exchange*, 25th ed. (London 1983) pp. 203 *et seq.*

[45] Ellinger, *Modern Banking Law*, p. 506; Megrah and Ryder, *Byles on Bills of Exchange*, p. 207; on US law, cf. section 3-302(2) and J. J. White and R. S. Summers, *Uniform Commercial Code*, 2nd ed. (St Paul, 1980), p. 568.

[46] Crawford, *Banking and Bills of Exchange*, pp. 1521 *et seq.*

[47] *Ibid.* 1523.

(2) forgery of the party's signature or signature by another without his authority, except in so far as he is estopped from denying his validity; ·
(3) fraud or illegality of such a nature as renders the expressed obligation of the party a nullity;
(4) the absence of effective delivery of a complete instrument or of a blank or incomplete instrument;
(5) material alteration of the instrument that releases the party;
(6) discharge of the instrument by payment in due course; renunciation at or after maturity; or by intentional or apparent cancellation at any time.

Authors who do not agree with this classification obviously do not disagree with the results. In the examples cited above they do not consider the instrument the drawer's bill at all (validly drawn and issued).[48]

The UCC explicitly provides for the following real defences against holders in due course:

(1) infancy, to the extent that it is a defence to a simple contract;
(2) such other incapacity, or duress, or illegality of the transaction as renders the obligation of the party a nullity;
(3) such misrepresentation as has induced the party to sign the instrument with neither knowledge nor reasonable opportunity to obtain knowledge of its character or its essential terms;
(4) discharge in insolvency proceedings;
(5) any other discharge of which the holder has notice when he takes the instrument.[49]

It can clearly be seen that there is a difference not only in the concepts under the Geneva Convention and the common law system but also within the common law system itself as far as statutory law is concerned. On the other hand, in the doctrine there seems to be an attempt to find an acceptable borderline for protection of the holder in due course v. protection of the liable parties. Dealing with these delicate questions in detail, however, would go beyond the scope of this article.

Conclusion with respect to forfaiting
From the point of view of international commercial law, the essence of the proceding discussion can be summed up in the following two statements:

(1) Mere personal defences are cut off under all legal systems provided the holder[50] has acted in good faith when negotiating the bill. This includes defences which are of greatest interest to international trade such as bad performance.
(2) Rights arising from defects of title are also cut off to a certain extent. There is no evidence that remaining differences between the legal systems have led commercial practice to evaluate the position of the holder differently depending on the applicable law.

[48] Megrah and Ryder, *Byles on Bills of Exchange*, p. 214.
[49] Sect. 3-305(2) UCC; for further details see C. M. Weber and R. E. Speitel, *Commercial Paper*, 3rd ed. (St Paul 1982) pp. 285 *et seq.*
[50] The *payee* can be protected under the Geneva Convention and under the UCC but not under the English concept of holder in due course (*supra* n. 45).

In regard to the use of bills of exchange in the context of forfaiting, it can be concluded that, as a holder of the bill, the forfaiter is protected against practically all defences arising from the underlying contract between the exporter and importer.

(iii) Guaranteeing third-party liability

In general, a forfaiter cannot bear the individual risk connected with a particular transaction.[51] Therefore the liability must be assumed by a third party in the importer's country who does not represent an individual risk. It was already mentioned that forfaiting requires a formally simple and legally safe way of guaranteeing the liability of a bank. In order to standardize the procedure, the best solution would be to have the bank back the bill of exchange instead of concluding a separate contract of guarantee.[52]

Geneva Convention

The Geneva Convention provides that liability under a bill of exchange shall be guaranteed by an aval[53] expressed by the words "good as aval"[54] or other equivalent phrase. An aval can be given by parties who have already signed the bill of exchange in another capacity or by third parties (Article 30(2)). Any signature on the face of the bill other than the drawee's or drawer's is considered to constitute an aval. The aval may be given for any party liable under the bill of exchange. If not specified, it is deemed[55] to be given for the drawer (Article 31(3)). The avaliser is liable in the same manner as the person whose obligation he guarantees (Article 32(1)). If, for instance, the aval is given for the drawer, protest is required (Articles 43 and 44).

Thus it follows that, under the Geneva Convention, the liability of a bank in the importer's country can be guaranteed by having the bank issue an aval for the importer (drawee).

Bills of Exchange Act and the UCC

On the other hand, the Bills of Exchange Act and the UCC[56] do not mention the aval.[57] As a result, confusion could arise if a party, for example, in the United

---

[51] See *supra*, section II.2.(a); Rowe, *Guarantees, Standby Letters of Credit and Other Securities*, p. 33.

[52] Separate guarantees would also lead to legal problems. The suretyship law of a certain state would govern and, as a rule, this is rather complicated, e.g., the provision on defences of the surety.

[53] Cf. Ripert and Roblot, *Traité Elémentaire de Droit Commercial*, nn. 2005 *et seq.*

[54] *Bon pour aval* or *als Bürge*.

[55] According to French case law, this presumption is not rebuttable; cf. Ripert and Roblot, *Traité Elémentaire de Droit Commercial*, p. 2008. Other Geneva Convention states do not follow this approach, cf. Baumbach and Hefermehl, *Wechselgesetz und Scheckgesetz*, Art. 31 WG n. 8 for German and Austrian law. For an overview see G. P. Portale "La 'Presunzione' die Avallo nelle Applicazioni Nazionali" *Vita Notarile* (1984) pp. 1323 *et seq.*

[56] On suretyship status according to Sect. 3 UCC, cf. Peters, "Suretyship under Article 3 of the Uniform Commercial Code" 77 *Yale LJ* (1968) pp. 833, 843.

[57] Ellinger, *Modern Banking Law*, p. 503 suggests with respect to Sect. 3-416 UCC that the aval is available in the UCC. This section affects the liability of the indorser who adds the words *Payment guaranteed*. Unlike the usual unqualified indorser, he is liable to a holder without any conditions precedent, i.e., he has no right to insist on either presentment for payment to the maker or drawee or notice of dishonour; cf. Weber and Speitel, *Commercial Paper*, p. 168. According to the Official Comment, the indorser's liability becomes indistinguishable from that of a co-maker. Even if these particular features are taken into account, further grounds are required to consider the indorsement identical to an aval; for a detailed comparison of the aval and an *anomalous indorsement*, cf. Crawford, *Banking and Bills of Exchange*, pp. 1621 *et seq.*

Kingdom would sign and deliver a bill of exchange with the words "good as aval".[58] In such a case it could be argued that by using the aval the parties have chosen the law of a state that is party to the Geneva Convention.[59] If one does not assume such a choice of law, the then applicable English law provides in section 56 of the Bills of Exchange Act[60] that persons who sign a bill otherwise than a drawer or acceptor incur the liabilities of an indorser to a holder in due course.[61] However, it appears that the effect of an indorsement is not identical to an aval as it does not create an obligation to previous parties but is solely for the benefit of subsequent holders.[62] Under English law the indorser will not be liable to a subsequent holder if the indorsed bill is subsequently nullified by an act of forgery[63] or other act.[64] Finally,. under English law,[65] an indorser can only be held liable after the holder has established the requisite proceedings on dishonour.[66] Even authors who suggest that a guarantee which is negotiable under English law should be admitted[67] strongly recommend that forfaiters take their security in a form more familiar to English lawyers whenever the instrument may be governed by English law.[68]

Nevertheless, there is no reason to be discouraged if an aval has been given under English law. Recently English case law has partially clarified the legal situation in the procedure commonly applied in forfaiting transactions.[69] As a rule, the drawer sends a bill which is payable to his order to the importer's country where it is signed by the importer himself (acceptor) and the guaranteeing bank.[70] Even if the bank's signature (intended as an aval) is given the effect of an indorsement (Section 56 BEA), the exporter who is supposed to be the beneficiary of the guarantee is not considered a subsequent holder; instead he is the *drawer* of the instrument, i.e., a *previous* party to the bill. The High Court,[71] however, has rather generously recognized a procedure which makes the guaranteeing bank liable to the drawer as an indorser: It may be held that the drawer has indorsed the instrument to the guarantor who, in turn, has indorsed the bill back to the drawer. Operating this device involves two factors:[72]

[58] In this case the conflict of laws rules of both the Geneva Convention and the Bills of Exchange Act would refer to English law.

[59] Davies and Grabiner, "Legal Issues in Trade Financing", pp. 222.

[60] Sect. 3-402 UCC contains a corresponding rule; for details see Weber and Speitel, *Commercial Paper*, p. 140 and White and Summers, *Uniform Commercial Code*, p. 504.

[61] For more details, cf. Crawford, *Banking and Bills of Exchange*, p. 1620; Davies and Grabiner, "Legal Issues in Trade Financing", p. 222; Megrah and Ryder, *Byles on Bills of Exchange*, p. 191.

[62] Megrah and Ryder, *Byles on Bills of Exchange*, p. 191; on the different position of Canadian case law, cf. Crawford, *Banking and Bills of Exchange*, p. 1621.

[63] Cf. the law in the U.S. in Sect. 3-404 UCC; also Weber and Speitel, *Commercial Paper*, p. 292 and Jäger, "Export Factoring and Forfaiting", p. 303.

[64] An aval is enforceable despite the guarantee that the liability is inoperative unless this is due to a defect of form.

[65] As to the UCC, cf. Sect. 3-416 and *supra*, n. 57.

[66] Cf. A. Berg, "Do Avals Work in England?" *IFLR* (March 1989) p. 29 and Jäger, "Export Factoring and Forfaiting", p. 303; this is not necessary in the case of an aval for the acceptor.

[67] Davies and Grabiner, "Legal Issues in Trade Financing", p. 223.

[68] *Ibid.* 223.

[69] Berg, "Do Avals Work in England?" p. 29.

[70] Cf. Rowe, *Guarantees, Standby Letters of Credit and Other Securities*, p. 33.

[71] *G&H Montage GmbH* v. *Irvani* 1 *WLR* (1988) p. 1285.

[72] Cf. Berg, "Do Avals Work in England?" p. 29.

- There has to be evidence that the purpose of the guarantor's indorsement was to make him liable to the drawer, not only to subsequent holders;
- If the drawer indorses the bill after the guarantor, the guarantor may be considered to have authorized the drawer to add his indorsement for the purpose of making the guarantor's indorsement operate in his favour.[73] The drawer's indorsement may then be treated as though it had preceded the guarantor's.

Obviously this decision is very favourable to the drawer relying on an aval which is given the effect of an indorsement. This reasoning enables him to recover under an aval of a bill payable to his order provided that there is evidence that the parties have agreed that the aval would cover the drawer.[74]

(c) Excluding Recourse under Bills of Exchange

Thus far we have seen the exporter in the position of a drawer who draws the instrument on the importer. The drawer may also be the payee who indorses the bill in favour of the forfaiter after a bank in the importer's country has given its aval.[75] As far as the forfaiter is concerned, the requirements of the transaction are thus fulfilled (documentation and cutting off defences).

From the exporter's point of view, however, there is a weak spot in this construction. Although the forfaiting itself is supposed to be without recourse, the exporter would be liable under the bill as drawer (and also as indorser). Any attempt to exclude the drawer's liability under the Geneva Convention is bound to fail: A stipulation by which the drawer releases himself from the guarantee of payment is deemed not to be written (Article 9(2)). It is evident that this provision does not keep the drawer from refusing payment if held liable by the non-recourse forfaiter.[76] This, however, would be a defence outside the bill of exchange, i.e., a mere personal defence and it could not be held against a third party who is holder in due course.

Parties to international transactions may attempt to exclude the drawer's liability by choosing a law outside the Geneva Convention (e.g., English or American law), thus assuring themselves of the right to limit the drawer's liability. English law, for instance, would govern if the drawer issues the bill in the United Kingdom. In cases before the courts of Geneva Convention states, choice of law issues related to liability are decided in accordance with Article 4(2) of the Geneva Convention for the settlement of certain conflict of laws in connection with bills of exchange and promissory notes.[77] According to this provision, the liability of the drawer would be governed by the law of the state where the party (except acceptor or maker)[78] has signed the bill. In order to subject the question of the drawer's liability to English

---

[73] Cf. Sect. 20 BEA concerning inchoate instruments: When a bill is wanting in any material aspect, the person in possession of it has a prima-facie authority to fill up the omission in any way he thinks fit.

[74] Berg, "Do Avals Work in England?" p. 30.

[75] Under English or US law the bank would have to indorse the bill (*supra*, section II.2.(b)) or issue a guarantee in addition to the bill.

[76] Cf. Rowe, *Guarantees, Standby Letters of Credit and Other Securities*, 35; Jäger, "Export Factoring and Forfaiting", p. 300.

[77] *League of Nations Treaty Series*, vol. CXLIII (1933-34), p. 319.

[78] Art. 4(1) of the Conflicts Convention: Application of the Law in the State of the Place of Performance.

law, a choice of law clause to this effect could be inserted in the underlying contract.[79]

The safest way to exclude the drawer's liability, however, is to use a promissory note instead of a draft.[80] The importer is the maker who signs the instrument and the exporter is the payee who indorses the instrument to the forfaiter. As to the indorser, the Geneva Convention provides for a clause excluding his liability for acceptance and payment (Article 15(1)).

3. The Bill of Exchange in Financing Transactions

Bills of exchange issued and delivered in connection with a trade transaction can be used to finance the proceeds at favourable terms (e.g., by discounting the bill).[81] Even if a bill of exchange is not involved in the trade transaction itself, the buyer may still use one to finance the price of the goods.[82]

Let us suppose that a European importer needs a considerable amount of US dollars to pay for imported goods. Under certain circumstances the most favourable method of financing would be for the importer to request his local bank to draw a bill of exchange on a US bank.[83] The acceptance by the US bank constitutes a *banker's acceptance*. It would be discounted either by the accepting bank, which would then sell the bill on the US market, or by the Federal Reserve Bank. In either case, a low interest rate would apply,[84] thus allowing the amount of the draft less the favourable discount[85] to be paid to the importer, who would return the full amount of the draft to the acceptor when the bill is due.

Economically speaking, in the case of banker's acceptances, bills of exchange are used as a means of securitization. Instead of the bank acting as an intermediary in a credit transaction, both parties are brought together for a short-term investment in securities (bill of exchange). The bank's role is limited to accepting the bill and managing the transaction.[86]

A similar procedure is applied in the United Kingdom[87] where bankers' acceptances are marketed by discount houses which, for example, have the bills discounted by the Bank of England.

---

[79] With respect to future litigation, one has to be sure that the courts of the foreign state will accept this choice of law.

[80] Cf. Rowe, *Guarantees, Standby Letters of Credit and Other Securities*, p. 35.

[81] See *supra*, section II.1.(b); Ellinger, *Modern Banking Law*, p. 494.

[82] Financing by acceptance credits is not limited to international trade transactions; cf. Ellinger, *Modern Banking Law*, p. 499: major international projects such as the financing of an oil rig and also purely domestic transactions; Lawrence, *supra* n. 17, at p. 47.

[83] In most cases this will be the US branch of his own bank.

[84] Federal Reserve rate or market rate.

[85] The customer has to draw a bill for a gross amount that would assure him of obtaining the required net; cf. Ellinger, *Modern Banking Law*, p. 494.

[86] Cf. *ibid*.

[87] *Ibid*.; Lawrence, "Bills of Exchange", p. 47.

4. The Trade Bill

If the bill of exchange is closely connected with a trade transaction, it is called a trade bill. In its simplest form, the trade bill is drawn on the buyer who also accepts it.[88] At maturity the seller or party who has discounted the instrument presents it to the buyer. This is the common practice in domestic trade, however, trade bills are being increasingly used in international transactions as well.

(a) Economic Reasons for the Use of Trade Bills

The costs of financing the transaction are higher when the parties rely on sophisticated devices such as letters of credit to secure payment. For one thing the banks must be paid for bearing the risk involved in such transactions. This money is well spent in the case of long-distance commercial relationships in which mutual trust has not yet been established between the parties. Here precautionary measures are required which necessarily entail higher costs. The situation is different if the parties are engaged in constant transboundary transactions, thus encouraging them to seek less costly ways of performing daily business operations. In such cases, the seller may be satisfied with the same procedure used in domestic transactions: a term bill is drawn on the buyer who accepts and pays at maturity. This practice has become rather common in the European Community and it should be safe to predict that its usage will become even more widespread as a result of the future single market (1992/93).

(b) Legal Risks

Trade bills involve no particular legal risks *per se*. For practical reasons, however, legal issues may arise more frequently. On the one hand, there is no bank supervision and thus the parties have to perform the formalities themselves. Inclined to overestimate the degree of international harmonization in this field, the parties may fall victim to differences in form and wording used in the respective countries.

Nevertheless, from a lawyer's point of view, the standard trade bill is still a rather safe device for international payments. It should also be emphasized that trade bills put the seller in a much better position than book debts;[89] if issues arise in an international transaction, the features of bills of exchange prove to be most valuable and effective.[90] A particular form of the trade bill, however, should be considered

---

[88] Cf. Ellinger, *Modern Banking Law*, p. 499; Rowe, *Guarantees, Standby Letters of Credit and Other Securities*, p. 7.

[89] In transboundary transactions the advantages of bills over book debts are of much greater importance than in domestic trade.

[90] e.g. in respect of proof and enforcement in summary proceedings.

delicate in the international context: the acceptor's bill[91] or bill-cheque procedure and its French and Belgian counterparts (*escompte indirect*[92] and *escompte-fournisseur*[93]).

(c) Particular Risks of Acceptor's Bills

Based on the situation in Germany,[94] the procedure can be described as follows: if the buyer is in a strong bargaining position, he may insist on paying the price by cheque in order to take advantage of the favourable terms in the contract of sale. In such case, the bill of exchange is issued as usual[95] but discounted by the acceptor (buyer) rather than by the seller (drawer). This discount provides the acceptor with the necessary means to pay the cheque. Technically speaking, the drawer may indorse the bill to the drawee who indorses it to the discounting bank.[96] Thus the bill of exchange seems to be reversed[97] in the sense that the drawee who is primarily liable under the bill holds and discounts it.

This practice is used by parties to transboundary transactions for the same reasons as in domestic trade. There may even be an additional advantage when using this procedure, i.e., the parties may be able to obtain more favourable terms by discounting the bill in the buyer's (acceptor's) rather than in the seller's country.

If the buyer (acceptor) is not able to pay the bill at maturity, it is often difficult to hold the drawer (seller) liable. From his point of view, the matter seems to be settled after the cheque has been paid[98] and he does not see why the drawee's bank should recover this amount. This psychological factor can easily be transposed to the legal level.

First of all, the drawer may deny his liability, claiming the procedure to be illegal and void in his country. In general, this argument is to be taken seriously. The legal systems now recognizing this or similar procedures previously expressed serious doubts as to whether the drawer can be held liable. Differing views have been taken on this issue in case law and in the doctrine.[99] Secondly, the drawer may refuse payment on the grounds that the discounting bank was well informed about its

[91] In German *Akzeptantenwechsel* or *umgedrehter Wechsel*.

[92] This procedure is very similar to the reversed bill as the *acceptor* discounts the bill with his bank. Reportedly it is used in France; cf. C. G. Winandy, "Les moyens de défense du tireur d'une lettre de change contre le recours exercé par le banquier escompteur d'un effet fournisseur", *Revue de la Banque* (1983) pp. 637, 640, 643. As to case-law see decision of the Cour de cassation of 23 June 1971, *Semaine juridique* (1972) II, 17040 n., by Gavalda. M. Cabrillac, *La lettre de change dans la jurisprudence*, 2nd ed. (Paris 1978) pp. 161 *et seq.* refers to this procedure as the *modèle allemand*.

[93] The supplier (drawer) discounts the bill with the bank of the *buyer* (acceptor); cf. Belgium Cour d'appel de Bruxelles, *Revue de la Banque* (1986) pp. 42 *et seq.* n., by Regout-Masson; on France see M. Cabrillac, *La lettre de change dans la jurisprudence*, 161.

[94] M. Thamm, "Rechtsprobleme beim Scheck/Wechsel-Verfahren", *ZIP* (1984) pp. 922 *et seq.*; P. Ulmer and I. Heinrich, "Das Wechsel-Scheck-Verfahren", *DB* (1972) pp. 1101 *et seq.* and pp. 1149 *et seq.*; BGH *WM* (1986) p. 547 = *WuB* I D 4. Wechselverkehr 5.86 Hueffer; LG Stuttgart *WM* (1987) p. 869 = *WuB* I D 4. Wechselverkehr 5.87 Reiser; cf. in English language U. Jahn, 6 *International Banking Law* (1987), pp. 66 reporting a decision of OLG Hamm.

[95] Drawn by the supplier and accepted by the buyer.

[96] The bill may also be payable to the order of the discounting bank.

[97] In German *umgedreht*.

[98] For a case in which the cheque was not honoured even though the bill was discounted, cf. Jahn, *supra*, n. 94, at p. 66.

[99] Cf. e.g. E. Hucko, "Missbrauch von Wechsel und Scheck", *DB* (1969) pp. 1135 and 592 *et seq.* (Germany) and M. Kwalo, "Der sogenannte Lieferantendiskont in der französischen Bankpraxis", *WM* (1969) pp. 678 *et seq.* (France).

client's financial situation.[100] If the drawee becomes insolvent, it is easy to suspect that the bank relied on the drawer's liability from the very beginning, thus implying that the discount was given "at his expense". Obviously this may involve potential liability on the part of the discounting bank.

If the drawer has good counsel, he may defend his position by referring to the rules on control of exchange in his country. Contrary to trade transactions, transboundary financial transactions are often prohibited or require permission of the authorities.[101] The drawer's position is rather strong as he can make a good point by saying that payment of the transaction was completed by cheque. The draft and liability of the drawer may well be considered part of a financial transaction, i.e., the drawee's financing the cover for the cheque. The bank will also have to realize that it cannot evade the restrictions on exchange control in the drawer's country. Even if the bank sues the drawer abroad, the courts will respect the exchange control rules under Article VIII(2b) of the Bretton Woods Agreement.[102]

Thus it follows that lawyers should be extremely cautious when giving advice on the use of these procedures in international trade. On the other hand, if this practice becomes more common, they may look forward to interesting litigation.

III. Brief Legal Guide to International Bills of Exchange

When a conflict arises in connection with a transboundary bill of exchange, lawyers are often forced to resort to rules of thumb. Since they know their own law, they may simply apply these rules, hoping the otherwise applicable foreign law would finally lead to the same results. Rather often it occurs that the results are even the same or similar. This is not surprising as bills of exchange share a common historical background and the various codifications have been influenced to a large extent by worldwide commercial usages. It goes without saying, however, that such an assessment cannot serve as a reliable basis for serious arguments and litigation. Lawyers have to clearly state which law applies and how the case is to be judged according to these rules. The following remarks should be regarded as a guideline to finding a suitable approach.

1. The Applicable Law

It is somewhat misleading to ask which law is to be applied to a bill of exchange. First of all, one must realize that the courts of different states will apply their respective rules on conflicts of law. Therefore, the applicable law can only be discussed in connection with the rules in certain countries where the case might be decided. As a first step the lawyer must find out which courts have international jurisdiction.

---

[100] Cour d'appel de Bruxelles, *Revue de la Banque* (1986) pp. 42 *et seq.*, n. by Regout-Masson.

[101] For an overview, see P. Bently (ed.), *A World Guide to Exchange Control Regulations* (London 1985); International Monetary Fund (ed.), *Exchange Arrangements and Exchange Restrictions*, Annual Report 1988.

[102] Cf. J. Gold, *The Fund Agreement in the Courts*, vol. 3 (New York 1986) pp. 55 *et seq.*

(a) International Jurisdiction

It is rather difficult to present a complete picture of international jurisdiction with respect to transactions involving parties in different states. It may be presumed that each party can be sued in the state where it is domiciled.[103] Beyond that, however, it is not easy to specify other connections which are sufficient to justify international jurisdiction. Presenting a detailed discussion of the various rules of international jurisdiction applied throughout the world would go far beyond the scope of this article. To illustrate how far this leads away from the transaction itself, it should suffice to say that in many countries international jurisdiction can be based on assets of the defendant which have no connection whatsoever with the particular case.[104] Other countries do not have such a rule but rely on the connection of doing business or physical presence of the defendant.[105] With respect to the future single market, a few remarks should be made on European international procedural law.

(i) Brussels Convention

Not only is the Brussels Convention on civil procedure[106] applicable in most of the member states of the European Community[107] but the recent Lugano Convention will make the same rules applicable in Austria, Finland, Iceland, Norway, Sweden and Switzerland as well.[108]

Jurisdiction based on defendant's domicile

According to the Brussels Convention, international jurisdiction is based primarily on the domicile of the defendant (Article 2). Although there are no rules specifically designed for bills of exchange, the special competence rules in Article 5 et seq. should be taken into consideration. Here one may find that parties to a bill of exchange can be sued in a state where they are not domiciled.

Forum solutionis

Article 5(1) provides a special jurisdictional ground with respect to contractual obligations, viz., the place of performance. At first glance, it is not easy to realize the full potential impact of this rule on jurisdictional issues involving liability. As regards the acceptor, he can be sued at the place of payment which may well be outside the state where he is domiciled. As far as the drawer is concerned, doubts may arise as to whether he is liable under a *contractual* obligation. It has already been pointed out that his liability cannot be excluded if the Geneva Convention applies (Article 9(2)).

---

[103] In the case of companies, their seat would be the equivalent.

[104] e.g., Austria, Greece, Sweden, Norway, Denmark, Japan, Quebec, Ontario, Hungary, Poland, Czechoslovakia, Turkey and Yugoslavia.

[105] Cf. A. A. Ehrenzweig and E. Jayme, *Private International Law*, vol. 2 (Leiden 1973) pp. 20 *et seq.*

[106] Convention on Jurisdiction and the Enforcement of Judgments in Civil and Commercial Matters of 1968 as amended by the 1978 Convention on Accession of Denmark, Ireland and the United Kingdom, *OJ* (1978), L. 304/77; cf. P. Kaye, *Civil Jurisdiction and Enforcement of Foreign Judgments* (Abingdon 1987) p. 3.

[107] Belgium, Federal Republic of Germany, France, Italy, Luxemburg, The Netherlands, Denmark and the United Kingdom; cf. in detail R. Welter, *Zwangsvollstreckung und Arrest in Forderungen–insbesondere Kontenpfändung–in Fällen mit Auslandsberührung* (Frankfurt 1988) p. 52, with further references.

[108] See F. Urlesberger, "Ein einheitliches Gerichtsstandsrecht für ganz Westeuropa mit Ausnahme Österreichs im Werden", 110 *JBl* (1988) 223; P. Volken, "Das EG/EFTA-Parallel-Übereinkommen über die gerichtliche Zuständigkeit und die Vollstreckung gerichtlicher Entscheidungen in Zivil- und Handelssachen", in *SJIR* 43 (1987) 97.

Therefore some authors conclude that the drawer's obligation is not contractual but *legal*.[109] If the liability of the drawer is nevertheless qualified as contractual, the holder may well be entitled to sue the drawer at his (the holder's) domicile. The place of performance has to be determined according to the applicable law (*lex causae* as opposed to the *lex fori*).[110] In the case of money debts, a number of legal systems regard the *creditor's* domicile as the place of performance.[111]

Disputes arising from the operations of a branch, agency or other establishment
If the liability under a bill of exchange is connected with the business of a branch, Article 5(5) of the Brussels Convention grants jurisdiction to the place where the branch is situated.[112]

Plurality of defendants
It can still be speculated as to which extent Article 6(1) of the Brussels Convention permits forum shopping. In cases where there is more than one defendant, this rule provides that a person domiciled in a Contracting State can be sued in the member state where one of them has his domicile.[113] Thus it appears that the holder, for example, is entitled to sue the domestic drawer and a foreign acceptor as a joint defendant, thus opening the door to forum shopping. A recent decision of the European Court attempts to limit the plaintiff's choice by requiring that the respective actions[114] be connected in the sense that it is expedient to hear and decide them together. A good point can be made by claiming that the instrument itself provides the necessary connection;[115] however, thus far Luxemburg case law still leaves some doubts as to the acceptability of this argument.

(ii) Inter-American Panama Convention
In a number of Latin American States[116] international jurisdiction in matters concerning bills of exchange is determined by a multilateral convention[117] which provides that the plaintiff may choose between the domicile of the liable party and the place of performance.[118]

(b) The Applicable Law under the Geneva Convention

The Geneva Conferences of 1930 deal not only with substantial law but also with conflicts of laws.[119] Members of the Convention of 7 June 1930 for the Settlement of Certain Conflicts of Laws in Connection with Bills of Exchange and Promissory

---

[109] A. Hueck and C. W. Canaris, *Recht der Wertpapiere*, 12th ed. (Munich 1986) 74; contra Baumbach and Hefermehl, *Wechselgesetz und Scheckgesetz*, Art. 9 WG n. 2.

[110] *Tessili* v. *Dunlop*, ECR (1976) p. 1473; cf. in detail P. Kaye, *supra* n. 106, at p. 515.

[111] England, Greece, Italy, The Netherlands, Portugal, Switzerland and the United States.

[112] Cf. Kaye, *Civil Jurisdiction and Enforcement of Foreign Judgments* pp. 589 *et seq.*

[113] *Ibid.* 635 *et seq.*

[114] *WM* 1988, 1736 = *WuB* VII B 1. Art. 6 EuGVÜ 1.89 Welter.

[115] Welter, *Zwangsvollstreckung und Arrest in Forderungen*, with further references.

[116] Argentina, Chile, Costa Rica, Dominican Republic, Ecuador, Guatemala, Honduras, Mexico, Panama, Paraguay, Peru, El Salvador, Uruguay and Venezuela.

[117] Inter-American Convention of Panama concerning Bills of Exchange, Cheques and Invoices.

[118] W. Frisch Philipp, "Die Interamerikanischen Abkommen von Panama über Wechsel, Schecks und Fakturen", *RIW/AWD* (1979) p. 525.

[119] *League of Nations Treaty Series*, vol. CXLIII (1933-1934) p. 319.

Notes include Australia, Belgium, Brazil, Denmark, Germany, Finland, France, Greece, Italy, Japan, Luxembourg, Monaco, Netherlands, Norway, Austria, Poland, Portugal, Sweden, Switzerland, USSR and Hungary. Other states which are not regular members have nevertheless incorporated the Convention into their law.[120]

Thus it follows that lawyers in these countries can easily determine which law will be applied by the courts of another member state. They must simply consult their own law and apply it accordingly.[121]

In determining the applicable law, the Convention does not adopt the approach of a single law but rather that of several laws.[122] Thus it is worthwhile to note the solutions set forth in the Convention for the following matters:

- Capacity (Article 2): As a rule, the capacity of a person to bind himself by a bill of exchange is determined by the national law.[123]
- Form (Article 3): The form of any contract arising from a bill of exchange or promissory note is governed by the laws of the territory in which the contract has been signed.[124]
- Intrinsic validity (Article 4): The legal effect of the obligations of the acceptor or the maker of a promissory note is determined by the place of payment. All other obligations are governed by the law of the state where the party has signed the bill.
- Delays as to recourse (Article 5): Delays as to the exercise of recourse are determined by the place of the first issue.
- Form and delays for protest (Article 8): These are governed by the laws of the state where protest has to be made. It should be noted, however, that Article 8 does not deal with the question of whether formal protest is required or not. This matter is dealt with in Article 4 in connection with the legal effect.[125]

(c) The Applicable Law under the Bills of Exchange Act

As in the Geneva Convention, the solution of several laws is adopted in the Bills of Exchange Act.[126] Section 72 deals with the following conflicts of laws issues:

- Formal validity (Section 72(1) BEA): The validity of a bill as regards requisites of form is determined by the law of the place of issue. This is the place where first delivery took place and thus may differ from the place of signature.[127] If a bill is sent after signature to a foreign country, the bill will be considered to have been issued there.[128] Validity as regards requisites of form of supervening contracts such as acceptance or indorsement is determined by the law of the place where such contract was made. Again, if a bill is sent abroad, the contract becomes

---

[120] e.g. Yugoslavia.

[121] i.e. in the sense of considering domestic and foreign bills or parties from the point of view of the forum abroad.

[122] Cf. A. V. Dicey and J. H. C. Morris, *The Conflict of Laws*, vol. 2, 11th ed. (London 1987) p. 881.

[123] Cf. in detail Megrah and Ryder, *Byles on Bills of Exchange*, p. 340.

[124] Cf. in detail *ibid.* 334.

[125] Baumbach and Hefermehl, *Wechselgesetz und Scheckgesetz*, Art. 97 WG n. 1.

[126] Dicey and Morris, *The Conflict of Laws*, vol. 2, p. 881.

[127] Megrah and Ryder, *Byles on Bills of Exchange*, p. 334.

[128] Dicey and Morris, *The Conflict of Laws*, vol. 2, p. 886.

complete upon its arrival at destination.[129] Within the United Kingdom, however, a bill which conforms to domestic rules may be considered formally valid without regard to foreign law (Section 72(1)(b)).[130]

- Intrinsic validity (Section 72(2)): The interpretation of the drawing, indorsement or acceptance is governed by the law of the place where such contract is made.[131] Even though there is some doubt as to the scope of this provision,[132] it may be presumed that interpretation includes the legal effects of the instrument, thus excluding the general conflicts rule which would refer to the *lex loci solutiones*.[133] Therefore the liability of all parties to the instrument is subject to the law where the respective contracts were made. Contrary to the Geneva Convention,[134] the place of payment does not come into play in determining the applicable law.

- Duties of holder (Section 72(3)): The duties of the holder with respect to presentment for acceptance or payment and the necessity for or sufficiency of a protest or notice of dishonour are determined by the law of the place where the act is done or the bill is dishonoured.[135] Thus it follows that, contrary to the Geneva Convention, the necessity for protest is determined by the law of the place of payment.[136]

The BEA also deals with exchange rates (Section 72(4)) and the date of maturity (Section 72(5)). As regards other matters not covered by the Act,[137] recourse is to be taken to the ordinary conflicts rules.[138]

It should be noted that similar rules will be applied in Australia, Canada,[139] New Zealand and South Africa.[140]

(d) The Applicable Law under the UCC

Lawyers who are used to applying the Geneva Convention or the Bills of Exchange Act will find familiar rules in the Restatement, Conflict of Laws 2d (1971).[141] To a large extent the rules in §§ 240 *et seq.* are essentially identical to those of the Geneva Convention. On the other hand, the restatement principles do not prevail when the subject-matter is governed by a statute containing conflicts of laws rules.[142] This is the case, for example, in Section 1-105(1) UCC which contains conflicts rules for all

[129] *Ibid.* 884, 885.
[130] For details see Megrah and Ryder, *Byles on Bills of Exchange*, p. 332.
[131] Dicey and Morris, *The Conflict of Laws*, vol. 2, p. 889: the place of delivery.
[132] For details see Megrah and Ryder, *Byles on Bills of Exchange*, p. 332.
[133] Contra Dicey and Morris, *The Conflict of Laws*, vol. 2, p. 892.
[134] See *supra*, section III.1.(c).
[135] For further details see Dicey and Morris, *The Conflict of Laws*, vol. 2, pp. 898 *et seq.* and Crawford, *Banking and Bills of Exchange*, pp. 1722 *et seq.* on widespread criticism of this section.
[136] Dicey and Morris, *The Conflict of Laws*, vol. 2, p. 889: the place of delivery.
[137] e.g. capacity, interest, limitation of actions and prescription, set-off, foreign discharge.
[138] See Megrah and Ryder, *Byles on Bills of Exchange*, pp. 342 *et seq.*, and Crawford, *Banking and Bills of Exchange*, pp. 1729 *et seq.*
[139] For details, see Crawford, *Banking and Bills of Exchange*, pp. 1710 *et seq.*
[140] Megrah and Ryder, *Byles on Bills of Exchange*, p. 331.
[141] This restatement is a systematization of case-law organized by the American Law Institute and drafted by eminent law teachers in collaboration with a group of advisors (teachers, practitioners and judges).
[142] § 6(1) Restatement Conflicts of Laws 2d.

transactions covered in the UCC, including the law of negotiable instruments (Section 3 UCC).

Since these conflict of laws rules are not specifically designed for negotiable instruments, the approach of the UCC is remarkably different in that it follows the single law rather than the several laws doctrine. Failing a choice of law, the law of the forum state (i.e., the UCC) shall apply provided the *transaction*[143] bears an *appropriate relation* to this state, thus extending the application of the UCC to particular obligations[144] closely linked with other jurisdictions. On the international level, however, there is a tendency to apply Section 1-105(1) UCC rather cautiously.[145]

(e) Inter-American Panama Convention

In a number of Latin American States[146] matters relating to the conflicts of laws are governed by the Panama Convention of 1972 which has already been mentioned. To a large extent these conflicts rules correspond to those of the Geneva Convention; however, the liabilities of the maker and the acceptor are determined by the place where the contract was made, not by the place of payment.[147]

2. Applying Foreign Law in Matters involving Bills of Exchange

One might be lucky to solve the particular issue by discovering that international procedural law and the applicable conflicts law lead to his own domestic law. Often enough, however, the law of a foreign country is involved. Since a detailed survey of the various national laws cannot be presented here, the following guidelines will have to suffice.

International harmonization can be relied on to a certain extent and thus it seems appropriate to choose one's own legal system as a starting-point. From there, one should attempt to establish in which relevant points the foreign law differs. If, for example, the law of a Geneva Convention State applies, a civil law lawyer will be able to apply his own law after verifying that none of the reservations of the Geneva Convention are involved.[148]

It may occur that both civil law and common law lawyers are forced to apply a law outside their own system. For this purpose the comparison of key points made by M. Rowe is helpful.[149] In this context only the most important points are mentioned in the brief outline below:

---

[143] i.e. the instrument.

[144] e.g. of a foreign indorser.

[145] Barclays Discount Bank Ltd. v. *Lewis*, 743–F2d 722 [39 UCC Rep 916] (9th Cir 1984); *United Overseas Bank* v. *Veneers, Inc.*, 375 F. Supp. 596, 601 [14 UCC Rep 1349] (D Md 1974); cf. F. H. Miller and A. C. Harroll, *The Law of Modern Payment Systems and Notes* (Norman, Okla. 1985) p. 24.

[146] Costa Rica, Chile, Dominican Republic, Ecuador, Guatemala, Mexico, Panama, Paraguay, Peru and Uruguay.

[147] Cf. in detail Frisch Philipp, "Die Interamerikanischen Abkommen von Panama über Wechsel, Schecks und Fakturen", pp. 520 *et seq.*

[148] Supp. II to the Geneva Convention on the uniform law enumerates 22 reservations which, however, do not impair the essential elements of the uniform law of bills of exchange.

[149] Rowe, *Guarantees, Standby Letters of Credit and Other Securities*, pp. 90 *et seq.*

Formal requirements
- Geneva Convention: the term *bill of exchange* in the language of the instrument;
- BEA: unconditional order in writing, addressed by one person to another;
- UCC: unconditional order in writing, signed by a drawer.

How negotiated
- Geneva Convention: by indorsement, even if the bill is not expressly drawn to order;
- BEA: by indorsement and delivery if made to order; by delivery alone for a bearer instrument;
- UCC: see BEA

Guaranteeing payment
- Geneva Convention: aval;
- BEA: backing the bill as an indorser; the Act provides that where a person signs a bill otherwise than as drawer or acceptor, he thereby incurs the liabilities of an indorser to a holder in due course;
- UCC: see BEA; a party can indicate on the bill that he will pay if it is dishonoured by the primary liable party ("payment guaranteed").

Procedure on dishonour
- Geneva Convention: formal protest required; in addition, the holder must give notice to his indorsee and to the drawer;
- BEA: as a rule, notice must be given to each drawer and indorser; protest is required only for foreign bills;
- UCC: see BEA.

Excluding the right of recourse against drawer
- Geneva Convention: no release from guaranteeing payment;
- BEA: release is admitted;
- UCC: see BEA.

Protection of holder against defences
See II.2.(a) "Cutting off defences"

Effect of fraud[150]
- Geneva Convention: a forged or otherwise ineffective signature is not binding; nonetheless, the obligations of the other parties are valid;
- BEA: in the case of a forged indorsement, there can be no holder, especially no holder in due course;[151] the risk of loss by forgery is borne by the person who dealt with the forger ("know your indorser"). In addition,[152] forgery of one's signature is a real defence available even against the holder in due course;[153]
- UCC: see BEA.[154]

---

[150] For a detailed comparison see UN-document A/CN.9/CN.9/213, Art. 23, 3-10.

[151] Megrah and Ryder, *Byles on Bills of Exchange*, p. 256; Crawford, *Banking and Bills of Exchange*, p. 1371; Ellinger, *Modern Banking Law*, p. 504.

[152] Forgery of a signature other than the indorser's (e.g., the drawer's or acceptor's).

[153] Crawford and Falconbridge, *Banking and Bills of Exchange*, p. 1368.

[154] For more details, cf. Weber and Speitel, *Commercial Paper*, p. 292.

7

Choice-of-Law Issues Related to International Financial Transactions with Special Emphasis on Party Autonomy and its Restrictions

Petar Šarčević

I. Introductory Remarks

A book on international contracts and payments would not be complete without mentioning recent developments in the conflict of laws in jurisdictions of the major financial centres: London, Frankfurt, Zurich and New York. Over the past decade the attempt to introduce a greater degree of predictability into the field of conflict of laws has resulted in a "proliferation of statutory choice-of-law materials".[1]

The trend to codify choice-of-law rules has included contractual relations as well, as a result of which the courts of various national legal systems no longer decide each case on its merits on the basis of case law alone. In Europe the most significant attempt to harmonize the approach to contract conflicts by establishing uniform statutory choice-of-law rules is the adoption of the EC Convention on the Law Applicable to Contractual Obligations, the so-called Rome Convention of 19 June 1980 (hereinafter: Rome Convention or EC Convention).[2] At present, Germany, Belgium, Denmark, France, Italy, Luxemburg and Great Britain have incorporated the Rome Convention into their legal systems. By enacting the Contracts (Applicable Law) Act 1990 (in force since 1 February 1991), Great Britain largely replaced her choice-of-law rules in contract with the uniform EEC code. This step by Great Britain is all the more significant because, in moving her contract choice-of-law rules into closer harmony with those of her European partners, it marks "a breakdown of the cohesion of approach commonly found between many common

---

[1] R. J. Weintraub's comment in the preface to the 3rd edition of his *Commentary on the Conflict of Laws* (Mineola, New York 1986) applies to the US; however, this is also the case in other countries as well. Several years earlier Morris emphasized the increasing tendency for statutes to replace common law. Preface to the 10th edn. of Dicey and Morris, *The Conflict of Laws* (London 1980), pp. i, ix.

[2] Published in *OJ* L266 of 9 October 1980.

International Contracts and Payments (Šarčević, Volken, eds.; 1 85333 615 7; © Graham & Trotman, 1991; pub. Graham & Trotman; printed in Great Britain), pp. 109-123.

law jurisdictions".[3] Commenting on the new trend in the United Kingdom, Young remarked: "The days of the common law proper law of the contract are numbered".[4]

The Rome Convention became effective in Germany by virtue of the Law of 25 July 1986 concerning German Private International Law,[5] which reproduces the text of the uniform EEC code as if it were a national law. As Jayme points out, "by incorporating the Convention into the national statute, the German legislator hoped to facilitate the judges in their daily work".[6] Here Jayme is referring to the fact that, pursuant to Article 2, the Rome Convention is to be applied "regardless of whether the law applicable to the contract is the law of a Contracting State". Prior to the enactment of the PIL Act, choice-of-law rules in contract had not been codified in Germany. As in Great Britain, each case had been decided on the basis of a smoothly elaborated case law.[7] Similarly, contract conflicts were decided in Switzerland on the basis of an important body of case law[8] until the subject-matter was finally codified in the Swiss Private International Law Act, which entered into force on 1 January 1989 after 15 years of preparation and parliamentary deliberation.[9]

Finally, a special statutory measure enacted by the state of New York is important for the development of contract choice-of-law rules in general and in particular for parties to international financial transactions who stipulate New York law as the governing law. In order to protect its position as a financial and judicial centre, the state of New York enacted new legislation in 1984 to eliminate uncertainty as to the validity and enforceability of clauses which designate New York law as the governing law and state and federal courts sitting in Manhattan as a forum for deciding issues not directly involving the United States and New York.

II. Party Autonomy

A distinction is made between party autonomy in the sense of the parties' choice of law to govern the contract and the mere incorporation of a foreign law into the contract. In addition to their right to select the law applicable to the contract, the parties also have the right to incorporate provisions of a foreign law into the contract, not as a law but rather, for example, as a specific text incorporated into the contents of the contract. The incorporation of foreign law "presupposes that the [applicable

---

[3] P. M. North, "Reform but not Revolution–General Course on Private International Law", *Rec. des Cours* (1990 I), p. 153.

[4] J. Young, "An EEC Choice of Law Code for Contracts", *Int'l. Banking L.* (April 1991), p. 445.

[5] BGBl. (1986 I), p. 1142.

[6] E. Jayme, "The Rome Convention on the Law Applicable to Contractual Obligations (1980)" in P. Šarčević (ed.), *International Contracts and Conflicts of Laws (London, Dordrecht, Boston 1990), p. 91.*

[7] B. von Hoffmann, "Assessment of the E.E.C. Convention from a German Point of View" in P. M. North (ed.), *Contract Conflicts (Amsterdam, New York, Oxford 1982), p. 221.*

[8] See A. von Overbeck, "Contracts: The Swiss Draft Statute compared with the E.E.C. Convention" in P. M. North (ed.), *Contract Conflicts, supra* n. 7, at p. 269.

[9] On the history and genesis of the Swiss PIL Act, see the Introduction to *Switzerland's Private International Law Statute 1987*, introduced, translated and annotated by P. A. Karrer and K. W. Arnold (Deventer, Boston 1989), pp. 8-12.

law] differs from the law to which reference is made and derives its validity from the provisions of the [applicable law] and not from the conflict rules of the forum".[10]

1. Test of the Existence and Validity of Consent

The parties' right to choose the applicable law and the conditions for establishing the existence and validity of the parties' consent as to their choice of law are determined pursuant to the choice-of-law rules of the law of the forum. It is completely irrelevant whether the choice-of-law rules of the chosen law permit such selection.[11] In this context, the question often arises whether the parties' consent as to the choice of law constitutes a special agreement independent of the main contract.

The Swiss view on this matter clearly confirms that such agreement, which they refer to as an agreement of party consent (*Verweisungsvertrag*), is an independent agreement in which the parties declare a certain legal system applicable.[12] This, however, raises the question of how to determine whether such agreement has actually materialized.[13] There are several approaches to this problem. In accordance with the idea that subjective rights are derived from the objective legal system, Schnitzer concludes that an agreement of party consent can be considered materialized if the objective legal system permits the parties to make such a choice. As he points out, party autonomy is derivative in the conflict of laws just as the freedom to contract is in substantive law.[14] According to the *lex fori* approach, an agreement of party consent is deemed materialized in accordance with the law designated applicable by the choice-of-law rules of the *lex fori*.[15] The most widely accepted approach, however, is the *lex autonomiae* method, i.e., the existence and validity of party consent is determined pursuant to rules of the applicable law.[16]

This solution has also been adopted in Article 8(1) of the Rome Convention, which provides that the existence and validity of a contract shall be determined by the law which would govern it under the Convention, i.e., the applicable law. This also applies to the consent of the parties as to the choice of the applicable law.[17]

2. Express Choice, Inferred Choice, or No Choice

In European legal scholarship the view still commonly prevails that the consent of the parties can be either express or tacit (inferred, implied); if neither an express nor inferred choice has materialized, then no choice has been made at all. The tripartite division of choice of law has come under attack, particularly by scholars who argue that inference should not qualify as a choice of law. In particular, North raises the

[10] O. Lando, "Contracts", *International Encyclopedia of Comparative Law*, Vol. III (Tübingen, Mouton, The Hague, Paris 1976), p. 13.

[11] K. Siehr, "Die Parteiautonomie im Internationalen Privatrecht", *FS Max Keller* (Zurich 1990), p. 486.

[12] I. Schwander, "Zur Rechtswahl im IPR des Schuldvertragsrechts", *FS Max Keller, supra* n. 11, at p. 474; see also the literature he mentions in n. 6.

[13] K. Siehr, *supra* n. 11, at p. 493.

[14] A. Schnitzer, *Handbuch des Internationalen Privatrechts* Vol. II (Basel 1958), p. 628.

[15] K. Siehr, *supra* n. 11, at p. 493; see also his n. 45.

[16] C. Reithmann and D. Martiny, *Internationales Vertragsrecht*, 4th edn. (Cologne 1988), p. 176, No. 161; see Siehr's explanation of the development of these theories, *supra* n. 11, at p. 493 and n. 47.

[17] See M. Giuliano and P. Lagarde, "Report on the Convention on the Law Applicable to Contractual Obligations" in P. M. North, *Contract Conflicts, supra* n. 7, at p. 382.

question of whether a choice can be made by a means short of an express contractual provision:

"How far is an "inferred" choice really to be regarded as a choice at all? Should there continue to be this tripartite division into express choice, inferred choice and no choice? Is the second not really the third, but one where identification of the most closely connected law may be relatively easy?"[18]

North's implication that the only alternative to express choice is no choice is not only practised in some states but is also statute law. For example, Article 24(1) of the Turkish PIL Act requires that the applicable law be expressly chosen by the parties.[19]

On the other hand, the view is also held that inference is of such importance that it deserves to be treated independently of express choice as a special category of choice of law. In the United States, for example, inference is recognized and offered special treatment by the courts: "The presence of a choice-of-court clause . . . and the presence of other factors in the contract may lead a court to conclude that the parties made an implied choice of law".[20]

Although it would be of interest to elaborate on this matter, the purpose of this chapter is not to evaluate the tripartite division. Instead, it is viewed as a fact which is widely recognized by the courts and is even regulated by statute law. For example, legal scholarship and case law in England,[21] Germany,[22] and Switzerland[23] clearly indicate readiness to accept inference as a choice of law under various circumstances. Moreover, inference is recognized as a choice of law in Article 3(1) of the Rome Convention which stipulates that "the choice must be express or *demonstrated with reasonable certainty by the terms of the contract or the circumstances of the case*" [emphasis added]. Similarly, Article 116(2) of the Swiss PIL Act states that "the choice of law must be express or *clearly evident from the terms of the contract or the circumstances*" [emphasis added].

III. The Parties' Freedom of Choice

More important for our purpose is the basic principle embodied in party autonomy— the parties' freedom to choose the applicable law. Back in 1970 Lando wrote that party autonomy is "so widely accepted by the countries of the world that it belongs to the common core of the legal systems. Differences only exist concerning the limits of the freedom of the parties".[24] Today Lando's statement is still true; however, the emphasis has shifted from the general principle itself to the restrictions or, as he called

[18] P.M. North, *supra* n. 3, at p. 156.

[19] Act No. 2675 on the International Private and Procedural Law of 22 May 1982, *Resmi Gazette* No. 17701.

[20] E. F. Scoles and P. Hay, *Conflict of Laws* (St. Paul, Minn. 1982), p. 633.

[21] G. A. Penn, A. M. Shea and A. Arora, *The Law and Practice of International Banking* (London 1987), p. 8; e.g., *Compagnie d'Armement Maritime S.A.* v. *Compagnie Tunisien de Navigation S.A.* (1971) A.C. 572, p. 595.

[22] C. Reithmann and D. Martiny, *supra* n. 16, at p. 63; e.g., BGH 6 Feb. 1970 in *BGHZ* 53, pp. 189-191.

[23] F. Vischer and A. von Planta, *Internationales Privatrecht* (Basel and Frankfurt-on-Main 1982), p. 19; e.g., *BGE* 87 II (1961), p. 200; see also Botschaft zum Bundesgesetz über das internationale Privatrecht vom 10. November 1982, No. 82072 p. 146.

[24] O. Lando, "Contracts", *supra* n. 10, at p. 3.

it, "the limits of the freedom of the parties". This raises a series of questions: How free are the parties to determine the applicable law? In other words, can they choose any legal system to govern the contract? Moreover, once they have specified the applicable law, to what extent will it actually be applied by the courts?

1. Increasing the Parties' Freedom of Choice

The question of whether the parties are free to choose any legal system to govern the contract has long been a major choice-of-law issue. Over the past decade the general tendency in Europe has been to increase the parties' freedom of choice by removing the requirement of a territorial connection or reasonable interest for the choice of law. In Germany, for example, it was formerly held that parties of different states were basically free to choose a neutral law that had no connection to the transaction,[25] yet case law and legal scholarship show that, as a rule, some kind of "reasonable interest" was required to justify the choice of the parties.[26] Similarly, in Switzerland case law and legal scholarship required a "reasonable interest of the parties" to justify application of the chosen law.[27] On the other hand, English law has basically permitted parties to international contracts to choose any legal system to govern an international contract since at least *P & O Steam Navigation Co.* v. *Shoud* (1865).[28] Later in the widely cited case *Vita Food Products Inc.* v. *Unus Shipping Co. Ltd.* (1939), Lord Wright indicated that the contract does not have to have connections to English law. Thereafter, however, he acknowledged that the parties' freedom of choice is not unlimited by adding the following provisos: "provided the intention expressed is *bona fide* and legal, and provided there is no reason for avoiding the choice on the ground of public policy".[29]

A liberal approach has been adopted in Article 3(1) of the Rome Convention which places no restrictions whatsoever on the parties' freedom of choice: "A contract shall be governed by the law chosen by the parties." In this sense, von Hoffmann writes that the rule contains neither the usual requirements that the chosen law "must have a territorial connection with the contract nor that the choice of law must be *bona fide* and legal".[30] With the enactment of the Swiss PIL Act, the "reasonable interest" requirement was also removed from Swiss law.[31] Without a doubt this liberalizing gesture increased the parties' freedom of choice. On the other hand, the primary intention may have been unification rather than liberalization.

2. The Substantial Relationship Requirement in the US

In the U.S., the principle of party autonomy in section 187 of the Second Restatement of Conflict of Laws has been recognized as "the keystone of the Contracts Chapter";[32] however, this is followed by the substantial relationship restriction in subparagraph 2(a), which specifies that the choice-of-law clause will

---

[25] OLG Munich, *IPRax* (1986), p. 178.
[26] See B. von Hoffmann, *supra* n. 7, at p. 222.
[27] See *BGE* 102 II 143.
[28] P. Wood, *Law and Practice of International Finance* (London 1980), p. 7.
[29] (1939) A.C. 277 at p. 290.
[30] B. von Hoffmann, *supra* n. 7, at p. 222.
[31] See Botschaft zum Bundesgesetz über das internationale Privatrecht, *supra* n. 23, at p. 146.
[32] R. J. Weintraub, *Commentary*, *supra* n. 1, at p. 369.

not be effective if "the chosen state has no substantial relationship to the parties or the transaction and there is no other reasonable basis for the parties choice". Similarly, section 1-105(1) of the Uniform Commercial Code requires that the chosen law bear a "reasonable relationship to the parties or transaction".

This restriction is regarded as a serious limitation of the parties' freedom of choice as it authorizes the court to refuse a choice-of-law clause if the state whose law was chosen has no geographic contact with the transaction. For the purpose of establishing a geographic contact, it is considered insufficient if, for example, one of the contracting parties only has an office in the state of the chosen law.[33] According to the available materials, it appears that US courts have invoked the substantial relationship clause only in exceptional cases.[34] Although the courts have the discretion to decide whether to apply the disputed article, the possibility that a court would no longer honour the contractual stipulation of US law and in particular New York law began to discourage parties from stipulating New York law and New York courts for major contracts not directly involving the United States and New York. In order to retain its standing as a financial and judicial centre,[35] the state of New York finally modified its choice-of-law rules. On 19 July 1984 New York Governor Mario Cuomo signed Assembly Bill 7307-A, which is codified primarily as Title 14 of the New York Law of General Obligations. Among other things, Section 5-1401 provides:

"The parties to any contract, agreement or undertaking, contingent or otherwise, in consideration of, or relating to any obligation arising out of a transaction covering in the aggregate not less than two hundred fifty thousand dollars, including a transaction otherwise covered by subsection one of section 1-105 of the uniform commercial code, may agree that the law of this state shall govern their rights and duties in whole or in part, whether or not such contract, agreement or undertaking bears a reasonable relation to this state. This section shall not apply to any contract, agreement or undertaking (a) for labor or personal services, (b) relating to any transaction for personal, family or household services, or (c) to the extent provided to the contrary in subsection two of section 1-105 of the uniform commercial code."

By guaranteeing that its courts would not refuse choice-of-law clauses to apply New York law in cases involving $250,000 or more irrespective of the substantial relationship requirement, New York State succeeded in introducing certainty into its law, thus restoring its attractiveness as an applicable law for transactions such as bank loans, sales of goods and other. On the other hand, personal, family or household services and labour or personal services are excluded from the exception.

In addition, it was also necessary to assure that New York courts would not refuse to decide a case on the grounds of inconvenient forum. Therefore, section 5-1402 provides that, in cases involving at least $1,000,000, contracting parties who have stipulated New York law may also agree on the jurisdiction of New York courts. In cases where the parties consent to jurisdiction, the statute prohibits New York courts from dismissing the case on the grounds of inconvenient forum. Moreover, Section 5-1402 now permits foreign banks to sue in New York[36] and removes prior restrictions

---

[33] U. Stoll, *Die Rechtswahlvoraussetzungen und die Bestimmung des auf internationale Schuldverträge anwendbaren Rechts nach den allgemeinen Kollisionsregeln des US amerikanischen UCC und des deutschen Rechts (Frankfurt-on-Main, Bern, New York 1986), p. 160.*

[34] *Ibid.* 156-160. Stoll cites only five such cases.

[35] B. W. Rashkow, "Title 14, New York Choice of Law Rule for Contractual Disputes: Avoiding the Unreasonable Results", 71 *Cornell L. Rev.* (1985), p. 241.

[36] *Ibid.*; see his n. 104.

preventing foreign corporations, banks, or individuals from suing a foreign bank or corporation in New York if the parties have chosen New York law in accordance with section 5-1401 and have consented to New York jurisdiction under 5-1402.[37] In its relevant part, section 5-1402 reads as follows:

"1. Notwithstanding any act which limits or affects the right of a person to maintain an action or proceeding, including, but not limited to, paragraph (b) of section thirteen hundred fourteen of the business corporation law and subdivision two of section two hundred-b of the banking law, any person may maintain an action or proceeding against a foreign corporation, non-resident, or foreign state where the action or proceeding arises out of or relates to any contract, agreement or understanding for which a choice of New York law has been made in whole or in part pursuant to section 5-1401 and which (a) is a contract, agreement or undertaking, contingent or otherwise, in consideration of, or relating to any obligation arising out of a transaction covering in the aggregate, not less than one million dollars, and (b) which contains a provision or provisions whereby such foreign corporation or non-resident agrees to submit to the courts of this state."

3. Freezing of the Applicable Law (Versteinerungsklausel)

In bank-borrower relationships there are situations where the borrower's national law prohibits him from agreeing on the choice of a foreign law.[38] In cases where the law of the borrower applies, the question arises as to how the parties can protect themselves against possible changes that may occur in that law after the conclusion of the contract. In practice the attempt is made to introduce predictability into the relationship by incorporating a special clause which "freezes" the borrower's law as it was at the time the contract was concluded.

In England and Germany this is not regarded as a choice-of- law but rather as an incorporation-of-law clause. In this regard, Martiny maintains that the incorporation of law is a sufficient means of protecting the parties' interests in private transactions.[39]

IV. Restrictions on Party Autonomy

1. The Public Policy Exception (Ordre public)

Despite the tendency to increase the parties' freedom of choice by removing certain traditional restrictions, party autonomy is by no means unlimited. One of the classic restrictions which has remained is the public policy exception. A general public policy clause authorizes the courts to refuse to apply a rule of the applicable law if such application would be incompatible with the public policy of the forum. Public policy clauses in this sense are found in Article 16 of the Rome Convention, Article 17 of the Swiss PIL Act, and section 187(2)(b) of the Restatement Second.

The public policy exception has a negative function in that it authorizes the courts to stop the conflicts process by refusing to apply a rule or rules of the foreign law

---

[37] *Ibid.* 240.

[38] See P. Šarčević, "Rechtsfragen der Umschuldung", *Zeitschrift für das gesamte Kreditwesen* (1985), pp. 53-56.

[39] C. Reithmann and D. Martiny, *supra* n. 16, at p. 61; G. A. Penn, A. M. Shea and A. Arora, *supra* n. 21, at p. 7.

chosen by the parties or designated applicable by the forum's choice-of-law rules. When applying a foreign law, the court must first determine that there are no mandatory rules of the forum which warrant direct application (see below); thereafter it analyses the substantive rules of the foreign law to determine whether their application would be contrary to their own notion of public policy. By invoking the public policy clause, the court can exclude application of the foreign law in its entirety or individual rules thereof. In such cases, the substantive rules or rule of the *lex fori* are usually applied.

The elements constituting public policy vary from legal system to legal system. In regard to the United States, Weintraub comments that by invoking public policy, a court can refuse to apply a rule of the applicable law "as contrary to its own notion of justice and fairness".[40] In English law, the notion of public policy as a restricting force includes not only the general public policy mentioned above but also the idea that courts should not "entertain an action to enforce a foreign penal, revenue or public law". By focusing on the "foreign rule rather than its application in the English forum," this "helps to concentrate attention on particular characteristics which will move a court".[41]

2. Special Treatment of Certain Consumer Contracts and Related Loan Contracts

The fact that the parties' freedom of choice sometimes results in the abuse of that freedom led to the realization there is a need to protect one of the parties depending on the nature and purpose of the transaction. In regard to consumer contracts, Philip remarks: "Therefore, it has not been found possible to give the parties the same degree of freedom to choose the applicable law as has been given to the parties in other types of contracts."[42]

As a means of protecting consumers, Article 120(2) of the Swiss PIL Act excludes the choice of law in contracts for goods and services intended for the consumer's personal use, that of his family, or other use not connected with his professional or business activity. Moreover, it designates that such transactions shall be governed by the law of the country in which the consumer has his habitual residence if:

"(a) the other party received the order in that country, (b) if there was an offer or advertisement in that country prior to the conclusion of the contract and if the legal formalities required for the conclusion of the contract were performed by the consumer in that country, or (c) if the other party prompted the consumer to go abroad and place his order there."

The Swiss provision is based on Article 5 of the Rome Convention; however, there are important differences. First of all, instead of excluding the choice of law in such transactions, the Rome Convention protects the consumer by guaranteeing him recourse to the consumer protection measures provided by the mandatory rules of the state where the consumer has his habitual residence:

[40] R. J. Weintraub, *Commentary, supra* n. 1, p. 81.
[41] D. Jackson, "Mandatory Rules and Rule of 'ordre public'", in P. M. North, *Contract Conflicts, supra* n. 7, at p. 69.
[42] A. Philip, "Mandatory Rules, Public Law (Political Rules) and the Choice of Law in the E.E.C. Convention on the Law Applicable to Contractual Obligations", in P. M. North, *Contract Obligations, supra* n. 7, at p. 91.

"a choice of law made by the parties shall not have the result of depriving the consumer of the protection afforded to him by the mandatory rules of the law of the country in which he has his habitual residence" (Art. 5(2)).

The circumstances of operation are basically the same as those in the Swiss PIL Act cited above. Moreover, Article 5(1) expressly states that the said article also applies to "a contract for the provision of credit for that object", i.e., for "the supply of goods or services to a person for a purpose which can be regarded as being outside his trade or profession". Although bank contracts are not expressly mentioned, Kropholler is of the opinion that they qualify as services in the sense of Article 5 if used for a purpose specified therein.[43] This is in keeping with the Convention on Jurisdiction and the Enforcement of Judgments in Civil and Commercial Matters which recognizes "a contract for a loan repayable by instalments, or for any other form of credit, made to finance the sale of goods" as belonging to the category of certain consumer contracts. On the other hand, the Convention on the Law Applicable to Certain Consumer Sales excludes sales "of stocks, shares, investment securities, negotiable instruments or money" from its scope.

3. Unequal Bargaining Power and the Choice of Law

As Giuliano and Lagarde point out, the drafters of the Rome Convention were guided in Article 5 by the idea that "the law of the buyer (the weaker party) should normally prevail over that of the seller".[44] This raises the question of whether some form of protection should be provided to the weaker party in other types of transactions such as international financial transactions.[45]

In commercial transactions it is not unusual for the economically stronger party to take advantage of his position to stipulate the applicable law most favourable to him. This often occurs when the weaker party is required to honour standard forms and conditions in which the choice of law is dictated by the stronger party. Although it is argued that the applicable law so designated is usually more developed, this does not justify the abuse of party autonomy. In such situations, the principle of party autonomy loses its significance because there is no real consent by the parties. Therefore, it has been proposed that choice-of-law clauses made without the real consent of both parties should be declared invalid.[46] Nonetheless, it is not to be expected that courts will intervene with the choice of law unless it is clear from the circumstances that the stronger party has abused the principle of party autonomy.

4. Evasion of Law: Old Problem, New Solutions

Another form of abuse of party autonomy occurs when the parties intentionally change or introduce new connecting factors in order to justify their choice of a foreign law that is more favourable. In such cases, the court may refuse to apply a foreign law chosen by the parties on the grounds of evasion of the law (*fraus legis*).

Today the evasion-of-law clause is sometimes regarded as a traditional correcting factor which is no longer needed. As a result, such clauses are not always in-

---

[43] J. Kropholler, *Internationales Privatrecht* (Tübingen 1990), p. 401.

[44] M. Giuliano and P. Lagarde, *supra* n. 17, at p. 377.

[45] P. Šarčević, "Real Interest Rates and the Debt Problem–A Legal Approach", *Droit des affaires internationales* (1985), pp. 861-862.

[46] P. H. Neuhaus, *Die Grundbegriffe des Internationalen Privatrechts* (Tübingen 1976), p. 257.

corporated into modern conflicts statutes.[47] Von Overbeck, for example, maintains that they are unnecessary because the same purpose is now achieved by other means.[48] In such cases, Swiss courts may refuse to honour the parties' choice of law on the grounds of the lack of good faith. As specified by Article 2(2) of the Swiss Civil Code, the parties must exercise their rights and fulfil their obligations in accordance with the principle of good faith.[49]

Other classic cases of evasion of law are now treated as a special category of evasion—evasion of the mandatory rules. For example, if the parties intentionally conclude their contract in Germany instead of Switzerland in order to evade the Swiss requirements in regard to the form of the transaction, German courts will not take account of the place where the contract was concluded but will apply the mandatory rules of Swiss law on the formal requirements for such transactions.[50]

The institution of evasion of law was not particularly well developed in English law;[51] nonetheless, English courts do not hesitate to refuse a choice-of-law clause if that law was chosen for the purpose of evading mandatory rules. Basically North believes that businessmen and their advisers usually have a sound reason for choosing a particular law to govern their contract. Thus he encourages courts to uphold the choice of the parties unless there is a good reason to refuse it. In his opinion, two reasons which are sufficient to justify judicial intervention with the parties' choice of law are lack of good faith and the evasion of mandatory rules.[52] The issue of evasion, however, is only one aspect of the complex system of mandatory rules, the major mechanism restricting party autonomy.

V. Mandatory Rules and the Choice of Law

Once the parties have designated the applicable law, the principle of party autonomy presupposes that the court will apply the substantive rules of that law. This raises the question of whether the court is expected to apply only the foreign rules of private law or those of public law as well. In the past, courts usually invoked the public policy exception as a means of refusing the application of public rules of the chosen or otherwise applicable law. Since the distinction between public and private law is of considerable importance in some jurisdictions and also has an effect on the operation of their choice-of-law rules, it is necessary to comment briefly on the characterization process. In other words, which criteria are used in various legal systems to characterize rules as either public or private?

---

[47] This does not mean that the evasion-of-law clause cannot be found in modern codifications. The respective legislation in the following countries/province contains such a clause: Spain (Art. 12(4)), Yugoslavia (Art. 5), Hungary (Art. 8), Portugal (Art. 21), and Quebec (Art. 6).

[48] A. von Overbeck, "Les questions générales du droit international privé à la lumière des codifications et projects récents", *Rec. des Cours* III, (1983), p. 208.

[49] See M. Keller and K. Siehr, *Allgemeine Lehren des Internationalen Privatrechts* (Zurich 1986), p. 526.

[50] C. Reithmann and D. Martiny, *supra* n. 16, at p. 320.

[51] Dicey and Morris on *The Conflict of Laws* (London 1973), p. 730.

[52] P. M. North, "Reform but not Revolution", *supra* n. 3, at p. 167.

1. Private Law and Public Law Rules

In many countries no consensus has been reached on the meaning of public law.[53] In civil law countries, of which France is the classic example, public law usually encompasses relationships between the State and individuals, whereas relationships between individuals belong to private law. Accordingly, penal law, revenue law, monetary law, social security law, administrative law and procedure are regarded as belonging to public law. In some civil law countries there is neither a constitutional nor a statutory definition of public and private law. Nonetheless, in the Netherlands, for example, the term "public law" is frequently used in practice to indicate "either the involvement of the State "as such" in a given legal relationship or the fact that public interests are at stake".[54]

Although a distinction is made between public and private law in other countries, it is not always clear which criterion is used. In this regard, the Swiss Federal Court emphasized in 1983 that the distinction between public and private law should be made on a case-by-case basis using the "most suitable" criteria in light of the circumstances of the particular case.[55] In Swiss legal scholarship there are various theories on how to determine the "most suitable" criteria for characterizing rules of law as private or public. According to the so-called subordination theory, relationships between individuals of equal status are governed by private law, whereas public law governs relationships involving the hierarchical subordination of individuals under the power of the state. The interest theory entertains the view that rules of private law are enacted for the purpose of protecting private interests as opposed to rules of public law which are intended to protect public interests. Sometimes all rules of law enacted for the purpose of serving the State and the execution of its power are characterized as belonging to public law. In Switzerland the rules of the *lex fori* (Swiss law) are also used to determine the nature of foreign rules of law. The reasoning for this is simple: all matters concerning the scope of application of Swiss choice-of-law rules are governed by domestic law.

If a court characterizes a rule of foreign applicable law as public, the question arises as to whether it will apply such rule. In the past, rules characterized as public were most commonly refused on the ground that their application is territorially limited. Thereafter, however, extraterritorial application was extended to such rules as well. This induced the Swiss Federal Court finally to depart from its earlier view that Swiss courts do not need to apply foreign public law rules except in cases where Swiss law requires that such rules also be taken into account. Today Swiss courts apply the substantive rules of the chosen law regardless of whether they belong to private or public law. In this sense, Article 13 of the Swiss PIL Act provides that the reference to a foreign law includes all provisions applicable to the facts under that law. The application of a rule of foreign law is not precluded solely because the rule is attributed the character of public law.

[0] K. Lipstein, "Conflict of Laws and Public Law", General Report at the XIIth International Congress of Comparative Law held at Melbourne and Sidney (1986), p. 1.

[54] C. Van Rooj, "Conflict of Laws and Public Law", Dutch national report at the XIIth International Congress of Comparative Law held at Melbourne and Sidney (1986), p. 2.

[55] Decision of 3 June 1983 in *Schweizerischer Treuhändler-Verband* v. *Schweizerische Nationalbank, BGE* 109 I6 146, at 149; see P. Šarčević and T. Burckhardt, "Conflict of Laws and Public Law", *Swiss Reports Presented at the XIIth International Congress of Comparative Law* (Zurich 1987), p. 139.

This development was fully in keeping with the basic principle of party autonomy. In effect, it strengthened the parties' choice of law and promised greater predictability in international transactions. At the same time, however, an adequate protective mechanism was required to prevent abuse. This seemed to be provided by the traditional public policy exclusion. At least that was the idea expressed as early as 1975 in a resolution of the *Institut de droit international* stating that the choice of a foreign law includes its public law rules as well, provided such rules are compatible with the public policy of the particular state. Nonetheless, many considered the protection provided by the public policy exclusion insufficient for this purpose, thus leading to the introduction of a mechanism of special mandatory rules.

2. Internationally Binding Mandatory Rules

In order to protect their interests countries introduced mandatory rules of a unilateral character which provide "that certain rules of their own law shall always apply under certain circumstances and in spite of the choice-of-law rules".[56] Subject to application without recourse to the choice-of-law rules of the *lex fori*, these special mandatory rules are known in legal scholarship as *rules of direct application (lois de police, lois d'application immédiate, Eingriffsnormen, selbstgerechte Sachnormen)*. From the point of view of private international law, Schwander defines rules of direct application as substantive rules of a municipal law which, by virtue of their special purpose, are applied in relationships with a foreign element irrespective of the choice-of-law rules.[57] Putting it a bit differently, Keller and Siehr define rules of direct application as internationally binding substantive rules which must be applied under certain factual conditions.[58] In this chapter the term "mandatory rules" is used in this restricted sense to refer to such internationally binding rules.

In an attempt to determine which mandatory rules of a legal system are internationally binding, Francescakis remarks that such rules are of primary importance in the regulation of the "social life" of a state.[59] According to Lipstein, if not specified otherwise by international treaty, "absolute binding rules" (as he refers to them) include rules of criminal law, labour law and revenue law, expropriation and confiscation rules, social security regulations, currency regulations, import and export regulations, antitrust legislation, trade regulations in general, and all administrative and financial regulations which affect civil, family and labour law.[60] From this list it is evident that internationally binding mandatory rules include not only public but also private law rules.

As a rule, the courts should apply the internationally binding mandatory rules of the law chosen by the parties or otherwise applicable law. Recent legislation, however, provides for a restricting mechanism which permits the courts to exclude application of the mandatory rules of the *lex causae* and to apply the mandatory rules of their own or even another law instead.

---

[56] A. Philip, *supra* n. 7, at p. 102.

[57] I. Schwander, *Internationales Privatrecht* (St. Gallen 1985), p. 161.

[58] M. Keller and K. Siehr, *supra* n. 49, at p. 244.

[59] Cited in I. Schwander, *Internationales Privatrecht, supra* n. 49, at p. 244.

[60] K. Lipstein, *supra* n. 53, at p. 7.

3. Direct Application of Mandatory Rules of the Forum

Article 7 of the Rome Convention authorizes courts to derogate from the application of the mandatory rules of the *lex causae* in certain circumstances and to apply those of another law instead. In particular, Article 7(2) provides that nothing in the Convention shall restrict the application of the rules of the law of the forum in situations where they are mandatory irrespective of the law otherwise applicable to the contract. Commenting on the far-reaching implications of this rule, Philip remarks that "it makes it possible for the participating states to apply their own law to the extent that they see fit".[61] More specific, the decision whether and to what extent courts will apply Article 7(2) depends on the rules of the *lex fori* providing for the exclusive application of domestic law.[62]

Article 18 of the Swiss PIL Code contains a similar provision which provides for the exclusive application of mandatory rules of Swiss law if such follows from the nature of their purpose:

"The Code is subject to those mandatory provisions of Swiss law which, by reason of their particular purpose, are applicable regardless of the law designated by this Code".

In regard to international financial transactions, it is generally accepted, among other things, that the parties cannot derogate from the currency regulations of the *lex fori*. This includes any regulations prohibiting the flow of currency abroad, i.e., restricting the amount of domestic currency which can be taken out of the country. The scope of application of such regulations is directly related to their purpose, i.e., the preservation of the country's balance of payments. In such situations, however, the task of the court is not to determine whether the country's balance of payments is threatened by the conditions of a particular contract but to investigate whether that contract in general could have an adverse effect on the foreign exchange market of that country.[63]

4. Direct Application of Mandatory Rules of Third Countries

In addition to applying the mandatory rules of the *lex fori*, courts may also replace the mandatory rules of the chosen law with those of third countries having a close connection with the situation. Article 7(1) of the Rome Convention reads as follows:

"When applying under this Convention the law of a country, effect may be given to the mandatory rules of the law of another country with which the situation has a close connection, if and in so far as, under the law of the latter country, those rules must be applied whatever the law applicable to the contract. In considering whether to give effect to these mandatory rules, regard shall be had to their nature and purpose and to the consequences of their application or non-application."

A similar rule can be found in Article 19 of the Swiss PIL Code. The Swiss rule differs from that of the Rome Convention in two aspects. Firstly, the scope of application of the Swiss rule is broader in that it applies not only to contractual but to all legal relationships.[64] Secondly, in addition to the conditions of operation cited in Article 7(1) of the Rome Convention, the Swiss rule stipulates that a mandatory provision of

---

[61] A. Philip, *supra* n. 7, at p. 102.
[62] *Ibid.* 101.
[63] C. Reithmann and D. Martiny, *supra* n. 16, at p. 293.
[64] P. Šarčević and T. Burckhardt, *supra* n. 55, at p. 154.

a law other than the applicable law may be taken into account if interests of a party are at stake which are deemed worthy of protection and manifestly preponderant by the standards of Swiss law.[65]

The principal condition for applying the mandatory rule of a third country is found in all three of the above rules: the existence of a close connection between the situation and the law of the third country. There are several situations in which the close connection with the law of a third country would be justified. For example, if the parties have chosen the applicable law and that law is different from the law that would otherwise have been applicable under the particular Act, then the situation is closely connected with that law. In fact, as Philip adds, the situation is "most closely connected with that law".[66] There are, however, other possibilities as well. Above all, the *lex loci solutionis* should be taken into account and with good reason. As Lipstein points out, the law of the foreign country where the contract is to be performed can "effectively control and thereby prohibit the execution of the contract".[67] Therefore, French, Belgian, English and Israeli law approve the idea of applying the mandatory rules of the *lex loci solutionis* even if that law is not applicable.[68] Another possibility is the *lex loci contractus;* however, since the place of contracting can be fortuitous, some countries reject the application of the mandatory rules of that law as irrelevant (e.g., England).

Furthermore, in international financial transactions, the law of the debtor's residence could also be taken into account. The reason is obvious: if the decision is to be enforced at the place of the seat of the debtor's business or the place of his residence, the mandatory rules of that law should be considered so as to assure consistency with its public policy. On the other hand, this is sometimes deemed necessary only if the debtor owns assets in the country of his residence. Another possibility is the law of the creditor's residence. According to Lipstein, the mandatory rules of the law of the creditor's residence may have a direct influence on the performance of the contract. If not respected, the creditor could be prevented from performing his contractual obligations.[69]

In regard to case law, the frequently cited decision of the Dutch *Hoge Raad* of 13 May 1966 in the *Alnati* case should be mentioned as it served as the impetus for the EC countries to include a provision in the Rome Convention justifying the application of the mandatory rules of a third country in certain circumstances.[70]

---

[65] A. von Overbeck, "Contracts", *supra* n. 8, at p. 271; see also P. Šarčević and T. Burckhardt, *supra* n. 55, at pp. 154-155.

[66] A. Philip, *supra* n. 7, at p. 103.

[67] K. Lipstein, *supra* n. 53, at p. 10.

[68] *Ibid.* 11.

[69] *Ibid*

[70] The *Alnati* case involved the carriage of goods (potatoes) from Antwerpen to Rio de Janeiro by a Dutch carrier under a bill of lading stipulating Dutch law as the applicable law. After having confirmed the parties' choice of Dutch law in the bill of lading, the Hoge Raad established that there were no mandatory rules to be considered under Dutch law and none under Brazilian law as well. On the other hand, Article 91 of the Belgian Commercial Code provided that the Hague Rules (i.e., the Belgian version) were directly applicable in all cases involving the carriage of goods originating at a Belgian port. Although the Hoge Raad applied Dutch law in the end, it follows from their reasoning that there may be mandatory rules of a foreign law which are so important to that law that their application by a foreign court is justified despite the choice of a different law by the parties. See details in J. C. Schultsz, "Dutch Antecedents and Parallels to Article 7 of the EEC Convention of 1980", 47 *RabelsZ* (1983), pp. 267-283.

This case shows how difficult the decision-making process is when the court must decide whether to give priority to the mandatory rules of a third legal system. From the wording of Article 7(1) of the Rome Convention–"effect may be given"–it is clear that the court may exercise its discretion in deciding whether or not such rules should be applied. However, the criteria on which it is to base its decision are vague: when making its decision the court shall take into account the nature and purpose of such mandatory rules and the consequence of their application or non-application. In view of the uncertainty Article 7(1) creates by conferring discretionary power upon the court without providing precise criteria for evaluating the circumstances, some experts proposed that the Contracting States be permitted to place a reservation on this article. This proposal was honoured in Article 22(1)(a) of the Convention. Both Germany and Great Britain used this reservation, as a result of which Article 7(1) was not incorporated into the German PIL Act and the British Contracts (Applicable Law) Act 1990.

VI. Concluding Remarks

The general trend in the conflict of laws in the jurisdictions of four of the major financial centres (London, New York, Frankfurt and Zurich) confirms that over the past decade an increasing number of statutory choice-of-law materials has been enacted to govern contractual relations. Although the intention has been to provide a greater degree of predictability by increasing the parties' freedom to choose the applicable law, the results have shown that absolute freedom of the parties' choice of law is a fiction. Although some of the traditional restrictions on party autonomy have been removed, others have been retained and new ones added in order to prevent abuse of the principle of party autonomy. This paradoxical situation characterizes the true nature of party autonomy: the greater the freedom of the parties' choice, the more restrictions are needed to balance that freedom.[71]

In particular, the principle of party autonomy is undermined by provisions authorizing the courts to apply the mandatory rules of the *lex fori* and even those of third countries irrespective of the parties' choice of law. Since such restrictions create uncertainty, it is necessary to investigate to what extent the courts have the right to intervene with the parties' choice of law. In order to assure predictability in international financial transactions, the parties and their advisers must take account of these restrictions when selecting the law to govern their contract.

---

[71] K. Siehr, *supra* n. 11, at p. 510.

8

Legal Opinions in International Transactions

Paul Volken

The multifold progress in international communication techniques has made our globe smaller and shortened distances. All the more we are astonished if we discover, even within communities of equal economic standing, concepts and ideas that are important to one but almost unknown to the other community. Legal opinions are such a concept. Whereas such legal technique is unknown to most lawyers trained in civil law , in other jurisdictions, namely in the USA, the conclusion and finalization of a commercial transaction has become almost unthinkable without being prepared and/or accompanied by one or more legal opinions.[1]

The concept of legal opinions comes from the common law.[2] Mainly in the USA where they have been strongly advocated, legal opinions have become common ground for the commercial world. And since the early seventies the US judiciary has developed an increasing body of case[3] law accompanied by regular legal writing[4] on the topic.[5]

---

[1] See e.g. J. J. Fuld, infra, n. 4, at 915: "Today, in important business transactions such as sales of businesses, mergers, bank loans or sales of securities, legal opinions are almost always required as a condition precedent to the closing of the transaction."

[2] See M. Gruson, and M. Kutschera, Legal Opinions in Corporate Transactions: Foreign Response to U.S. Opinion Requests, Report of the Subcommittee on Legal Opinions . . . of the International Bar Association (London 1987).

[3] In the sixties and the seventies various malpractice cases were decided in California; see e.g.: Lucas v. Hamm, 56 Cal. 2d 583, (1961) 15 *Cal. Rptr.* 821; Smith v. Lewis, 13 Cal. 3d 349, (1975) 118 *Cal. Rptr.* 621; Horne v. Peckham, 97 Cal. App. 3d 404, (1979) 158 *Cal. Rptr.* 714; Davis v. Damrell, 119 Cal. App. 3d 883, (1981) 174 *Cal. Rptr.* 257. According to Fuld, "Lawyers' Standards and Responsibilities in Rendering Opinions" (1978), 33 *Bus. Law.*, 1295, at p. 1298: "[C]onscientious lawyers are deeply concerned today when delivering opinions . . . There is a cumulative effect: Opinions are being requested in increasing types of transactions, the requested opinions are being increasingly broadened as to scope, the class of persons who may rely on lawyers' opinions may be expanding, and lawyers are being increasingly sued on expanding theories."

[4] Among the earliest publications were: Fuld, "Legal Opinions in Business transactions: An Attempt to Bring Some Order Out of Some Chaos" (1973), 28 *Bus. Law.*, p.915; J. P. Freeman, "Opinion Letters and Professionalism" (1973) *Duke, L. J.*, p. 371; G. W. Bermant, "The Role of the Opinion Counsel: A

International Contracts and Payments (Šarčević, Volken, eds.; 1 85333 615 7; © Graham & Trotman, 1991; pub. Graham & Trotman; printed in Great Britain), pp. 125-140.

In international transactions the seller of goods, the lender of money and the offerer of technical know-how often have a tendency to handle their business the very same way as they do in their day-by-day activities. As a consequence it follows that e.g. a Midtown Manhattan Bank, in preparing a loan agreement, follows the same steps of proceedings and asks for the same kind of documents, no matter whether the money lent goes just across the Hudson River or is intended to be used on the other side of the Atlantic. All that the Manhattan lender wants is to be sure that its loan contract is a valid, legally binding instrument and that the borrower is bound to repay the loan with interest at maturity.

In the New Jersey case, the Manhattan money-lender gets the required guaranties and controls by asking for a legal opinion on the validity of the loan agreement both under the law of New York and New Jersey. And if the money is supposed to go to France or Italy, or to Yugoslavia, our money-lender in New York wants to receive the very same pieces of paper certifying that the transaction is also valid and binding as to the law of the borrower's country.

There are basically three ways to face the demands of our Manhattan money-lender. The first would be to convince him that, under European law, a legal opinion of the kind he asks for is a meaningless piece of paper. But as the requesting side might not be in a position to dictate modalities, such a solution seems not to be sound. A second way would be what American legal scholars have characterized as the globalization of the American legal profession. An American lawyer would then opine on Austrian, Czechoslovakian or Hungarian law. The obvious variant to this are lawyers coming from, and practising in the countries in question who familiarize themselves with the concept of legal opinions in order to give an appropriate response to the demands of legal opining as to their domestic legal system.

The present chapter aims to make lawyers from both sides of the Atlantic aware of the conceptual differences when establishing the content of a given legal solution. Thus the North-American lawyer might better understand why his European counterpart sometimes has difficulties in understanding his demands, and the European lawyer might easier grasp what kind of statements his North-American colleague is looking for.

Cont.
Tentative Reevaluation" (1974), 49 *Cal. St. B. J.*, p. 132; R. W. Jennings, "The Corporate Lawyer's Responsibilities and Liabilities in Pending Legal Opinions" (1975) 30 *Bus. Law.*, p. 73; W. L. Landau, "Legal Opinions Rendered in Securities Transactions" (1976) 8 *Inst. on Sec. Reg.* p. 3. Since then publications cover most fields where legal opinions are regularly used. For a detailed recent bibliography see W. L. Estey, *Legal Opinions in Commercial Transactions* (Toronto 1990), pp. 299-304.

[5] Individual legal writing was followed rather early by committee reports; see e.g.: "Subcommittee on Opinion Writing of the Massachusetts Bar Association Committee on Corporate, Banking and Business Law, Omnibus Opinion for Use in Loan Transactions" (1975), *Mass. L.Q.*, p. 193; id., "Omnibus Opinion for Use by Seller's Counsel in the Sale of Closely-Held Business" (1976), 61 *Mass. L.Q.*, p. 108; "Association of the Bar of the City of New York, Report by Special Committee on Lawyers' Role in Securities Transactions" (1978), 32 *Bus. Law.*, p. 1879; "Special Comm. on Legal Opinions in Commercial Transactions, New York County Lawyers' Ass'n, Legal Opinions to Third Parties: An Easier Path" (1979), 34 *Bus. Law.*, p. 1891 and "An Addendum" (1981), 36 *Bus. Law.*, p. 1981; "Committee on Corporations of the Business Law Section of the State Bar of California, Report regarding Legal Opinions in Business Transactions" (1983), 14 *Pacific L.J.*, p. 1001; "Joint Committee of the Real Property Law Section of the State Bar of California and the Real Property Section of the Los Angeles Bar Association, Legal Opinions in California Real Estate Transactions" (1987) 42 *Bus. Law.*, p. 1139.

To this end, the present chapter contains two parts, each of which is divided into four sections.

The first part deals with the concept of legal opinions: it describes the legal nature of such opinions, makes some references to comparable instruments, stresses their principal functions and main purposes, and mentions the areas of law where legal opinions are commonly utilized.

The second part addresses the framing of legal opinions and tries to go systematically through the substantive elements of a legal opinion. In the United States, it is now more or less agreed what legal opinions are, what they say and what they do. The agreement includes the legal matters for which such opinions are required, the topics to be addressed and the language to be used. Recent developments are moving towards the use of standard clauses with an agreed understanding of what such clauses are supposed to mean and/or to say.

The chapter will close with a list citing the principal points of a legal opinion.

I. The Legal Opinion

1. Legal Nature

As a rule, a legal opinion is a written document, prepared by a legal counsel in connection with a given transaction and expressing a lawyer's legal conclusions with respect to one or more legal issues involved in that transaction.[6]

In commercial matters two types of opinions are frequent: the transaction opinion and the reasoned opinion.[7]

Transaction opinions are rendered at the completion of a commercial transaction, and they report on the nature of the transaction accomplished and its legal consequences. Such an opinion can exist of a simple report on the different technical steps undertaken by the lawyer; it can also take a more formal character where, besides the mere technicalities, more detailed information is given about the particular measures undertaken by the lawyer about the assumptions, qualifications or limitations he made, or about the possible legal consequences that might follow from the transaction.[8]

On the other hand, reasoned opinions contain a detailed analysis of the law involved in a particular situation. They can aim at the interpretation of a given statutory rule, they can explain the possible meaning of particular provision in a

---

[6] According to Black's Law Dictionary, 5th ed. (1979), at 985, a legal opinion is a "document prepared by an attorney for his client, embodying his understanding of the law as applicable to a state of facts submitted to him for [a given] purpose". And the Report of the Committee on Corporations of the Californian State Bar stated (*supra*, n. 5, at 1004-5): "In the context of business transactions, a legal opinion can be more accurately defined as a formal writing prepared by a lawyer, expressing the lawyer's informed understanding of the legal principles generally applicable to a specific transaction or to a particular aspect of such a transaction."

[7] See Estey (*supra*, n. 4), at 17.

[8] See ibid. 18.

contract, or they may, as a consequence of an interpretation, give advice as to a possible course of action.[9]

A transaction opinion usually includes a statement saying that a legally binding, enforceable contract has been formed between the parties to the transaction. But in more complex dealings many difficult legal issues may be involved. They may affect a borrower's obligation to repay the loan; they may also affect the lender's remedies with respect to collateral security, or they may have some influence on the successful promotion of the borrower's projects. As some of the issues may involve unusual and uncertain legal concepts, extensive factual or legal analysis could be required so that the transaction opinion might be combined with a reasoned opinion.

It is understandable that in doubtful cases no prudent lender is prepared to advance funds to his borrower without being convinced that the obligation to repay is legally binding on the borrower. With the legal opinion the lender seeks such assurance. To this end, he requests a reasoned statement from the borrower's counsel or at least from a practising lawyer in the borrower's country confirming that even the lender and his counsel (or a practising lawyer in that country) believe that the obligation of repayment is enforceable under the law of the borrower's country.[10]

2. Functions and Purposes

Lawyers may be involved in international transactions in different ways. On the one hand, they are asked to advise generally on a transaction and to see that their client gets adequate protection by the terms of a contract. On the other hand, they have to provide legal opinions by which they confirm the legal validity of the contract document.

As to legal opinions in particular, they may be requested for different reasons. For example, opinions are prepared at the request of the lawyer's client in order to inform him about the probable legal consequences of a contemplated transaction. Other opinions are prepared in order to satisfy the requirements stipulated under the agreed terms of negotiations between the parties to a transaction and their legal counsel. But legal opinions may also be requested for submission to an administrative authority or to a third party, either directly or in an annual report.[11]

In each of these cases such opinions may serve different purposes. They may e.g. underline that an intended course of action is lawful and that certain expected legal consequences will follow or certain undesirable results will be prevented by the proposed course of action. They may also confirm that certain legal relationships have been created; they may warn against undesirable legal risks, they may help to

[9] See e.g. Bermant (*supra*, n. 4), at 134: "A typical example of the reasoned opinion occurs in transactions where a lender desires legal assurance that the borrower does not have [e.g.] the defence of usury available to it, often in complex financing arrangements . . .In such event, the lawyer's opinion might well discuss the theory of usury . . . and then arrive at the conclusion that "although the issue is not without doubt, we are of the opinion that the transaction when viewed as a whole does not involve the imposition of usurious interest.""

[10] See S. Fitzgibbon and W. Glazer, "Legal Opinions on Incorporation, Good Standing, and Qualification to Business" (1986), 41 *Bus. Law.*, p. 461: "Legal opinions are short . . . and look simple. But they are an essential element of almost all major corporate financial transactions. In an opinion for such a transaction, the lawyer confirms that the transaction is what it is meant to be from a legal point of view."

[11] See e.g. Report of the Committee on Corporations of the Californian State Bar (*supra*, n. 5, at 1005).

resolve textual uncertainties in a contract; they may satisfy important contractual or statutory requirements in view of the closing of a transaction or they may provide a defence against an allegation of wrongful conduct, etc. In short, legal opinions may serve multifold purposes inside and outside formal legal proceedings.

3. Comparable Instruments

Where a representative of the civil law is confronted with a legal opinion coming from the common law, he might ask himself whether comparable instruments exist under the civil law system. The answer is yes and no.

If we understand the legal opinion as an instrument by which one contracting party seeks assurance as to the validity and the enforceability of another party's obligations, then a legal opinion might, in its functions, be compared with an instrument of assurance or guaranty.

In international transactions, there are numerous types of assurances or guaranties: the transport sector works e.g. with insurance contracts, the export business uses bills of lading, money-lenders have securities, bonds, collateral with real or personal security, construction builders prefer first demand guaranties and other sectors have recourse to export risk guaranties.

Legal opinions are not securities or guaranties of that kind. The legal opinion is a kind of expertise, a legal document based on special professional skill and knowledge.

Even so, legal opinions can be of considerable economic consequences. As the addressee of an opinion relies on its statements and acts accordingly, an imprecise, incomplete or even partially erroneous opinion can cause significant economic loss. As a consequence, the personal integrity and the professional renommée of the opinion writer is at stake and he might be held legally liable for the damage caused.[12]

4. Fields of Application

Especially in the USA, it seems to be generally accepted nowadays that, for a wide range of business activities, the legal opinion forms an important part of any transaction; almost nothing of substantial importance happens unless one or more legal opinions are submitted.[13] For example, in order to receive now loans, in 1988, Mexico issued Floating Rate Bonds guaranteed by zero-coupons from the United States Treasury. The prospectus was accompanied by a dozen opinions and similar statements, including legal opinions given by the Mexican and the United States Counsel of Mexico as well as the Mexican and the United States Counsel of the US Bank acting as an exchange agent.[14]

Legal opinions are used in different fields of business transactions such as corporate matters, sales of business, mergers, financing matters, loans or securities transactions. Other typical areas are real estate businesses, information to auditors,

---

[12] See Estey (*supra*, n. 4), at 255.

[13] See Fuld (*supra*, n. 4), at 914. Estey (*supra*, n. 4), at 1: "Many lawyers assume that a transaction opinion is among the most important documents to be delivered on closing."

[14] See Documents to the Invitation to Bids to purchase United Mexican States Collateralized Floating Bonds, March 1988, Exhibits C to F.

dealings with the S.E.C., statements intended to tax authorities or other state agencies.[15]

In the USA, nine out of ten legal opinions relate to domestic matters or to cases that are international in the US sense of the term only, i.e. cases which relate to two or more sister states but not to other countries.

In view of the widespread use of legal opinions, several years ago the US legal profession started to deal in a more systematic way with legal opinions in an attempt to create some order out of some chaos.[16] Over the last fifteen years different Bar Associations established special committees to analyse particular aspects of possible practices in the preparing and drafting of legal opinions.[17]

So far, general and special reports have been prepared by the American Bar Association (ABA) Committee on Ethics and Professional Responsibility. Recently, the ABA created a special Committee on Legal Opinions. Other reports came from the New York Bar Association, the Bar of the City of New York, the Massachusetts Bar Association and the Texas Bar Association; especially active was the Business Law Section of the State Bar of California.[18]

The aim of the different reports was to develop commonly acceptable principles as to the structure of legal opinions, their content, their language and standardized terminology.[19] The second part of this chapter takes a closer look at these questions.

II. The Characteristics of Legal Opinions

Although various committee reports and articles published thus far stress different elements and emphasize different clauses, they generally agree on the basic structure common to all kinds of legal opinions.[20] This structure consists of essentially four parts which can be called the preliminaries, the surroundings, the substance and the closing part.

---

[15] See Fuld (*supra*, n. 4), at 915; Fitzgibbon and Glazer, "Legal Opinions in Corporate Transactions: Opinions Relating to Security Interests in Personal Property" (1989) 44 *Bus. Law.*, pp. 655-656; see also Estey (*supra*, n. 4), for commercial opinions at 129, for real estate opinions at 171.

[16] See Fuld (*supra*, n. 4), at 915.

[17] See *supra*, n. 5.

[18] See *supra*, n. 5; add: "American Bar Association, Committee on Ethics and Professional Responsibility, Professional Ethics Opinions" (1974) 60 *A.B.A.J.*, p. 488; "Committee on Audit Inquiry Responses Regarding Initial Implementation, ABA Statement of Policy regarding Lawyer's Responses to Auditors' Request for Information" (1976), 32 *Bus. Law.*, p. 177; Report Regarding Legal Opinions in Personal Property Secured Transactions, Uniform Commercial Code Committee of the Business Law Section of the State Bar of California (1989), 44 *Bus. Law.*, p. 791.

[19] Most of the Committee Reports referred to in nn. 5 and 18 contain structured models for the drafting of legal opinions; see e.g. the three "Reports of the State Bar of California regarding Legal Opinions in Business Transactions" ((1983), 14 *Pac. L.J.*, p. 1001), ". . . in Real Estate Transactions" ((1987), 42 *Bus. Law.*, p. 1139) and ". . . in Secured Transactions" (1989), 44 *Bus. Law.*, p. 791).

[20] See also Estey (*supra*, n. 4), at 34: "Many law firms have now produced various standard forms of opinions. These may take the form of a full opinion for use in a particular type of transaction . . . There appear to be at least two principal reasons for this initiative: (1) firms are becoming more zealous . . . in attempting to achieve a consistency . . . among opinions . . .; and (2) the custom that lawyers on both sides of a transaction drive to deliver on closing substantially similar, if not identical, opinions."

1. The Preliminaries

In the preliminary part we normally find five elements, i.e. the date on which the opinion was prepared, the addressee of the opinion, the counsel's role in the underlying transaction, some reference to the transaction in the context of which the opinion was given, as well as some references to definitions and qualifications.[21]

The Date

Legal opinions normally bear the date of the day when they were delivered, for the opinion speaks as of that date. In complex transactions it is, however, often required that the opinion bear the date of the closing day of the principal transaction. If the opinion is dated prior to that day, the opining lawyer might not be responsible for matters which have occurred between the two dates, e.g. the changing of a local statute.[22]

In international transactions, it is usually not possible to have all relevant documents prepared on the day of closing, nor will all local counsel be able to attend the closing. In such cases most attached documents including the relevant legal opinions will be prepared beforehand, and at the day of the closing the opining counsel will confirm his opinion and authorize its dating. Thus, possible liability for modifications, in local law, lies with the local counsel.

The Addressee

Legal opinions usually identify their addresses either by indicating their names or by specifying the appropriate group or class of persons (the sellers, buyers, purchasers). As a rule, only addressees are entitled to rely on the opinion. Although non-addressees may acknowledge an opinion, if they rely on it, they normally do so at their own risk. Sometimes counsel indicate in the opinion whether non-addressees are permitted to rely on the opinion and, if so, under what circumstances and to what extent.[23]

The Role of Counsel

In their opinions, lawyers normally state the capacity in which they act, and on behalf of which party the opinion is given. Often the lawyer specifies his function as that of a general, a special or a local counsel, or simply as counsel to one of the parties to the transaction.

The term "general counsel" indicates that there is a substantial, complex relationship between the lawyer and his client. Such counsel may be handling a variety of matters for that client; in particular, he might be responsible for the whole transaction in which a particular legal opinion was required.

A special counsel usually deals with a specialized topic or field of law (taxes, patents or bankruptcy), and represents a client in a specific case or a particular matter.

---

[21] See e.g. Report of the Committee on Corporations of the Californian State Bar (*supra*, n. 5), at 1014.

[22] Fuld (*supra*, n. 4), at 919.

[23] Cf. n. 22, at 920.

Local (or international) counsel are lawyers outside the (main) jurisdiction of the client. Most of their cases are international transactions where they deal with the law of another jurisdiction.

Whether a lawyer acts as a general, special or local counsel has some impact on his standard of care and liability: the more familiar he is with the aspects on which the opinion is given, the higher his level of liability will be.[24]

The Underlying Transaction

The introductory paragraph of a legal opinion also refers to the transaction in the context of which such opinion is given (e.g. we have acted as counsel in connection with the issuance of a new series of shares by corporation X).[25] In the same context, the opinion usually mentions the documents on which it is based, and indicates the reasons why the opinion was given.[26] All these elements might become important if divergent views should arise with respect to the meaning of the language and the content of an opinion, or some of its statements.

Definitions

The same applies to possible definitions and qualifications in the opinion. Such elements should be clearly expressed and accurately explained.[27]

Sometimes the underlying agreement or some of its annexes might already provide definitions. In such cases it is advisable to use the same definitions for the opinion, and the opinion should make express reference to the agreement or document in question.

2. The Surroundings

After the preliminary matters mentioned in the first paragraph, the legal opinion refers to a set of surrounding factors. For example, reference is made to the counsel's role in the underlying transaction or to a series of assumptions on which the opinion is based. Other factors relate to the documents investigated and to special or local opinions given on specific matters of the transaction.

Counsel's Role

As already mentioned (*supra*, "The Role of Counsel"), the opining lawyer normally indicates at the beginning of the opinion the capacity in which he was required to act. The statement usually specifies whether the lawyer was acting as a general, a special or local counsel, and whether he prepared his opinion as a corporate, fiscal or a securities lawyer.

In the same context, the opining counsel usually discloses his relationship to the addressee, indicating whether, and if so, in what capacity he was involved in the underlying transaction.[28] Such statements are particularly helpful where the quality

---

[24] Cf. n. 21, at 1015/1016.
[25] Estey (*supra*, n. 4), at 35.
[26] Ibid. 36.
[27] See Report of the Committee on Corporations of the Californian State Bar (*supra*, n. 5), at 1016.
[28] Estey (*supra*, n. 4), at 34.

of an opinion depends on impartiality or where, on the contrary, thorough knowledge of the client's business is required.

Assumptions

Of equal, if not greater importance are the assumptions under which a legal opinion is given. Assumptions are normally made with respect to certain facts or elements. For example, if counsel has to examine a set of documents, he may expressly assume that all documents submitted to him are authentic, or that copies are complete and conform to the original documents. As to facts, counsel may assume that the statements made in the documents are complete and correspond with reality.[29]

Sometimes a legal opinion is asked to reassure the addressee that the underlying transaction (in preparation) will be binding on the counsel's client. Such an assurance presupposes that the other contracting party, will also be bound by the planned transaction. Therefore, legal opinions sometimes state that the issuing counsel assumes due authorization, execution and delivery by the other party, as well as the fact that the basic documents are valid and binding on that party.

The text mentioned reflects the importance of adequate assumptions, for if one of the assumptions fails, the sense of the entire legal opinion may be affected. Therefore, before relying on counsel's conclusions, the addresses should carefully check and verify the assumptions.[30]

In the same context the term "qualification" may be mentioned. Whereas in private international law qualification stands for a process of interpretation, a qualified legal opinion is the opposite of an unconditional and unrestricted legal opinion based on crystal-clear law.

If the legal rule on which a counsel has to opine is controversial and he takes a stand in favour of one theory, his opinion is deemed to be qualified.[31] As to the party to an international transaction, any qualification means legal risk; therefore the client or addressee of an opinion should be informed about such qualifications.

Documents Investigated

In most cases, legal opinions are based on factual matters. A legal counsel who has to verify such facts may rely on documentary proof. Some opinions give a detailed overview of the documents that have been examined; others mention just the title of such documents, or make a general statement that such documents have been examined and such investigations as deemed relevant have been made.

Sometimes, the list of documents includes certificates from a government agency indicating the good standing of a corporation or stating that fiscal duties were fulfilled.[32] If the certificate is dated prior to the closing of the transaction, a supplement to cover the intermediate period of time may be required.

---

[29] See Fuld (supra, n. 4), at 921.

[30] See Legal Opinion in California Real Estate Transactions (1987), 42 Bus. Law., p. 1148.

[31] See Fuld, "Lawyers' Standards and Responsibilities in Rendering Opinions" (1978), 33 Bus. Law., 1306; see also Estey (supra, n. 4), at 30, 31.

[32] Report of the Committee on Corporations of the Californian State Bar (supra, n. 5), at 1019 and 1023.

Special Opinions, Local Opinions

As a rule, legal opinions are restricted to specific matters; they serve as an assurance from a legal point of view but do not guarantee that a particular transaction is economically sound. If an opinion affirms that a transaction is binding in accordance with its terms, such statement is only of help if the terms of the transaction themselves are sound. Inappropriate contract terms cannot be improved through legal opinions, not even by the strongest opinion language.

A legal opinion should only deal with the national law of its author, and it should be restricted to legal topics with which the author is familiar. If some of the questions put to the legal counsel refer to special matters such as tax law or the law on intellectual property, then the assistance of a special counsel might be advisable. Similarly, if questions of foreign law are involved, a local counsel of the country in question should be engaged to answer such questions.[33]

If, in preparing his opinion, a legal counsel realizes that a special or local opinion is needed to clarify a particular question, he may request such an opinion, and then either refer to it or integrate the special counsel's conclusions into his own opinion. On the other hand he may give a qualified opinion and expressly limit the conclusions to his domestic law. In my opinion, counsel at the very least has the duty to draw the addressee's attention to the particular problem.[34]

Once a special or local opinion has been given, the general (or principal) counsel has to choose between two approaches. One course of action is to indicate the particular problem by expressly excluding it from his opinion. The other is to request a particular opinion, and then either to make a simple reference to such special opinion or to integrate its results into the general opinion.[35]

The decision on the appropriate course of action depends on how much risk the general counsel is prepared to bear. For him the safest way is to give a qualified opinion. In the case of a simple reference his liability may be restricted to *a culpa in eligendo*, whereas in the case of an integrated opinion, he might be liable for possible errors made by a special, or local, counsel.[36]

3. The Substance

Whereas the preliminary aspects and the surrounding clauses are identical for most, if not all types of legal opinions, this is no longer true in regard to the substantive

[33] Cf. n. 32, at 1027.

[34] In the same sense M. W. Jonin, "The Lawyer's Responsibility for Foreign Law and Foreign Lawyers" (1982), 16 *Int. Law.*, p. 696: "The client relies on the lawyer for legal advice and services. The lawyer is, generally, better able than the client to recognize when a matter involves aspects of foreign law."

[35] According to A. N. Field and R. H. Ryan (*Legal Opinions in Corporate Transactions* (New York 1988), p. 2) the more common practice is for principal counsel to incorporate local counsel's opinion rather than have it delivered to the client separately as an independent opinion.

[36] See also Gruson and Kutschera (*supra*, n. 2), at 516 where it is stated that "Principal Counsel does not discharge his duties to his client by simply obtaining some opinion from Foreign Counsel. Principal Counsel must make a diligent effort to uncover legal problems that might exist under the relevant Foreign Law and must ascertain that these problems have been addressed and resolved."

clauses.[37] In this section, the content of the clauses depends on the purpose of the opinion, on the nature of the transaction, and on the parties concerned.

The following presentation applies mainly to borrowing and lending between private corporations.

In such cases, the legal opinion usually starts with statements concerning the corporate status; it then concentrates on the essentials of the transaction and its enforceability, and ends with some proposals for possible remedies.

The Corporate Status

The substantive part of a legal opinion dealing with money-lending might start with a clause of the following nature:

"The X-corporation has been duly incorporated and is duly organized, validly existing and in good standing under the laws of State A; in addition it is duly qualified to do business and is in good standing as a foreign corporation in States X, Y and Z."[38]

The terms "duly incorporated", "duly organized", "validly existing", "in good standing" and "duly qualified" need further explanation.

All these terms are from the common law, most of them being US legal language. If a request to act as local counsel is made from the US, the addressee of the local opinion needs to be informed in exactly such terms; otherwise a local opinion might not be operative.

A civil lawyer's task will then be twofold: first, he has to understand what his clients mean by such "strange" terminology; and second, he should be able to adjust such terminology to the appropriate terms of his own domestic legal system. In short, the European lawyer will not only be an opinion writer, but he will have to do some comparative work as well. In addition, he may have to make some adaptations or adjustments. Such task may easily lead to what the US terminology calls a qualified local opinion. After these preliminary remarks we return to the terms mentioned above.

"Duly incorporated" indicates that all the steps required to create a corporation and to realize its specified purposes have been undertaken according to the law of the state or country in which the corporation is deemed to exist.[39]

As to European law in general and Swiss law in particular, this means that all steps required for the founding of a corporation have been fulfilled, i.e. the statutes and by-laws have been accepted by the meeting of the founders, the required capital has been provided, the shares have been taken over by the statutory number of shareholders, and the corporation has been registered at the Registrar's Office in the place of incorporation.[40]

---

[37] For this very reason the State Bar of California has prepared different reports which deal with Business Transactions (1983) 14 *Pac. L. J.*, p. 1001), Real Estate Transactions (1987) 42 *Bus. Law.*, p. 1139) and Secured Transactions (1989) 44 *Bus. Law.*, p. 791).

[38] See e.g. "Report of the State Bar of California regarding Business Transactions" (1983), 14 *Pac. L. J.*) (*supra*, n. 37), at 1031.

[39] See e.g. "Report of the State Bar of California regarding Business Transactions" (*supra*, n. 37), at 1031; Fitzgibbon and Glazer (*supra*, n. 10), at 468.

[40] As to European law see Art. 2 of the First EC directive of 9 March 1968 on the co-ordination of company law.

In order to establish these facts, a local counsel in Europe would ask the Register of Commerce at the place of incorporation to issue a certificate of registration. Such a document is issued with a *praesumptio iuris pro veritate* and thus establishes full proof of the duly incorporated requirement.[41]

Under US law the term "duly organized" refers to matters such as the proper election of the directors and other officers, holding of the first meeting, regular adoption of the statutes and by-laws, authorization and issuance of stock or shares, payment of a minimum amount of capital and similar matters relating to the starting of a business.

Under US law, the duly organized requirement is more important than the duly incorporated test, for a corporation which is duly organized must have been duly incorporated.[42]

Under European law, the two terms are somewhat different. It is true that an enterprise cannot be duly incorporated without having been duly organized, but such organization may, and in practice often does change afterwards with respect to the required minimum of capital and membership.[43] A legal opinion must therefore verify these elements not only at the time of the founding, but also at the date of issuance of the opinion.

If a corporation is duly incorporated and duly organized, it also fulfils the requirement of validly existing. This term has no independent meaning, at least not in corporate matters; but things might be different as to contracts or agreements.[44]

The term "good standing" refers to the fiscal situation of a company. It indicates that the company has duly performed its tax obligations in the state of its corporation and the state where it does its business. Therefore, the state authorities have no reason to revoke its corporate status.[45]

The term "duly qualified" concerns a specific US interstate problem. In the US a corporation may be incorporated under the law of one sister state,[46] but carry out its business in one or more other states.

In Europe, things are different. If a company wants to do business in different countries, it needs a local establishment in each such country. As each such establishment normally takes the legal form of an independent local corporation, we have a so-called multinational corporation.

Corporate Power

Another substantive clause refers to the powers of a corporation; it normally has the following structure:

"The corporation has the corporate power and authority to enter into and perform the X-agreement. The execution, delivery and performance of the X-agreement has been duly authorized by all corporate action, and the X-agreement has been duly executed by the corporation."[47]

[41] See e.g. Art. 641 Swiss Code of Obligations.

[42] See Report of the State Bar of California (*supra*, n. 37), at 1032; see also Fitzgibbon and Glazer (*supra*, n. 10), at 468-469.

[43] See e.g. Art. 625 para. 2 and Art. 633 para. 2 Swiss Code of Obligations.

[44] See Fitzgibbon and Glazer (*supra*, n. 10), at 470-471.

[45] Ibid.: "Good standing certificates are available in most states but mean different things . . . Some states issue a single certificate relating both to the payment of taxes and to other matter, such as filing of periodic reports with the state secretary."

[46] Many corporations are incorporated under the laws of Willmington, Delaware, but have their principle place of business elsewhere.

[47] See similar clauses in Report of the State Bar of California (*supra*, n. 37), at 1035.

In this clause there are two elements of particular interest.

The first element (corporate power and authority) indicates that the corporation is entitled to be active in the particular field, and that such undertaking falls within the scope of activities provided for in its statutes and by-laws. This clause acts as an assurance against the famous *ultra vires* doctrine.

The second element (duly authorized by corporate action) relates to the question of corporate authorization. It underlines that the appropriate corporate body was acting and confirms that this body was empowered to perform such acts, either by law, by statutes and by-laws or even by an authorization received from the competent corporate body.[48]

Transactions

In case a corporation wants to issue new shares, the transaction will probably be accompanied by a legal opinion in which, among others, this special power might be expressly addressed. A possible standard clause would read as follows:

" The corporation's authorized capital stock consists of X. shares, par value of Y-$ per share. The shares have been duly authorized and validly issued and they are fully paid and non-assessable."[49]

When applied to stock, the term "duly authorized" means that under the applicable law, as well as under its statutes and by-laws, this corporation has the power to issue shares. The term also indicates that all corporate action necessary to authorize such issuance has been undertaken.

The power to issue shares contains at least two aspects: first, the power to issue a given number of shares and, second, the power to issue such shares at a particular price.[50]

Shares are validly issued, if the issuance was duly authorized, if payment was made as indicated by the value, and if the certificates evidencing such shares were properly executed. In addition, the necessary technicalities and official authorizations must be met.

Fully paid means that the amount required by the corporate action authorizing the issuance has been paid in full. The clause also implies that such amount was sufficient.

The legally binding clause refers to the validity of the underlying agreement and certifies that this agreement was neither void nor *ultra vires*, nor in conflict with any rule of law. If the agreement is legally binding upon both parties to the transaction, it must also be enforceable before a court; this leads to the next set of clauses.

Enforceability

According to the enforceability clause, an agreement can be enforced by a legal action before a court.[51] An agreement may be legally binding without being enforceable, e.g. if one party is a state or an international organization which has not waived its immunity. The term "enforceability" may be used in different contexts.

---

[48] See Fuld (1973) (*supra* n. 4), at 927.
[49] See Estey (*supra*, n. 4), at 87.
[50] Ibid. 88, 89.
[51] See Fuld (*supra*, n. 4), at 929-931; Report (*supra*, n. 37), at 1037.

Specifically enforceable refers to the common law and its equitable remedy of specific performance. The effect of such clause is similar to what a civil lawyer might call a performance *in natura*.

The no-conflict-rule covers and prevents conflicts with other statutory or negotiated texts mentioned in the clause. The following language might be used:

The execution and delivery of the agreement do not and will not conflict with,
- *any law of States X,*
- *the certificate of incorporation or the by-laws of the corporation or with*
- *any agreement, instrument, judgment or decree known to us and to which the corporation is a party or is subject.[52]*

If the documents mentioned in the clause are not in the possession of the opining lawyer, he must rely on information received from the company or certificates issued by official authorities.

The no-litigation statement indicates the absence of any pending court or arbitration proceedings. In this respect, again, the opining counsel will have to rely on information provided by the client.

In order to limit personal liability as to such statements, as a safeguard, counsels usually add, the knowledge exception "known to us".[53]

Official Consents

In export or international financing transactions, consent, licences and/or authorizations from state agencies may be required. The opining counsel should verify whether such authorizations have been obtained and whether they duly authorise execution of the agreement. The positive result of such control may be stated in the opinion as follows:

"All consents and authorizations of governmental or official authorities of State A have been obtained for the entry into and the performance of the agreement."[54]

Remedies

The substantive part of a legal opinion may also contain a remedy clause declaring that:

"The agreement is a legal, valid and binding obligation of the corporation and is enforceable against the corporation in accordance with the terms of the agreement, except as may be limited by bankruptcy, insolvency or similar laws affecting the enforcement of the creditors rights in general. In addition, the enforceability of the corporations obligations under the agreement is subject to the general principles of equity."[55]

As already mentioned, the language in legal opinions resembles that of incoterms. This is especially true in regard to the remedy clauses. In this sense, opinion counsel nowadays give LVB or EAT assurances or they make a BKE or an EPL reservation.[56]

---

[52] See Report (*supra*, n. 37), at 1047; Estey (*supra*, n. 4), at 143.

[53] Report (*supra*, n. 37), at 1057; Fuld (*supra*, n. 4), at 941.

[54] See Estey (*supra*, n. 4), at 82.

[55] See Report (*supra*, n. 37), at 1037, 1039.

[56] LVB: Legal, Valid and Binding; EAT: Enforceable in Accordance with its Terms; BKE: Bankruptcy Exception; EPL: Equitable Principles Limitation reservation.

With an LVB clause counsel tends to limit his possible liability; therefore, he restricts his statements to the terms of the agreement. If these terms are unsatisfactory, the impact of a LVB or an EAT clause is manifest.

In addition to the two limitation clauses there are also two exception clauses.

The Bankruptcy Exception (BKE) refers to the function of this procedure. In all jurisdictions bankruptcy is intended to defeat the enforcement of an obligation under certain circumstances. Even in a simple obligation to pay, bankruptcy proceedings tend to release the bankrupt debtor from his obligation to pay. As a consequence, the creditors are deprived from any remedy. Instead, bankruptcy proceedings prescribe a global solution to settle all assets and debts.[57]

The Equitable Principles Limitation (EPL) tends to exempt debtors from the obligation to respond to a duty stipulated in the agreement. Under the common law principle of equity, there may be valid reasons not to perform such duty.[58]

The Closing Part

As in all the other parts of a legal opinion, there is also a set of standard clauses frequently used in the closing part.[59]

The Legal Form Clause

The legal form clause reads as follows: "The agreement is in proper legal form for enforcement in the court." Clauses of this type confirm that the conditions are satisfied, thus permitting one to exercise a particular right.

Filings

In most cases a registration or filing relates to export control, exchange control or similar questions. A possible wording of such a clause might be: "No filings or registration with a public agency is necessary in regard to the making, validity or enforceability of the agreement."

Stamp Duties, Taxes

Another element of the closing part usually states whether the agreement to be concluded has to satisfy stamp duties. This might be the case in the field of securities or bonds. In the same context reference should be made to the question whether some special tax duty is to be taken into account under foreign law .

Other Agreements

Depending on the legal nature of the underlying transaction, a legal opinion might have to deal with various other matters such as the *pari passu* ranking, the judgment clause, the immunity clause, the no-adverse-consequences clause, the application of the proper law or the adherence to securities regulations.

Signature

Common to all legal opinion, is the final personal signature of the opining counsel.

[57] See Report (*supra*, n. 37), at 1038, 1039.

[58] Ibid. 1040.

[59] As to the closing part see "Report by New York County Lawyers' Association. Legal Opinion to Third Parties: An Easier Path" (1979) 34 *Bus. Law.*, p. 1891.

Appendix

Typical Elements of a Legal Opinion

1. The Preliminaries
   1.1 Date
   1.2 Addressee
   1.3 Role of Counsel
   1.4 Underlying Transaction
   1.5 Definitions

2. The Surroundings
   2.1 Counsel's Role in Underlying Transaction
   2.2 Assumptions
   2.3 Documents Investigated
   2.4 Special Opinions

3. The Substance
   3.1 Corporate Status
      Duly incorporated, duly organized
      Validly existing
      Good standing
      Duly qualified
   3.2 Corporate Power
   3.3 Transaction
      Duly authorized
      Validly issued
      Legally binding
   3.4 Enforceability
      Specifically enforceable
      No-conflict, no-litigation
      Knowledge exception
   3.5 Official Consents
   3.6 Remedies
      Bankruptcy exception
      Equitable principles

4. The Closing Part
   4.1 Legal Form
   4.2 Filings
   4.3 Stamp Duties, Taxes
   4.4 Other Agreements
   4.5 Signature

Index